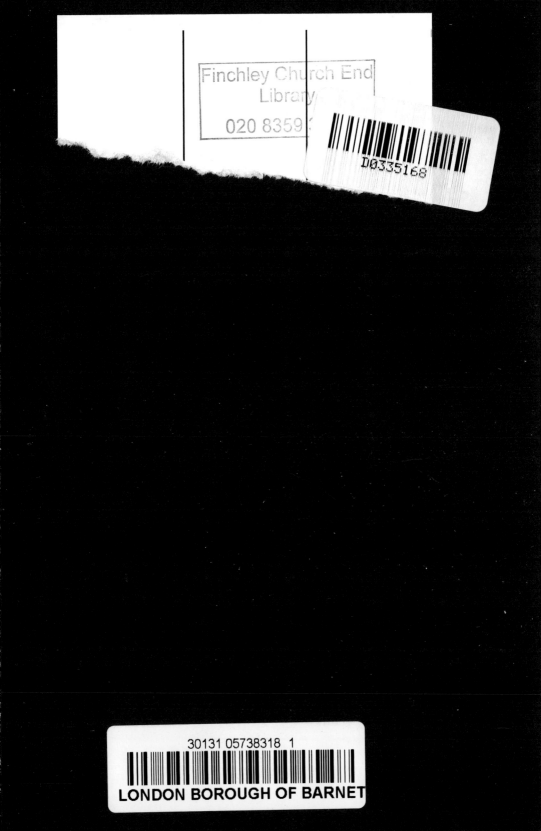

THE
END
OF THE
ROAD

JACK COOKE

THE
END
OF THE
ROAD

**A journey around
Britain in search
of the dead**

MUDLARK

Mudlark
HarperCollins*Publishers*
1 London Bridge Street
London SE1 9GF

www.harpercollins.co.uk

HarperCollins*Publishers*
1st Floor, Watermarque Building, Ringsend Road
Dublin 4, Ireland

First published by Mudlark 2021

1 3 5 7 9 10 8 6 4 2

© Jack Cooke 2021

Jack Cooke asserts the moral right to
be identified as the author of this work

A catalogue record of this book is
available from the British Library

ISBN 978-0-00-829470-0

Printed and bound in Great Britain by
CPI Group (UK) Ltd, Croydon

MIX
Paper from
responsible sources
FSC™ C007454

This book is produced from independently certified FSC™ paper
to ensure responsible forest management.

For more information visit: www.harpercollins.co.uk/green

To my father and son

CONTENTS

To bring the dead to life
Is no great magic.
Few are wholly dead:
Blow on a dead man's embers
And a live flame will start.

Robert Graves

Eternity is not something that begins after you are dead.
It is going on all the time. We are in it now.

Charlotte Perkins Gilman

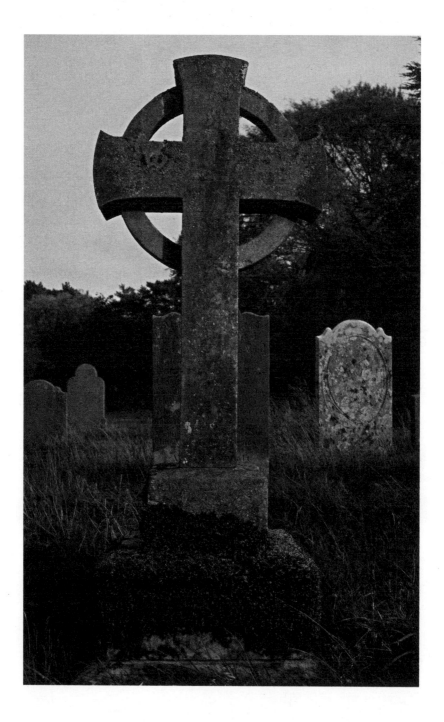

PROLOGUE

One dismal morning I walked into my local churchyard on a whim. I had no faith to carry me over the threshold, only the echoes of a few 'Our Fathers' and the lyrics of half-remembered hymns. Yet the church beckoned to me each time I passed it, alone inside its brick walls and guarding the remains of a thousand people I'd never met.

It began to rain as I reached for the latch on the churchyard gate. A rabbit bolted from behind a tombstone and disappeared beneath a stone cross, using the dead to hide from the living. In the church porch, gargoyles pulled faces at me from the safety of high pedestals.

The door was heavy and I had to lean into it. It swung slowly inward to reveal a dim and private world, the village noticeboard rustling softly as I passed, flyers for second-hand lawnmowers competing with curry nights in the pub. The air inside smelt of wood polish and damp prayer books. It felt close, heavy with the weight of expectation. The pews were empty and silent, save for flies that buzzed belly-up under the windows.

I reached a corner of the church where the shadows held their own communion. A large memorial stood with its back to the windows, pressed hard into the join between two walls. Amid this gloom knelt the figure of a man, his knees on a stone pillow and his hands joined together in prayer. The paint on his face had faded like an old doll's make-up and his gaze wandered among the ceiling beams.

Beneath him was a statue of his wife. The carving was much smaller and barely reached to my waist. Only the woman's back could be seen, a great sweep of black drapery rising to a hood like a cobra's silhouette. The form beneath the folds was thin and angular, unnaturally pinched in at the shoulders.

To look upon her face I had to squeeze between the memorial steps and the wall of the church, until we came nose to nose. In contrast to her husband, the woman's gaze was direct, meeting my own. Her hair was drawn back from a high forehead, the stone scalp framed by the hood's sinister fork. A sharp nose ended in a small, tight-lipped mouth, oddly twisted at the corners. Her hands had been amputated at the wrist by neglect or vandalism, and I imagined them as forbidding as the rest of her – thin, talon-like. Where her husband's epitaph ran the length of several stone tablets, the woman's read only, *Here lies Elizabeth Read.*

Turning away from this fearful effigy I noticed a small stone flower, the size of my palm, had fallen from the tomb's ceiling and lay unbroken on the floor. I picked it up and turned it over in my hands, wondering if I had just missed this moment in time.

I emerged from this reverie to find my eyes drawn again to the hooded form of Elizabeth Read. If the statue were a true likeness, she must have inspired as much dread in life as in death. Something brushed against the windows of the church, the shadow of tall weeds dancing against the glass, and I left the building to escape my own irrational fear.

In the churchyard, memories were less well preserved, the grave markers eroding like the coastline hidden beyond the boundary wall. The wind was in the east and I could hear breakers on the beach a mile distant, the great undertow sounding like it swept in among the graves. I counted two hundred tombstones listing forward or backward, as if their occupants were constantly rearranging themselves. The ground beneath them teemed with older bones, generations stacked in the soil.

Returning through the iron gates I paused by neighbouring graves. The first was the headstone of a sailor lost at sea, *I harbour here below*, the second a fresh grave not two weeks old, with the funeral flowers withered inside their wrappings.

The visit to the church reminded me how divorced I was from death. I inhabited a high-turnover world, a place of constant change that continued without pause or reflection. I ignored the dead because they interrupted life.

The possibility of dying was also easy to obscure with the act of living. Daily routine, a young family, good health; all of these provided a means of disregarding death. It existed only in the distant past and future, peripheral, made up of news-paper columns and other people's tragedies. In my sheltered world people died out of sight and bodies vanished beyond doors and curtains, magicked from hospital wards to morgues to crematoriums, or closed coffins. Death was expedited, the whole process sped up, with digital memories supplanting deathbed vigils. Any bond my ancestors had with the deceased was broken.

Most of us live in denial of death. We practise unconscious alchemy, loath to accept our own mortality and searching for ways to prolong life in an age of modern medicine. Those already dead and buried are to be skirted around, side-stepped, wherever possible put to the back of our minds. The 'respect' we accord them is also a way of establishing distance between them and us. In spite of our common fate we disso-ciate ourselves.

That night, when I went to bed and turned on my side, I found myself thinking once more of Elizabeth Read and the drowned sailor. I lay in a foetal position with my knees one on top of the other, a thin layer of skin separating the joints and flesh pressed hard between bones. As if for the very first time, I became acutely conscious of my own skeleton rubbing against itself.

I got little sleep and stumbled into a bath at sunrise. After washing I pulled the plug but felt too tired to climb out. My body slowly settled as the water ran away, floating limbs becoming deadweight and lifeless. As the last of the water drained through the plughole, I found myself beached in a ceramic coffin and realised I had become morbidly obsessed, preoccupied with the thought of all those men and women underground.

The idea of someone absconding to another world did not sit well with me. If there was any kind of human soul it did not fly off to heaven or hell but became an integral part of the landscape. I could not reconcile myself with total absence. For me the dead had gone to ground; their atoms synonymous with the earth and the living things in which they were reconstituted. They still had a role, not in some imagined afterlife, but in the traces they left behind.

Lying alone in the empty bath, I made up my mind to go looking for the dead, to visit them at their points of departure and pay my respects. Instead of avoiding them I would seek them out. I would abandon the living, my wife and children, and become a *taphophile*, a tomb tourist, embarking on a journey that would take me the length and breadth of the British Isles. I decided to confine myself to these islands, where everything is necessarily condensed and we all live in close proximity to a corpse.

My tour would actually be a detour, from the relentless pace of life itself. I would strike out for the past, pulling hard against the currents of the future. The whole country is made up of memorials, from roadside graves to skyline monuments, and I began to construct a grand tour of the dead, a pilgrimage to see those long underground. The headstones would serve as my highway markers, a road map yet to be drawn.

I would visit heroes and villains, kings and outcasts, explorers, eccentrics, mummies and monks. Some stood rank and file in uniform cemetery rows, others lay in small churchyards or buried in lonelier places still. By winding my way from tomb to tomb I would attempt to hang onto their memory a moment longer and salvage something from all the scattered history beneath our feet; the ways we choose to be remembered and how others choose to remember us. I did not believe the dead possessed voices but I wanted to give them one, or listen in to what I could.

To this end, I set out with a mixture of fear and morbid fascination. A natural fear of facing what we all dread but a hope that I might distil something from the past; a sense of peace, belonging, or acceptance. At the very least a good story.

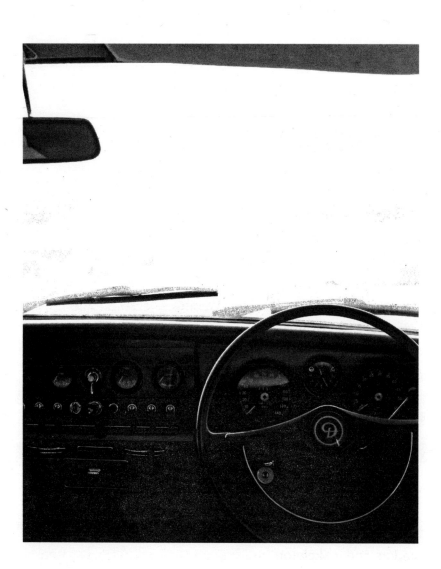

A VEHICLE FOR THE DEAD

I bought the hearse from John Lakey, a Bristol undertaker with auburn hair and stubble and the build of an old-world wrestler.

After plotting my tomb tour I needed a suitable mode of transport, something I could live out of, sleep in, and use to travel to all corners of the country. My journey was an attempt to connect to the dead, and driving a hearse seemed a way of throwing myself in at the deep end.

The hearse also appealed to me as a kind of time machine, capable of moving forward and sliding backward simultaneously. It was ponderous enough to slow the pace of modern life and it was dignified, a vehicle in which the stories of the departed could accrue like imaginary passengers.

Lakey meets me at Bristol Parkway station, waving from the window of a black Passat with bat stickers stuck to the fenders and a skeleton nodding on the dash. He's wearing a Slayer T-shirt and smoking an e-cigarette.

He drives with his hands resting on his knees, speeding through the steep back roads of suburban Bristol. As he expertly ushers other drivers into parking lots and hedge-rows, I question him about his life as an undertaker.

'It's a good job. You see some things, but it's a good job.'

Lakey has worked for the Co-op funeral home for fourteen years, a period in which it slowly cannibalised a series of smaller family firms and built itself into one of the largest corpse handlers in the country. As we turn a corner and narrowly avoid a large scaffold truck, the man behind the wheel becomes philosophical.

'I guess you could say I'm a shepherd. A shepherd of people.'

Another HGV blasts us with its horn and mounts the kerb. *'Jesus Christ,'* I mouth silently. The shepherd drives on, and after an uneventful mile my grip relaxes on the door handle. The world goes by in a rainbow blur.

We pull up by a row of pebbledash garages. One of them belongs to Lakey's mum and, apparently, she wants it back. He squats down by a huge steel lock on the door and spends five minutes beating it before the bolt loosens. The door springs up and at first I see nothing at all. Then, like some hideous beetle emerging from a hole, the hearse materialises.

It fills the garage, eighteen foot long and barely squeezed between the walls. It looks suffocated, a great swollen body wedged into the bay and weighing three metric tonnes. It certainly has presence.

The undertaker performs a surprising feat of athleticism, sucking in his chest and tip-toeing along the front wing before dropping through the driver's window. The handbrake releases with a heavy clank and the car rolls forward into the sun.

Lakey motions for me to have a look, with the air of a steward inviting a guest on board a luxury liner. I open the passenger door and a mist of rust drifts out across the concrete. Inside, the car is as dark and hollow as a grandfather clock. I lift up the floor carpet and am surprised to find daylight through a ragged hole in the foot well. The steward leans in over my shoulder.

'You'll need to cut out the floor panels, the boot and some of the middle.' He pauses. 'Obviously.'

I look suitably impressed. 'Leaving what?'

The hearse came off the production line in the winter of '72, less than a mile from the hospital I was born in thirteen years later. These points of origin no longer exist; the car factory abandoned, and the labour ward demolished and turned into flats. In this instance, man has fared better than machine.

Lakey stretches forward and turns the ignition. The engine makes a brave attempt to come to life, idles for a moment, then coughs silent again. The windscreen wipers flap twice before one falls off and disappears under the wheel.

At this point in the negotiations, Lakey's mum appears with two cups of tea, perhaps in an attempt to seal the deal. Lakey climbs into the back of the hearse and places his tea on the coffin deck.

'One time I was working a funeral when I stepped out the car and something grabbed my ankle.' He makes a pincer-grip motion with his hand.

His mum rolls her eyes. 'You caught your trouser leg.'

Lakey tries again. 'Another time, I was filling the fuel tanks when my whole arm suddenly went numb.'

'You probably hit your funny bone.'

So saying, the cynic leaves me with the mystic, retreating back into a neighbouring house. After checking the hearse over for other faults (worn wheels, patched pipes, innumerable missing parts), Lakey leads me into the garage to go over the car's paperwork. The far end is stacked with coffins in several sizes and levels of trim, and I stop to look at them.

'Cast-offs. Some of them were dropped, one or two I got cheap but couldn't sell on.'

He lifts a thick folder from a filing cabinet, and a great wedge of old MOTs and garage invoices falls out, like the medical records of a terminally ill patient. The hearse has been condemned, and in three months it will undergo and fail a road test. It awaits its own interment in the scrapyard – the only other tabled offer is from a man wanting to break the car up for parts.

At the back of the folder is a collection of photographs. Lakey pulls one out, a black and white shot of a funeral cortège showing a line of hearses processing between crowds.

'That's my hearse carrying Ronnie Kray to Chingford Cemetery.'

Whether or not Lakey can verify this claim, his hearse has ferried many men and women to their final destinations. It's a Daimler, the chosen means of conveyance for generations of royals, rock stars and ordinary folk, a rare beast from an age of no seat belts and silver ashtrays. The same marque that took Princess Diana to her temple up the cordoned-off M1, bystanders chasing the hearse along the empty motorway; the same as carried my grandfather to his grave, nine years before I was born.

I leaf through the folder and the car's history unravels itself: a stint ferrying bodies across the Highlands, a spell committing the Cornish dead to their graves, an interlude in Surrey. The last body the hearse buried was in 2008. The service sheet for the funeral is still in the glove compartment, a portrait of the dead woman bordered by lilies. Going back through the years at an average of three funerals a week, the coach has made thousands of trips to the graveside and crematorium.

Will she carry me on one final journey? I return to the driver's seat. Sitting on the worn leather and with the polished wood of the coffin deck stretched out at my back, the weight of memory seems to lie as thick as the rust in the footwell. I lean forward and adjust the rear-view mirror. The garage fills with the smoke of the vaping undertaker and the past seems to open up behind me.

After a week of protracted negotiation, the keys to the hearse are finally mine. The car has been delivered cross-country to a local welder in Suffolk, who does his best to patch her up, melting a mixture of aluminium and steel to the body and chassis. I collect the hearse from a warehouse where it has temporarily been stored, the building rising like a tin-clad temple out of the flat landscape.

Nothing moves in the yard. I'm dropped off at reception, where a row of pot plants lines the office windows. I peer inside – the room is bathed in green, as if a forest has sprouted between the desks and filing cabinets. A man sits in a corner eating a sandwich, and when I tap on the window he swivels round to stare blindly at the light. Moments later he emerges, smiling, with cress between his teeth and gripping my hand in fingers laced with flames, blue lightning and the open aorta of a bleeding heart.

Together we put our shoulders to the great warehouse door and it slides slowly open. I'm motioned towards the back of a cavernous space, a dimly lit corridor leading between packing crates and parked fork-lift trucks. As I wander alone into the darkest recesses, enormous coils of steel and cellophane-wrapped boxes emerge from the gloom. My footsteps echo on the concrete floor and strange thermals blow in from nowhere. At the far end, the hearse has been wedged between several tonnes of onions, crates stacked thirty feet high on either side.

I squeeze inside, and the whole car is perfumed with onion. Starting up the engine is like coaxing an old man out of a favourite armchair. I turn twin ignition keys and the petrol pumps make consumptive noises, pushing fuel along the car's extended underbelly. After several attempts the hearse is wrestled from its deep vegetable dreams.

Cautiously, I sidle out from the onion towers and back down the valley of containers, the cold engine faltering in the shadows. The warehouse door forms a stark square of light at the end of the tunnel. As I pass through, the interior of the hearse glows with the fire of a new spring day.

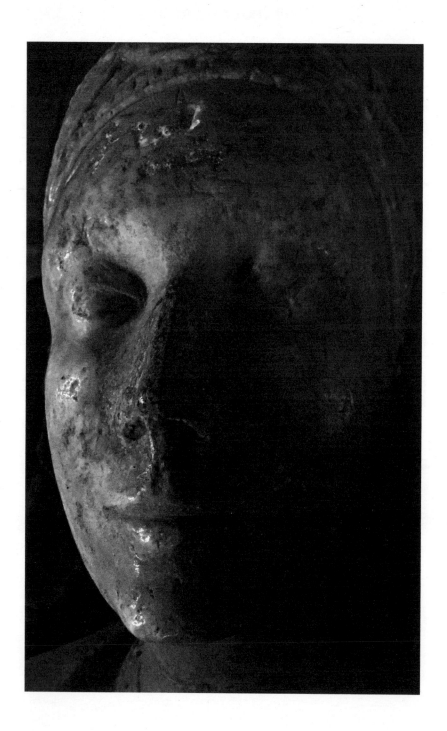

Chapter One

It seems fitting to go looking for the dead on a beautiful morning when the whole world is returning to life. The hearse slips quietly along overgrown Suffolk lanes, coasting between stands of blackthorn and nettles. At junctions with busier roads I wait for lines of speeding courier vans to pass by, as if England's interior is one enormous racing track for Parcelforce, UPS and DPD. I feel like a phantom, gliding over crossroads then disappearing again down dwindling lanes.

I've abandoned the wisdom of satellites for a road map as thick as a pulpit gospel, an old atlas filled with signs and symbols that never made it onto a computer database. To this I've added my own landmarks, the many tombs I've set out to see. Where possible I'm sticking obstinately to back roads, the byways that make up the in-between. Thomas Hardy once described lonely roads as possessing 'a tomb-like stillness', and they will fit my purpose well.

Every so often the car makes a distinct *cracking* sound, as if someone sits beside me on the driver's bench flexing their knuckles. It takes a few miles for my shoulders to relax, steering three tonnes of metal without a seat belt. I drive so slowly that the noise of a garden wind chime can be heard through the open window.

It's surprising to find out who's buried within a few miles of your own home. I'm starting my journey on the edge of England, where the oldest graveyards spit their dead into the sea.

I grew up in Suffolk but never realised how like a skull the coast of East Anglia is. One side of the Wash forms the bone at the skull's base, rising to the dome across the beaches of north Norfolk. The tilted forehead extends south from Great Yarmouth to Walberswick, before the complex estuaries of Suffolk and Essex describe the nose, mouth and chin. The county lines appear like skull sutures dividing plates of bone.

I'm headed for a village that rests squarely in the skull's eye socket, the near mythical Dunwich, a once prosperous place that has slowly slipped into the sea. Like a child's sandcastle dissolving wave by wave, the buildings of the medieval town have crumbled to leave a last line of houses, a pub and a solitary church. It's a good beginning, this ghost town an apt reminder of my own impermanence.

As I cross Dunwich Heath a strong wind rocks the hearse on its axles. The road to the coast is narrow but glimmers with the light of the approaching sea. Hawthorn bushes detonate on the verge, blossom-heavy arms erupting like shell fragments from an explosion, and after ten miles the engine is radiating a fierce heat into the driver compartment, the gloss black paint of the hearse acting as an incubator and turning the interior into a cauldron. I'm grateful not to be wearing an undertaker's three-piece suit.

The hearse drags its heels along the final mile to the sea. At the height of its power there were eight churches in Dunwich, a handful of chapels and a monastery. Entering the village, I park under the massive, flint-topped walls of Greyfriars, the monastery ruin that shares the cliff top with All Saints', the last of the medieval churches to fall to the sea. A corner of its churchyard still survives on the lip of the cliff overlooking the beach.

Inside the monastic compound the only sign of life is a man grooming a horse, sheltering from the sun in a stable tied into the monastery walls. As I walk towards the cliff path the sound of the sea burrows through the empty arches of the monks' refectory building.

The remains of Pales Dyke edge the cliff top, a ditch that once served as a medieval sea defence. The monks were Franciscans, first settling here in 1289. As a child I had an illustrated book, *St Francis of Assisi*, which told the saint's story through pictures of a shoeless man talking to the birds of the air and the fishes of the sea. I try to imagine a 13th-century monk standing here and communing with a shoal of herring.

The last of the ground that formed the adjacent churchyard is cordoned off behind a wooden fence. I follow alongside until it branches out towards the brink, channelling me like a tourist to a much-touted view. At the end of this promontory stands a single grave, lost in a thick coppice of thorn that clings stubbornly to the cliff edge. A sign on the fence reads, '*The Last Grave of All Saints*'.

I hop over the railings to examine this local celebrity. The gravestone has broad shoulders and conjures an image of a similarly thickset man. A beetle basks on the stone lettering: *In memory of Jacob Forster who departed this life March 12th 1796 aged 38 years.* Behind the grave the cliff edge is a clean line, snapped off like a chocolate bar. Gaps in the thorn show the brown mass of the North Sea washing the beach far below.

The church Jacob was buried beside fell into disuse the year he was born. From 1758 no services were held, only baptisms and funerals. The graveyard crept closer to the cliff with every winter storm, but the inhabitants of Dunwich continued to bury their dead here. They had grown accustomed to their ancestors being swallowed by the sea.

At the base of his grave someone has left a tribute, a dried bunch of holly and yew held together with a single red ribbon. I'm surprised to find 'the last grave' is not alone and the broken stub of another headstone projects from the ground six feet behind it, while a third lies choked in weeds. Examining the back of Forster's grave, I discover a fresh pile of gravel heaped against it. Jacob's memory has been reinforced, propped up in an attempt to safeguard his celebrity. It seems the Suffolk tourist board shares my desire to hang on to the dead.

Returning over the fence, I descend the cliff path to the sea and double back along the beach. The shore is overflowing by the car park, day-trippers drawn like wasps to the waste bins and ice cream stalls, making it a few feet onto the shingle before collapsing under the weight of windbreaks and beach towels.

I trace a line beneath the cliff back towards the remnants of All Saints'. The crowd thins until I walk alone among clumps of flowering sea kale. The graveyard housed a radar station for much of the 1940s and, reaching the spot directly below Forster's grave, the cliff's base is littered with relics of wartime defences, steel 'hedgehogs' and concrete blocks.

The cliff is chequered with landslips and collapsed walls of clay and crag. Bones from the graveyard occasionally spill down onto the beach to be picked up and stored by locals, a village ossuary accruing in cottage windows and back gardens. I watch a jack rabbit return to a burrow under the cliff edge and wonder if he inhabits tunnels framed by human bones.

The body-snatching tides that claimed Dunwich have eroded other churchyards along England's east coast. Thirty miles north from here the fishing village of Eccles-on-Sea suffered a similar fate. In 1570 a storm tore through the high street and ripped the roof off the Norman church of St Mary's. The ruined building was soon pulled down and only the tower remained, standing above the sand dunes that bordered the village. An accidental lighthouse, it served as a sailors' landmark for the next three hundred years.

Another storm in the 19th century dissolved the dunes and left the tower stranded in the middle of the beach. Before the lonely edifice finally collapsed it became a famous tourist attraction. In *Norfolk Life*, Lillias Rider-Haggard recalled visiting as a child and bearing witness to an extraordinary event:

One September day years ago, when the tower of
Eccles Church still stood ... there came a north-easterly
gale and a 'scour' which swept the sand from the old
graveyard, leaving the long outlines of the graves
washed clean by the sea. In one lay an almost perfect
skeleton embedded in the clay, the hollow-eyed skull
gazing up at the limitless sweep of sky.

This vivid description shows what a lasting impression the
bodies on the beach made on Rider-Haggard, a memory that
stayed with her for the rest of her life.

Another St Mary's, in Whitby, North Yorkshire, has fought
a long-standing battle to prevent its dead from falling onto
the town below. Not even Bram Stoker, who used the churchyard as a setting for his famous *Dracula* novel, could have
envisaged the kind of gothic horror that unfolded in 2012
when heavy rainfall caused human bones to fall from their
clifftop graveyard and batter the roofs and back yards of the
sea-front buildings.

Before returning to the baking heat of the hearse, I decide
to explore the Dunwich of old by going for a swim. The drop-
off is steep and I sink into windswept water, the cliff rising
and falling with the swell. To the south a strange white edifice
bobs above the waves like a giant beach ball. This is a landmark of my Suffolk childhood, the enormous dome of Sizewell
B nuclear power station. The reactor sits hunkered down in
sand dunes but from my vantage point it seems to have come
untethered, floating off towards Holland. My dad had a
theory that the water was three degrees warmer in front of

the reactor – anything that took the edge off the North Sea seemed a good idea.

Material from Sizewell's outflow is borne towards the underwater ruins of Dunwich on every ebb tide. I float in a shallow sea, a mixture of medieval stone and bone jostling around beneath my feet. The traces of the old town extend for over a mile offshore but are near invisible in the murky water.

This has not deterred explorers from trying to find the lost churches under the sea. Strapping weights to their belts, divers have walked the seabed with arms outstretched, clutching at flint and mortar ruins like blind men feeling their way into the past. In 2008 one diver reported finding himself in a room with walls on every side, unable to see what medieval dead end he'd wandered into. Some of these divers have reconstructed the ruins in haunting sketches, pictures of things they felt but never saw.

I'm roused by a wave that rolls in over my head, causing me to inhale the sea through my nose. I sneeze salt water and look for the shore. At first, I can see nothing across the contours of the waves and experience a dizzying dread of deep water. Then I spot the cliff, an irregular line that's shrunk to a third of its former size.

I've drifted a long way out and start swimming hard for the beach. Regaining the shore, I climb exhausted from the surf, staggering up the shingle and collapsing like one more splayed skeleton beneath the old graveyard. Lifting my head, I find myself surrounded by the scattered egg cases of sharks – bull huss and lesser-spotted dogfish. I pick one up, a bubble-like leather pouch with four horns projecting at the corners. There is an old east coast tale that when fishermen die they become seagulls, but it looks as though the souls of All Saints' are being reincarnated as sharks.

I'm wind-dry within five minutes and dress before returning along the shingle and back through the ruined friary to the hearse. I drive past the Ship Inn and stop at the 'new' church in Dunwich, built in 1832 as All Saints' slowly crumbled into the sea.

St James stands above the marshes inland from the beach, next to the remains of a lepers' chapel and medieval hospital, an indication of how remote from the old town centre it once was. Near the gate into the graveyard is the last buttress of All Saints', rescued from the cliff top and placed here as a reminder of what went before. It sticks out above the graves, flint-cobbled and broken off on one side, still bearing the 19th-century graffiti of tourists who visited the doomed church. Their scrawls seem to cry out in chorus, 'Dunwich was here'.

When the buttress was moved to St James, some surviving headstones accompanied it, transplanted from the old churchyard to the new. I have a hunt around the graves for John Brinkley Easey, a headstone I remember from picture postcards of the town. My search proves fruitless. There was a trade in hauling the last headstones off the beach, to sell or reuse, and Easey's memorial probably ended as paving in someone's front garden.

I return to the hearse and turn inland, pulling clear of the village and the coast. Thistledown blows across the windscreen and the road shimmers in the heat. It seems the residents of Dunwich have attained their own kind of immortality, bones ground into fragments to mingle with the ever-shifting sand.

In the early hours of 17 June 1917 a strange light flickered through drawn curtains in the Suffolk village of Theberton. The light intensified until it coloured bedroom walls blood red and sodium yellow, as if hell fires raged outside every window. People stumbled outside, half-dressed, and stood with their faces turned to the sky.

High above the village an enormous zeppelin, six hundred feet long, was on fire. At first the blaze was as silent as the stars all around it. Then the roar of the flames reached the ears of those gathering below. A woman woken by the sound described a noise like a tractor ploughing through the sky.

The zeppelin took fully five minutes to fall to earth, a great Chinese lantern drifting low over the village. As it fell its fabric was torn away by the flames, exposing the metal endoskeleton. While it was still several hundred feet above the ground the frame buckled, forming a huge burning 'V' in the dawn sky. The awestruck villagers were watching death in slow motion. Above them, eighteen German airmen fought for their lives beneath the airship's burning underbelly.

I turn into Theberton past 'Wild About Birds', a store selling every conceivable avian delight, and follow a low brick wall along Church Road. St Peter's lies cheek by jowl with the village hall, and I draw up in the car park between two pink camper vans. I've come looking for the graves of the men who fell from the sky over a century ago.

Stepping into the churchyard, I pass sarcophagi erupting with the shoots of a dozen weeds, more like plant pots than coffins. Perhaps this is the true measure of a grave's success, the body that proves most fertile.

A carving of a woman's head watches me from the church eaves, her face wrapped in thick folds of drapery. Only the eyes and nose remain visible, and beneath her chin a mountain of owl pellets is piled high against the wall, her headgear vital protection against the bird that uses her for a latrine. I stoop and pick up one of the dried pellets and break it open. Entombed within are the minute bones of the owl's prey: mice, shrews and voles. I wonder how many hundreds lie here in this miniature cemetery, a microcosm of the churchyard beyond.

Inside the porch I find the zeppelin's ghost. Part of the wreckage hangs in a glass display case on the wall, aluminium struts bolted together like a primitive cross covered with cobwebs. Beneath the case a row of photographs show the crop field on Holly Tree Farm where the airship fell. Soldiers climb through the wreckage like children lost in a maze, nervously grinning at the camera. In one photograph the airship's nose cone is being lifted intact from the wreck. It looks like the fallen dome of a great Victorian glasshouse, a piece of the Crystal Palace lost in the middle of a field.

The twenty-five tonnes of the zeppelin's frame were cut up and carted off to be studied by British engineers. On the way, scraps fell off the back of trucks and were eagerly picked up by sightseers who had arrived in the wake of the crash. Souvenirs were fashioned out of the wreckage: candlesticks, rings, ashtrays, even the statue of a carthorse. Parts of this German giant live on in the kitchens and parlours of Suffolk cottages.

As I stand looking up at the zeppelin cross, an elderly man with his arms full of prayer books emerges from inside the church.

'Hullo,' he says cheerily. 'Looking for the Germans?'

He explains that the war memorial lies on the other side of the road. I thank him and make to leave, but he catches hold of my arm.

'You've got to see John Fenn first,' he says, grinning with a flash of dentures.

Just outside the porch a table tomb hugs the wall, with a jar of daffodils framing the first lines of an inscription:

> Here is a stone to sit upon,
> under which lies in hopes to rise
> … honest John Fenn.

Not many graves invite you to perch on them, but the old man motions me to climb up. Feeling slightly foolish, I lift myself onto the slab and dangle my feet. The tomb faces south and the stone is warm from the morning sun. Strands of ivy tickle the back of my neck as my impromptu guide narrates the occupant's story.

'Fenn was rector here at St Peter's at the outset of the English Civil War. His loyalty to King Charles got him booted out of his own church.'

The man pats the lid of the tomb affectionately.

'Fenn's revenge was this tomb outside the door of the place that turned its back on him.'

My guide is ancient and yet as animated as a child telling a favourite story. He puts down his armful of prayer books and joins me on the table tomb. We sit side by side, the old and young brooding over the grave. He points out a buttress beside the tomb with a medieval mass dial scratched into the stone, indicating the service times before the advent of clocks. Four hundred and forty-five years of weary parishioners have sat on John Fenn.

I bid the old man farewell beneath a gargoyle, designed to channel rainwater into an iron grate at the grave's base. In heavy weather a small waterfall must arch over the rector's bones. The memorial to the zeppelin crew lies in an extension of the graveyard and a large, chestnut-coloured cat bolts past me as I open the gate. At the back of the burial ground is a sheet of tin attached to wooden slats with a line from Romans: *Who art thou that judgest another man's servant?* The badly burned bodies of the airmen were buried here under sixteen matching stones.

Whatever afterlife the German aviators believed in, it could have hardly involved more extreme visions of heaven and hell than those they witnessed in the sky above Suffolk. The ill-fated zeppelin – painted jet black for night flying and shaped like a super-sized bomb – began its journey in the heart of a German forest. From the open windows of their gondola the aviators had a god-like perspective on the earth, watching thunderstorms play out and tracing patterns on the

JACK COOKE

sea. It was a cold kind of paradise, where they wrapped themselves in fur coats and fought to catch every breath.

The distant remove of this other world evaporated over England. Artillery searchlights probed the sky and hundreds of guns lit up the dark landscape below, shells exploding on every side of the fragile hull. At the same time the Germans released their bombs, their dull thud punctuating the cacophony of the artillery.

Although the zeppelin survived the ground barrage its engines began to fail and it dropped to lower altitude, attempting to catch tailwinds that would deliver it home across the North Sea. This brought it within the range of British pilots, and three different planes pursued the stricken airship across the dawn sky. Firing round after round of incendiary bullets, one of them struck his target and the zeppelin's gas cells burst into flame.

Standing in the forward gondola as the zeppelin fell earthward, trapped in a cage of red-hot metal with flames and gas pouring in on all sides, Lieutenant Otto Meith later recalled locking eyes with his captain:

> Absolute silence reigned [...] Only the roar of the flames was audible. Not a man had left his post. Everyone stood waiting for the great experience – the end.

Meith was one of only two survivors pulled from the wreck. The zeppelin's commander, Franz Eichler, threw himself from the front of the burning gondola with four others, and their bodies were found in a neat line stretched out across a corn-field, like toy soldiers discarded by a child.

The crew's graves remained undisturbed for half a century. Then in the 1970s a new cemetery was built at Cannock Chase in Staffordshire to house German war dead scattered around the British Isles. All over the country bodies were exhumed, nearly five thousand dug up from small graveyards like this.

A thin fence divides the former graves from the back gardens of a housing terrace, and boys play football behind the panels. Fifty years in Suffolk soil had reduced the zeppelin crew to a few solitary relics. Soil and bone were moved to the Midlands, carted in containers along newly built motorways to rest among their kin. The ground around the memorial is now occupied with the fresh graves of Suffolk farmers.

As I drive out of Theberton on Pretty Road I stop by the village sign. A model of the church has been painted matt grey with yellow windows, glowing as if lit by candlelight. A tall oak fans out in silhouette behind the roofline and the whole scene has an atmosphere of first light. At the very edge of the frame something else intrudes, a strange conical shape drifting east in the empty spaces beyond the village.

Under the noonday sun the road has become a drawing board for shadows. Telegraph wires fragment the lane into geometry lessons and birds cast silhouettes as they pass overhead. I drive beneath an advertisement for 'The Harmony Healing Centre' next to an enormous silo of chicken shit. Further on, laundry blows on a washing line as I bounce over a railway crossing.

At thirty-three years old I'm already in decline. My physical peak has come and gone, and I failed to notice. In another decade my brain cells will start to die in droves. Already, parts of my body seem to be undergoing necrosis; my feet yellowed and calloused. After a certain age we are all in the process of dying and unless we're forced to contemplate death by its imminence, or the loss of a loved one, we do our best to ignore it. It was high time I took the process seriously.

On the outskirts of Ipswich I pass another hearse travelling in the opposite direction, a motorbike with a coffin carried along in a sidecar. It reminds me of the gravedigger in Ronald Blythe's *Akenfield*, riding a moped with a spade and fork tied to the rear ('Time's winged chariot with a two-stroke'). The machine is followed by a procession of men riding cruisers, choppers and touring motorbikes. We face each other at a traffic light. The bikers' engines grumble out of tune but explode with a common voice when the light turns green.

I'm hunting for a grave lost in suburbia, the memorial of a suicide buried beside the road. Burying people on the verge was common well into the 19th century, a means of rejection, labelling suicides as outcasts. Anyone who took their own life was considered unfit for Christian burial and the details of their lives stood little chance of enduring.

Ironically the shared memory of such events often led to the roads acquiring nicknames. *Deadman's Lane*, *Deadman's Bottom* and *Deadman's Cross* all attest to this practice, the common usage of such names eventually resulting in their adoption by mapmakers. Occasionally, the name of the individual would also survive. Such is the case with the grave I search for now.

I turn into Dobbs Lane past a Domino's pizza takeaway. The hearse is flanked by neat bungalows, front gardens full of manicured, bonsai-scale shrubberies. After half a mile the bungalows give way to woodland, lines of trees carved into tunnels by passing lorries. Although Dobbs's Christian name is uncertain, he shares with the rich and famous the honour of having a road named after him; instead of casting him into obscurity, his roadside burial has enshrined his legend. Dobbs's memory will be recalled by house numbers and signposts long after his contemporaries' headstones have crumbled.

I scan the road's margin for signs of the grave but a hedge of gorse and wild roses hides the interior. I'm working from an old photograph taken when the area was heathland and the road newly metalled; what was once a stretch of countryside is now a densely populated suburb. I slow down alongside a man in lime green jogging bottoms and ask him for directions. He jogs nervously on the spot before pointing into a copse of trees a hundred metres ahead.

A footpath leads into the wood opposite a hubcap caught in the hedge, like a silver medallion hanging among the roses. A number of lost-dog appeals have been stapled to the sign, seeking the return of 'Snowball', 'Daisy' and other missing canines.

Dobbs's grave lies among oaks a short distance from the road. The wood is full of birdsong and periodic screams from a primary school in Kesgrave. The burial has been cordoned off from the footpath by ornate iron railings, with a small gate set near the headstone. There's no lock, and when I lift the latch the gate swings inward, rustling dried leaves that have collected inside. Behind the enclosure is a mound in the grass, as if the grave diggings were left in place to grow over.

It seems Dobbs's death had something to do with sheep. One version of his story tells of an 18th-century shepherd who hanged himself when he lost his flock, another of a gypsy on the run for sheep theft who took his own life. Whatever the truth, for many years after Dobbs's committal shepherds were reputed to have tended the grave. The last drover has long since vanished from Kesgrave and the lane now echoes with engines instead of bleating lambs.

Curiously, the grave still survives, locals taking it upon themselves to preserve the memory of 'Gypsy Dobbs'. Between 1900 and 1909, two stones were placed on either end of the grave to permanently mark the spot. I squat down beside the headstone, which bears no inscription other than a deeply etched cross. The grave has clearly been vandalised as well as venerated, and a great V-shaped lump of rock has fallen from the face as if someone struck it with a hammer.

While I'm examining Dobbs's memorial, something stirs in the trees. A moment later a large black bull terrier erupts from the undergrowth, barking wildly, and bolts towards me. Reaching the grave, it leaps in an effort to hurdle the railings, falls to the ground, then starts grinding its teeth on the bars.

Instinctively, I back up against Dobbs. The dog begins conducting circuits around the grave, snarling and searching for a point of entry. I wonder if this is one of the lost dogs of Kesgrave, a wild creature living on the edge of Ipswich and subsisting on lone walkers. Tentatively, I try 'Down, Daisy' and 'Sit, Snowball', but these commands only seem to stoke the black dog's fury and it lets out a low, guttural growl from between bared fangs. Perhaps it's the spirit of Dobbs himself, outraged to find me sitting on his bones.

Just as I consider making a mad dash for the hearse, a woman appears on the footpath. I'm still cowering behind the gravestone. She looks at me with deep contempt before striding over and shackling the dog. The two of them disappear again without a word, the dog staring over its shoulder with bloodshot eyes. I remain with Dobbs for some time until I'm confident the beast and its mistress are gone.

Back in the safety of the hearse, I leave Dobbs Lane and drive to the nearby Bell Inn. The pub plays a part in Dobbs's story and I'm in need of something to settle my nerves. I order a cheese and pickle sandwich and find a table next to a window that looks onto the graveyard of a church, the very place where Dobbs might have been buried had he not taken his own life.

On another sultry day many years ago, this room played host to a group of men on their way home from harvest. After drinking heavily to celebrate the crop, one of them recounted the story of Dobbs's infamous burial. The others refused to believe him, deciding to visit the grave and satisfy themselves that there really was a body. On uncovering the corpse, one man was alleged to have removed a tooth from the skeleton's jaw and worn it as a pendant.

Today the Bell is decked out with slot machines and television sets and seems a far cry from a farmers' pub in a field by a lonely highway. But whatever has changed around him, Dobbs remains in his plot. The people of Kesgrave continue to guard his memory.

When I return to the hearse the bonnet has been covered in white lace, deposited by a satisfied-looking pigeon in the pub car park. I take this for a good omen.

I join the Ipswich ring road. As the traffic solidifies, I'm acutely aware of the constant threat of mechanical failure, my heart rate seeming to mimic the stuttering engine in the afternoon heat. I pull in to a filling station and open the bonnet, letting off a cloud of steam. The hearse is a thirsty beast and the primary fuel tank is nearly spent after my morning's grave-hopping. Even without the weight of a coffin, the car barely seems to scrape five miles to the gallon.

Back on the road, I pass the gates of Ipswich Old and New Cemeteries. An ice cream cone lies upended by the sign for the cemetery car park, an incongruous pink dribble between ranks of grey headstones. On top of the crematorium chapel a magpie admires its reflection in the polished steel of the chimney cap, and beyond, a line of men with strimmers process between the graves, clad in matching black khaki like Grim Reapers wielding petrol-powered scythes.

The two cemeteries are still open for burial but have largely been superseded by the Millennium Cemetery on the town's outskirts. Ipswich expels its dead further into the countryside with each passing generation. The town's original burial grounds were its medieval churchyards, now stranded on traffic islands in the centre. Once they would have been at the heart of town life, a space where children ran, laundry aired, chickens pecked, men brawled and drunks slept off their stupors. Today these graveyards have been squeezed by town planners until their headstones look like broken teeth waiting to be pulled.

The town's suburbs fade west of Washbrook and industrial estates are replaced with long lines of sentinel oaks. I struggle to negotiate the hearse through a series of tight roundabouts. The steering wheel is broader than the span of my shoulders and I grapple with it like a ship's wheel, battling the high seas of the A1214.

Miles go by through fields of spring barley that seem to have no horizon. The interior of the hearse has become a furnace once more and a police car slows to let me pass, the driver's gaze lingering on me as I sweat behind the wheel. The polished chrome of the coffin deck reflects the sunlight and even a corpse fresh from the morgue would soon spoil in this inescapable heat. I try pushing a button on the dashboard marked 'Air' but a sinister line of smoke issues from the socket. I hastily turn it off again.

On Saxon Lane I receive unexpected deliverance. I miss the warning sign, a deep puddle on an otherwise dry road, and get the full force of a crop irrigator through the open window. The windscreen is momentarily veiled, as if going through a car wash, and water drips off the steering and pools in my lap. I stop, step out of the car and shake myself like a dog.

There is no witness to my baptism, just the sun-stroked fields and the rhythmic tick of the irrigator.

Quietly steaming on a bank beside the road, I consult my map. I'm headed back in time from the 19th-century tombstones of the Ipswich cemeteries to something older, something almost forgotten. I'm bound for a land of knights and dragons, a place as arcane as the cemeteries were planned and plotted. Somewhere in this border country lies a small chapel with some peculiar relics.

Continuing on my way, a water meadow on one side of the road is home to a thatched cottage surrounded by pigs rooting in the mud. It's like an illustration from a Grimm Brothers' fairy tale and I half expect to see a witch sitting on the porch casually chewing on the thighbone of a child.

The directions I've scribbled on the margins of my map guide me into the village of Bures. The name derives from a Celtic word for boundary, and the houses straddle the county line between Suffolk and Essex. I turn up Cuckoo Hill beneath a Tudor-framed building that hangs over the street like a fat man's belly over a belt. The hearse grumbles up the incline and I pull in to the forecourt of a farmyard.

An ominous array of signage guards the entrance: *You are being watched* and *Beware of the Dog* above an illustration of an Alsatian with open jaws. Among these warnings is a hand-painted placard for the chapel car park, tucked in behind a warehouse covered in solar panels.

I park the hearse in suitably strange company, between an abandoned school bus on bricks and an ice cream truck with its shutters down. A dirt track leads off into the distance through a field of maize and I start walking, relieved not to be pursued by another deranged dog. The maize brings to mind an old nickname for this place, 'the chapel in the corn', and when I stop beside a bend in the track I find I've accrued a host of insect acolytes, flies circling my head and grasshoppers landing on my chest and arms. A little further on and the chapel appears behind a hedgerow.

In 855 this place is rumoured to have played host to the coronation of a Saxon king. The building is much changed since then, a jumble of mismatched parts like a jigsaw put together the wrong way. Sacked during the Reformation and split into cottages for farmhands, the chapel later became a storage barn filled with cattle feed. The cobbled exterior is interrupted by old, filled-in entrances, holes knocked through the walls to allow carts to be wheeled in and out, and a clapboard extension has been added to the west end. The chapel could easily be mistaken for a farm shed.

I enter through a small door in the north side of the building, and the temperature drops by ten degrees. The chapel is an oasis, cool and dark, and I stumble over an uneven floor as my eyes adjust to the gloom. Two massive shapes resolve in front of me, cramming the chapel's central aisle and overwhelming a scattering of chairs on either side. A third looms out of the corner, the space seeming to shrink around it.

These are the table tombs of long-dead nobles. They are disproportionate in size, filling the small chapel so that they overpower it. The tombs seem to belong under the high ceiling of a great cathedral and I feel as if I should go forward on bended knee. I walk over and reach out to touch the cold stone of the nearest tomb.

Originally these tombs sat beside nineteen others in a great mausoleum at Earls Colne Priory. They belonged to the de Vere dynasty, Earls of Oxford, who ruled this part of the country for many centuries. The tombs have not rested here long, and the odyssey of their survival is as curious as the building in which they now sit.

In the late 15th century the priory mausoleum was considered one of the greatest collections of effigies anywhere in England. When the monastery was dissolved the mausoleum was plundered and most of the tombs destroyed or damaged beyond repair. A 17th-century chronicler described the sad state of the old burial hall, 'razed to the ground … the bones of the ancient Earls left under the open air'.

And yet that was not the end of their story. Thirteen tombs survived either whole or in fragments. Ten of these languished in the ruins of the priory for the next hundred years until an antiquarian arranged to 'cart' them to London by water. The plan never came to pass, and another century came and went while the tombs further decayed. Sadly, in 1736 their remains were chopped into pieces to build new fireplaces at Earls Colne House.

Three of the tombs fared better. Taken from the mausoleum before the priory's destruction, they were placed in the parish church. Here they remained until 1825, when the vicar, keen to make space for improvements, threatened to bury the enormous tomb chests in his churchyard. Henry Cawardine, then living at Earls Colne House, had them moved to a new gallery of his own design. Here they sat gathering dust well into the 20th century, apparently used to hold tennis racquets.

The chapel, meanwhile, had continued as glorified farm storage, more ruinous with every passing year. In the 1920s a woman called Isabella Badcock and her brother-in-law, Colonel William Probert, began an ambitious restoration. The Proberts owned the land and the whole family pooled their talents to bring the chapel back from oblivion, reinstating the original layout and putting glass into the empty windows. In 1935, when the work was finally completed, Colonel Probert looked for something to crown this remodelled sanctuary. He settled on the three tomb chests languishing in the gallery at Earls Colne House.

How they were moved here remains a mystery. They may have been shipped on the now defunct railway that used to run through Bures. I try imagining this great procession, the knights' effigies riding in state on a steam train through the Suffolk countryside, then hauled up the hill to the chapel on flatbed trucks.

I examine the tomb closest to the altar. The 8th Earl of Oxford, Thomas de Vere, looks like he is suffocating inside his armour, eyes bulging and tongue sticking out above a chin encased in chain mail. The earl's face has been badly damaged, and much of his body is covered in graffiti. His calf is marked by a 16th-century scrawl that looks like it was dug out with a blunt knife.

The earl's stone biceps are highly polished, like a prize-fighter whose muscles have been felt by generations of admirers. And indeed he was, a distinguished soldier who fought many battles under Edward III, the king who started the Hundred Years' War with France.

The 11th Earl, Richard de Vere, also swung a sword from the saddle, commanding a large portion of Henry V's forces at Agincourt, a culmination of the conflict begun by his great-grandfather. His tomb sits behind the first, his head resting on a helmet with a magnificent boar on the crest, the de Vere family emblem.

I cross to the 5th Earl, Robert de Vere, relegated to a corner of the chapel. He stares at the ceiling with barely concealed contempt. His feet rest on another large boar, which looks lovingly at its master, iron pins projecting from the stone where it's missing an ear. On either side of Robert's jaw kneel his headless children. He died in 1296.

The earls have had various noses, arms and calves restored, cut off by the men who desecrated the mausoleum where they originally lay. The weepers' faces that line the tomb chests are all the more poignant for having melted away.

More impressive than any of these storied warriors is the figure of a woman lying beside the 11th Earl. Her forehead is heavily pitted and scarred, and there are deep cuts in her cheeks and eyelids. Her nose has also been struck off and replaced from the bridge down to the nostrils. In spite of this vandalism, and the passage of time, she remains incredibly beautiful. I'm spellbound, surprised to find myself physically attracted to the 626-year-old effigy of a dead woman. The earl's wife is the archetypal sleeping beauty, but it's a cold splendour and the countess invites no kiss to wake her. At her feet two collared hounds playfully snap at her skirts.

The other ornaments in the chapel are sparse. Beneath a ceiling of cracked lime plaster, the hollow capital of a magnificent column serves for a font and a cast concrete altar dates from the building's restoration.

As I make to leave, I find myself transfixed by light shining through the chapel's west window. The sun has penetrated through holes in the clapboard beyond and the stained glass puts on a kaleidoscopic display of orange and amber, colouring the cold effigies and warming their stone limbs.

Walking around the chapel's perimeter I find the final resting place of its principal restorers. Isabella Badcock and Colonel Probert lie against the southern wall, their humble graves contrasting with the grandeur of the tombs they helped to save. No effigies adorn their plot.

Beyond the chapel the hillside falls away into a valley, and on the far side an enormous dragon has been etched in chalk. This is another product of local legend, a monster said to have terrorised the village in the 14th century, slaughtering sheep and evading capture.

The modern dragon is the creation of Sir Geoffrey Probert, a man with an aquiline nose strikingly reminiscent of the dead knights. Sir Geoffrey is the colonel's great-grandson and revived the legend in 2012, painstakingly mowing the serpent's image into the field. Today the dragon seems more like a guardian of the dead than a medieval monster, ready to return should anyone dare disturb their peace.

The chapel, the dragon and the empty valley hold me in their thrall for an hour or more. I sign the 'guestbook', stored in a wooden box beneath an oak tree. As I lift the latch a swarm of earwigs bursts out across the lid and over my hands, and I dance around the tree trying to shake them off. Eventually I turn from the tombs and make my way back along the track, the sightless eyes of the countess following me through the corn.

Beyond Sudbury I cross over the River Stour, and the sun is low in the west as I drive through the village of Foxearth. I've lined the long windows of the coffin deck with reflective panels and the hearse sparkles when they catch the last light, as if a miracle of resurrection is going on behind them.

On the inside I have a single bed beneath the coffin deck. The hearse was made to accommodate any corpse, from a child's coffin to the burden of a giant. Consequently, there's ample space for a decent-sized mattress. On top of this I have my faithful sleeping bag, a snug fit reminiscent of the burial shrouds used in medieval England, sewn shut over those who could not afford coffins. Lying below deck and with the sleeping bag zipped up to my nose I am perfectly cocooned, a living mummy sandwiched between petrol tanks. If a thief tried to steal the hearse in the night, I'd only have to make sepulchral sounds from these hidden quarters. Anyone without a heart of steel should run screaming into the sunrise.

The outer panels of the coffin deck serve as bookshelves, with various maps, biographies and bedtime reading arranged in rows. *Death in England: An Illustrated History* shares shelf-space with *Funerals: And How to Improve Them* and J. B. Bradfield's guide to do-it-yourself burial. The enormous black bulk of *The Oxford Book of Death* acts as a bookend, propping up the rest. I've also stowed cooking essentials, a spare tyre, tool kit, traffic cone and fire extinguisher, and photographs of various (living) relatives. The fantastic volume of space makes the hearse an excellent packhorse and I've made it far comfier than it ever was for the deceased.

Leaving Foxearth, I find myself alone on an empty road. At day's end I'm looking for a lost wonder of the world, three burial mounds once given the grand title 'The Pyramids of Essex'. Today they're simply known as the Bartlow Hills, a footnote in out-of-print guidebooks.

Bartlow is a crossroads hamlet, a scattering of houses clinging to the junction between two roads, and I nearly drive in and out without noticing. Only the village sign catches my eye on an otherwise deserted lane, the image of three green hills swinging in the evening breeze beside a telephone booth. I park the hearse and wander on foot into a small clutch of houses.

Bartlow used to belong to Aubrey de Vere, forefather of the earls I've left lying in the chapel at Bures. The burial mounds were part of his inheritance, ancient barrows built in the 1st century AD and already a thousand years old by the time he came here. They represent a kind of mongrel burial, British nobles interred with Roman rituals but inside traditional barrows, as if reluctant to relinquish their old gods.

From my map I know the hills lie somewhere south of the village church. I find St Mary's set back from the road, propped up by an enormous round tower at one end. The path through the churchyard forks left and disappears through a gap in the perimeter wall. I shuffle between brick piers and onto a winding woodland track. In the undergrowth lie the remains of an old railway signal box, glass punched out of the windows and the wooden frame split at the corners. Bartlow was connected to a seven-mile stretch of railway in 1866, running across hayfields from Saffron Walden. The track cut straight through some of the original burial mounds, flattening them in the process and uncovering trenches containing the remains of a Roman cemetery. A century later and the branch line was already abandoned.

I step through a screen of trees, and there, rising above me with their sides in shadow and their summits in the sun, are the three ancient barrows. There's no signpost and everything is rampantly overgrown. The largest mound has a set of wooden steps half-hidden in the undergrowth, and I climb through cow parsley, hemlock and a dozen other flowering weeds, the air thick to breathe. I count sixty-three steps before emerging on the hilltop.

Early photographs show the hills well mown and capped with ash trees, shading the summits like giant parasols. Today they're crowned by sycamore shoots and long grass, and I have to wade through the undergrowth until, nearing the centre, I'm suddenly pitched forward into an unseen hole. I find myself flat on my face, surrounded by old beer cans and cigarette ends.

Clearly a favourite haunt for locals, this hidden hollow is the remains of one of the early excavations on the hill, when a team dug down from the top into the heart of the mound. The first recorded dig was by a man called Busick Harwood, who used the premise of a local treasure hunt to provide work for unemployed men. His team of tomb raiders dug into the top of the northernmost mound until they struck the cist buried in the middle. Unfortunately, whatever they found was pocketed or dispersed.

A few decades later, the task was taken up by an antiquarian called John Gage, assisted in his work by a middle-aged Michael Faraday, soon to wash his hands of grave digging to devote himself to his study of electricity. A series of digs through the 1830s and 40s explored all eight original mounds, including those that have since vanished.

Each hill was found to contain the remains of a single man or woman. The bones and ash of the cremated individuals had been placed in glass urns and bottles and secured in wooden chests. In one instance the chest was replaced with a brick vault. Alongside their mortal remains, the chests and vault contained sacrificial vessels and household goods. Some of these were beautifully intricate, such as a gold signet ring with an intaglio of two sheafs of wheat.

Alone in the hollow, I'm sitting on top of the richest of the surviving hills. The man interred here was buried in a bronze urn, enamelled with red, blue and green foliage. A folding iron chair of a type used by Roman magistrates was also recovered from his tomb chest. These precious finds were taken to Easton Lodge, twenty miles away, an Elizabethan timber-framed house that suffered a devastating fire two years later. After two millennia in the ground, all these grave goods were consumed in a single night. I try to picture this second cremation, the bronze urn melting in the blaze and bleeding into the ground.

The numerous burrowings, in-fills and excavations Hardwick, Gage and others made in the hills created a warren of unstable archaeology. So it was that in 1919 a visitor to the site recorded the following discovery:

> ... the old excavation tunnel of 1840 fell in at the entrance and going along it I found that the hill had been dug down from the top at some time and the shaft filled up with rubble. In this rubble lies a skeleton, largely cleared by rabbits. It is laid out on its back in a natural position, covered and surrounded with large flints.

The skeleton the visitor stumbled on was not an original burial. It seems that after an unsuccessful dig some centuries ago, the pit formed was used to dispose of an inconvenient body, as if the culprits hoped the corpse might be confused with ancient bones.

I have dinner in the Three Hills pub, back near the village crossroads. Like the village green, the pub also has a sign depicting its namesake attraction. This rendering shows a family in the foreground with their backs turned, a black dog beside them. The man and woman hold hands while their child points to the nearest barrow and the dog stares at something out of the frame. The whole scene is painted like a bad waxwork. The abiding impression is not of a happy family outing but the chance alignment of three people with the three mounds, as if the hills represent a premonition of their own interment.

I eat my meal at the bar, next to a man in motorcycle leathers. In the space of five minutes he has bared his soul to the pub, directing his story at no one in particular. He has a girlfriend twenty years his senior, wants to visit Iceland and loves nothing more than his 1957 Norton Manx motorcycle. When people enter or leave he starts up again, like a human slot machine waiting for loose change.

Returning to the hills in the last of the gloaming, I climb the southernmost mound. It is the wildest of the three, with the newly risen moon caught up in the cow parsley. I crawl on hands and knees up a steep path of exposed chalk and unroll my blanket in a bed of weeds. Lying down, I find myself surrounded by wild strawberries and pick a few to chew on. The fruit of the burial mound is sweet.

By the light of my head torch I read through the memoirs of Violet Maud Murkin, a woman who lived in Bartlow at the outset of the 20th century. She recalls the natural beauty of the hills as they were then, covered in bee orchids and 'ladies hair'. As a child she knew the area around the mounds as 'Three Hills Field', a place where the villagers held fairs and celebrated national events. When the barrows were first built they would also have served as a meeting place for ritual and rites now lost. Murkin records an unbroken tradition over two millennia, the hills retaining a role long after their original purpose was forgotten.

While Murkin was still living in Bartlow, a family called Brocklebank bought one of the big houses and most of the land around the village. Much of it was taken over by a shoot and the hills were enclosed. Murkin's writing speaks of loss, the hills taken from the village and allowed to grow wild for the sake of the shoot. In the 1960s, when she returned there as an old woman, she recalled, 'Those hills and fields we used to love were like a jungle.'

I turn off my torch and try to sleep, my imagination returning to the wooden chest that once lay under the hill. When the tombs were first prised open, iron lamps were found inside. The wicks were only partially burned, suggesting they had been left alight when the burials were sealed, like nightlights for fearful children. Perhaps they were intended to guide the way into the next world, a place populated by shared gods.

Waking intermittently, I watch the stars of the Plough revolve around the hill and the orange eye of Arcturus rise in the east. Its 37-year-old starlight competes with lines of jets flying out of Stansted airport. Dogs bark in the recesses of the village and cars speed past on the road beyond the treeline. I feel safe on my hilltop, invisible to the 21st century and cradled by an older order.

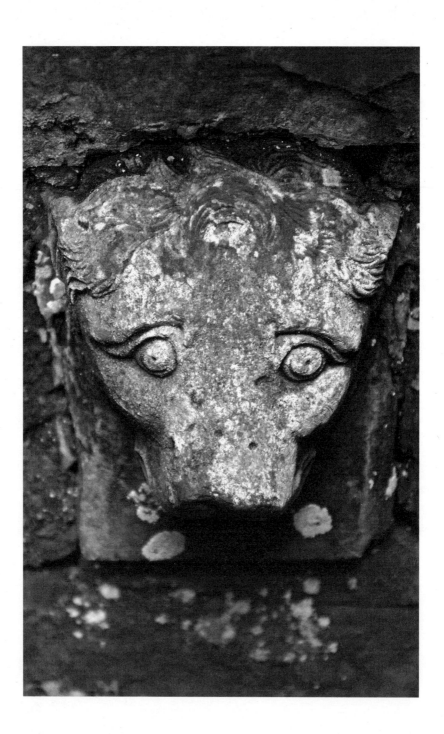

Chapter Two

· Willpower ·
· 'Into the Silent Land' ·
· A Night in the Cemetery ·

One winter's evening in 1712, two men walked home through the streets of Stevenage. Richard Tristram and Henry Trigg had been drinking at a favourite inn, and their feet slipped on icy cobbles as they made their way through the town.

Before they parted ways, they passed close to a churchyard. Faint lights shone from behind the wall and muffled sounds could be heard within. Curiosity got the better of the men. They crossed the road and climbed up to the lip of the wall to take a closer look. Inside the churchyard a lantern swayed above a grave. Figures moved in and out of the shadows and the rasp of spades on frozen ground echoed among the tombs.

What Tristram and Trigg witnessed was no supernatural apparition or graveyard ghoul. Far worse than these imagined horrors, the shadows they saw among the graves were men digging up the dead. They watched as a corpse was roughly pulled from a hole, hastily wrapped in a shroud and bundled into a cart.

The lantern-lit figures at work in Stevenage that night were body snatchers, later popularised as 'sack 'em ups' or 'resurrection men'. In the 18th century fresh corpses were in short supply for the teaching hospitals and anatomy schools springing up across England and Scotland. Tristram and Trigg lived in a time when body snatching was fast becoming a nationwide epidemic.

The grim spectacle they saw that winter's night made a deep and lasting impression. Both men swore a solemn pact never to let their own bodies suffer the same fate. The second day of my tomb tour begins with a quest to find their graves and discover whether or not they succeeded.

I descend from my hilltop encampment at first light. The burial mounds are wet with dew, and by the time I slip and slide my way to the bottom I'm soaked through. Drinking coffee on the tailgate of the hearse, I find my arms and face are covered with bites, courtesy of an entomological army living on the barrows.

The old coach takes some time to wake up, but eventually the engine ticks over and I return to the open road. The heavy morning mist clings to the fields and hollows outside Bartlow and the newly risen sun shines through the haze, edging the road with candyfloss. The ethereal atmosphere is soon dispelled by the sound of the gearbox, grinding with the indifference of false teeth.

Driving through the medieval streets of Saffron Walden, my head is full of yesterday's ghosts: Jacob Forster, Franz Eichler, the magnificent earls in their suits of armour. All these have paved my way and the hearse no longer seems empty. I imagine them side by side in the undertaker's seats behind me, the countess trying to avoid the shepherd Dobbs, his crook stowed under the coffin deck on which John Fenn is busy composing a sermon.

Outside Hitchin the air is laden with the smell of hot tar and the hearse skids on a freshly gravelled road, stones battering the underside like machine-gun volleys. I pull over in a lay-by filled with ankle-deep litter. Beyond the A602's constant tide of lorries and cars lies a sloping meadow with a scattering of sheep, the last farm on the outskirts of the town. Hidden somewhere in a corner of this field is the tomb of Richard Tristram.

Fear of the body snatchers forced people to go to great lengths to avoid relatives' graves being defiled. Large stones were placed on top of coffins to hinder digging and iron coffins with heavy locks were introduced, impregnable caskets for the recently deceased. 'Mortsafes' were also placed over tombs, latticeworks of iron bars hammered into the ground as if the dead were wild animals that needed to be caged. Once bodies had sufficiently decayed, the devices could be removed and reused. Sometimes iron straps were placed over the body itself, across the chest, waist, legs and ankles, shackling them to their coffins. Some graves even introduced booby traps, coffins rigged with spring-loaded guns.

All of these measures required money, and the poor remained easy prey for the resurrection men. A last resort was to stand vigil over newly dug graves, taking it in turn to watch over the departed. A few churches constructed special 'watchtowers' for this purpose, small, castle-like structures erected in the midst of the tombs. From here men could scan the graveyard from dusk till dawn.

Tristram devised his own scheme to escape the clutches of the body snatchers. He was a lawyer by trade, with an eye for detail, and his will made a series of specific requests. Rather than have his body consigned to a churchyard, he asked that his executors purchase land expressly for his burial and that this property be held in trust, watched over by successive generations. On Tristram's death in 1734 his son bought four acres in the parish and buried his father in open ground. For a period of one hundred and sixty-one years Tristram's tomb was guarded by the trustees, and any profits from the land were distributed to the poor. Then, in 1895, the field was sold.

I cross the busy road and follow a footpath alongside a stream bounding the field. A faded sign next to an electricity substation reads 'Rural Walk – no motorcycles please' and bags of dog shit hang neatly from tree branches like Christmas baubles. On the far side of the stream is what looks like a stone table, a hundred yards into the field next to a pile of sawn timber. I splash across and wrestle my way through a stand of nettles on the far bank.

The slab I saw from the footpath sits atop a brick base. The lettering cut into the stone is badly faded, but the Latin numerals 'XXXIV' can still be made out. At some point a corner has been prised off, later repaired with three iron braces now heavily rusted. A final demand made in Tristram's will was that he be buried within the sound of running water, but the stream I crossed to get here is inaudible over the constant traffic of the road. Tristram's epitaph once read 'Rest in Peace', but the sentiment has fittingly worn away.

I have a tea break sitting on the tomb while two buzzards circle low overhead. I hug my biscuits jealously, but the birds are after better pickings – the squashed rabbits and deer that pepper the A602. Sheep are all that the lawyer has for company, though they keep their distance at the field's other end. Woollen threads on the corners of the tomb reveal this is not always the case, the flock clearly fond of rubbing themselves on the dead man's memory.

A siren wails as an ambulance shoots past behind the hedge. In the field a breeze rustles the grass. Tristram's tomb exists in isolation, hidden in plain sight. The modern world rushes past a few feet away but never pauses. Perhaps this is exactly what he would have wished.

Having successfully located Tristram, I set out to hunt for his companion from that fateful night long ago. Henry Trigg – grocer, landlord, eccentric – chose a method of self-preservation that, as far as I know, has never been imitated.

Back on the road I come dangerously close to sliding into the business end of a cement truck. The hearse brakes like a horse, a four-hooves-in-the-sand sensation every time I squeeze the pedal. I queue into Stevenage through the serried ranks of the housing schemes that were wrapped around it in the 1950s, the tired buildings of the old town peeking from behind this post-war sprawl like an old woman in a crowd of teenagers. I park up behind Middle Row, a street that grew out of a market, stalls gradually replaced by buildings. I have to wedge the hearse into the only free slot, shunting back and forth until I'm safely stowed between a Volvo and a green Skoda.

Trigg desired that his body should rest not in the ground but in the air, balanced on the rafters of his barn, 'as to my body, I commit it to the west end of my hovel, to be decently laid there … upon the purlins'. He was so determined that his wishes be carried out that he left the majority of his estate to his brother, only on the condition that he fulfil these bizarre instructions.

How quickly legends spawn. The long-running *Gentleman's Magazine* published an article on Trigg's coffin only fifty years after his death. It alludes to the 'remains of a farmer' that left his worldly goods to his brother for a period of thirty years, at which point he claimed he would return to life. He 'also ordered his coffin to be affixed on a beam in the barn, locked, and the key to be inclosed, that he might let himself out'. As well as getting the date of Trigg's death wrong, the magazine suggested he believed in his own resurrection, not among the heavenly host but back where he began in Stevenage.

Middle Row is not as busy as it would have been in Henry Trigg's day, when hawkers lined the pavement selling their varied wares, and, walking through the thoroughfare, I sense that many of the shops had gone out of business. Through half-drawn shutters I glimpse a man squirrelled away under dim lights, imprisoned behind filing cabinets.

Trigg's old house on the high street is faceless from the front and flanked by an estate agent and the public toilets. I press my nose to the glass of the casement windows. Inside, the rooms are newly plastered and filled with paint pots and power tools. Skirting around to the rear of the building, I find a pair of steel gates opening onto a yard with parking bays and a builder's van drawn up next to the house. Squatting to one side is a lopsided barn, its timber frame sagging in the centre as if a great weight has being lying on the roof.

Trigg's will was carried out to the letter by his brother, eager to inherit, and his lofty grave became something of a local tourist attraction. In 1774 his former shop was sold and turned into a pub, the Old Castle Inn, but the coffin remained in place. Successive landlords milked the macabre attraction, and over the years locals couldn't resist climbing up to the coffin and stealing pieces of the skeleton as keepsakes: teeth, hair, even entire bones.

Stooping under the barn's low lintel I find a space crowded with sandbags, strips of insulation and stacks of breezeblock. The floor is covered in a thick layer of sawdust from a work-bench projecting into the yard. Expecting little, I shine a light into the rafters above me.

At first not much can be seen, the rafters cobwebbed and half hidden by stacks of cut timber. Then I see it, balanced across two joists, an unmistakable shape formed of wooden planks. The coffin has the aura of a forgotten museum display, an object shelved years ago and never dusted off. At some point the foot has been torn away and a pile of twigs protrudes from the open end. As I watch the head of a pigeon appears, like a cuckoo from a grandfather clock. It blinks furiously at me, then vanishes again.

By the time the East Herts Archaeological Society visited the coffin in the early 1900s, a third of the skeleton was already missing. The situation got worse, and over the course of the 20th century animal bones were substituted for missing parts. In 1999 the National Westminster bank bought the pub and discovered they had inherited what little remained of Henry Trigg. On the eve of the millennium his remaining bones were finally laid to rest, and the coffin was restored and replaced in its original position.

While I'm staring at the rafters, a man in overalls gets out of the van parked in the yard and strides over.

'This is private property,' he says, gesturing at the house and barn with a half-eaten Mars Bar.

'I just came to see the coffin.'

He pauses mid-chew. 'What coffin?'

I point above my head and the man steps in under the eaves and looks up. He seems unimpressed. I launch into the story of the body snatchers, Trigg's will and the legend of the coffin perched above us.

The man pretends to listen while checking his phone and finishing the Mars Bar. Suddenly the pigeon re-emerges from the coffin's broken toe and ruffles its feathers at us. As if this proves a point, the man folds his arms and sits down proprietorily on a stack of breezeblock.

'It's just a bird box, mate. You can't hang around here.'

I mumble 'thanks' and retreat back through the gates onto Church Lane. The builder's lack of interest is shared by the few shoppers I ask on the high street. No one seems to remember this man who lay 'buried' ten feet above their heads.

As I drive away from Stevenage I ruminate on the fate of Tristram and Trigg. In the end they only delayed the inevitable, escaping the body snatchers but enjoying a short-lived victory. No one can extend their will indefinitely beyond the grave.

The hearse rumbles through Datchworth with both windows wide open and a warm wind blowing across the dash. The leather of the driver's bench has moulded to my back and I feel conjoined to the car, as if fated to drive it for eternity.

On a stretch of Roman road beyond the village I perform my first ever overtake. The hearse begins to shake on its chassis as it approaches fifty miles an hour, a terrifying wobble, like a space rocket breaking up in the stratosphere. I draw alongside a hatchback and there is an agonising moment of stasis, the hearse neither gaining nor losing ground. I glance across at the driver, an elderly man with a shock of white hair, and he notices me for the first time with a look of complete incomprehension. Mercifully, he slows, and I regain the left-hand lane as a line of traffic rounds the corner ahead.

Perhaps the greatest single advantage of driving a hearse (and there are many) is that people are desperate to get out of my way. Whether out of respect or superstition, cars seem to scatter before me. On open roads traffic will hang back from the hearse, keeping its distance. In built-up areas drivers disappear down side streets to avoid any contact with my vehicle of ill omen. I drive through Hertfordshire much as Moses walked through the Red Sea, the way parting before and behind me.

Near Waltham Abbey I stray onto the westbound carriageway of Britain's busiest motorway. The M25 is a terrifying gear change after quiet country lanes, and the hearse roars down the slip road with my foot to the floor, just managing to squeeze between ranks of articulated lorries. I stick doggedly in the slow lane, ready to flee at the first available exit.

West of Enfield the sun seems to set the windscreen on fire and I can barely see ten feet ahead of me. I reach for the visor and disturb a large spider that has made a home behind it. The interloper performs a quick circuit around my outstretched hand then hastily retreats.

The sensation produced by this meeting of spider and skin causes me to spasm involuntarily. The hearse veers across two lanes of traffic and the wheels scream in protest. When I re-establish control, passing motorists pay their due to my driving with windscreen-muted expletives.

It's a strange thing to insult someone at seventy miles per hour from the inside of a sealed box. I watch a man with heavy eyebrows work the rage out of his system, jerking red-faced behind the wheel. We make eye contact but are locked in a paralysing silence – he might as well be shouting into a vacuum. I mime an apology by making the shape of a spider with my free hand. This so incenses the red-faced man that he abandons the pretence of driving altogether, using his whole body to express inaudible fury. Having thus removed both hands from the wheel his own car now veers erratically, pushing a third driver onto the hard shoulder. The epicentre of rage shifts as a new actor enters the pantomime.

I glance back at the sun visor and find my gaze returned eight-fold. Oblivious to the carnage it has caused, the spider has withdrawn to its lair in the join with the roof lining. It seems to be toying nervously with a strand of web.

Being very short of living company, I decide to let the spider stay. With its overheating engine, extreme body length and black livery, the hearse is likely to attract more than its fair share of flies. Here was a passenger offering companionship and pest control all at once. The spider took up little space and had no luggage of his own, other than what looked like a small, mummified moth. In many ways he or she was the perfect hitchhiker.

I reasoned, in a typically human and mawkish manner, that if I named this eight-legged freeloader I would be less likely to squash him in a moment of revulsion. To this end, and from here on in, the spider will be referred to as Enfield. Every traveller needs a familiar. Steinbeck had his dog, Stevenson bought a donkey, and I have Enfield, an arachnid of the open road.

Having successfully escaped the motorway, I coast downhill into the Thames Valley. So far, my tomb tour has dealt only with burials, but now I'm headed towards London's oldest crematorium, a place that has been burning bodies since 1902.

The approach to Golders Green Crematorium lies along Hoop Lane. A few pebbledash houses peter out before the compound takes over, bounded by a brick wall. I park the hearse centre-stage, next to a set of gates that leads into one of many courtyards. The shadows of chapels and columbariums loom over me as I step onto the kerb.

The crematorium has a Lombardy, red-brick design that makes it look like it should be perched on an Italian hillside instead of stuck in a north London suburb. I enter through the gates and pause to watch a man digging out a drain beneath the inscription 'The Earth and The Spirit abideth forever.' Owned by the London Cremation Company, no one else in the city has been in the business as long.

The buildings have steadily expanded over the years, with new halls and chapels added like LEGO sets to the original structure. I begin in the west cloister, wandering along a wall covered by hundreds of memorial tablets. Beneath them are plastic stands with paper inserts; pay-and-display parking for the dead, single-day permits to lay flowers for the recently cremated.

The memorials cover an eclectic range of lettering and styles. There are beautiful bronze plaques from the 1920s next to rows made from marble and stone. Some stand out from the crowd – the Watkins family memorial has elaborate bronze lockers for individual ashes, each with its own key; a memorial to the artist Mabel Spinks is inset with her own ceramic tiles.

The placement of many memorials seems entirely random, the accidental death of an organist commemorated next to the life of a celebrated explorer. Others cluster together for solidarity, such as a section reserved for members of the Communist Party of Great Britain. Trade unionists Arthur and Ethel Horner are immortalised side by side: *'Their God was a man covered with coal dust.'*

At the opposite end of the crematorium's arcades another group have staked a claim to exclusivity. On four facing walls are the memorials of 'musician's corner', a celebrity A–Z of the harmonious dead. British jazz giants rub shoulders with glam rock gods, Ronnie Scott sharing brick and mortar with Marc Bolan. At chest height is a plaque to Vivian Stanshall, the charismatic singer-songwriter who burnt himself to death in an act of drunken self-immolation. His epitaph? *Imagination is all I've ever called home.*

I step out from under the arcades into the south-facing gardens. Afternoon sunshine has transformed the crematorium from grim repository to stately home. In a rose bed of scattered ashes, two gardeners wielding pruning shears help an elderly man search for a friend's remains. They move slowly, bent double, until one of them gestures triumphantly, waving his hands in the air like a child in a playground.

I pause halfway up the slope that inclines away from the crematorium. Paths have been mown in the grass to delineate 'dispersal areas', and I waver, unsure of which to follow first. A man in the obligatory crematorium black approaches me.

'Can I help, sir?'

Like all men who wear uniform, he has an air of unnatural incubation, as if whatever lies under his stiff jacket and tie has metamorphosed. I look indecisively at the paths.

'What would you recommend?'

The question doesn't seem to surprise him. He launches into a list of the crematorium's principal attractions, gesturing with his arms at distant corners of the grounds.

'There's the Lutyens mausoleum, of course. You can't miss that.'

'Very grand, is it?'

'Very expensive,' he replies, making a cash sign between thumb and forefinger and winking knowingly.

I follow his directions between borders of ash-fed flowers and find the mausoleum squatting against the crematorium boundary. A stone fence encircles the whole structure like a fortification, and yellow ragwort sprouts from the roof. Looking through the gates, I can see two urns side by side on a pedestal above a stone basin. The dome was conceived with a hole in the middle, to let rainwater fall and pool beneath the memorials. At some point the opening was glazed over, and the basin lies empty while the walls sprout mildew. The mausoleum no longer breathes.

Beyond the Lutyens edifice I come face to face with a colossal statue towering over the path. A hooded bronze figure holds the body of a girl and lifts her arms aloft, bearing her into the afterlife. A title at the base reads, *Into the Silent Land*.

The statue used to have pride of place in the gardens but the wife of a former superintendent developed a mortal fear of it. She lived on site and awoke each morning to find the hooded giant shrouded in mist, as if borne aloft and floating towards her. Her nerves already fractured by the constant company of ovens and ash, the statue seemed to follow her wherever she went. Hence its consignment to this obscure corner, screened by trees and cheap panel fencing.

I leave the statue and walk across to the 'Chapel of Memory', a high-ceilinged room set aside for the bereaved. Marigolds, primroses and lilies spill out from the chapel's aisles, a rainbow of colour contained by sombre stonework and heavy furnishings. The chapel smells like a florist's shop floor, and feeling drugged, I flop down in one of the empty pews.

No sooner have I done so than I realise I'm not alone. A hunched figure occupies a seat a few rows in front, a brown overcoat drawn up over their head. Their shoulders heave and a sudden sob fills the chapel. The flowers seem to glow more vividly than before, as if electrified by the sound of grief. I get up, embarrassed, and quietly exit.

Adjacent to the chapel is a 'Hall of Memory', a three-storeyed columbarium. Galleries surround a central light well, with frosted glass balconies and urns lining the walls. The whole space has the aura of a library, its occupants like books on a shelf.

The hall was finished in 1939, and some of the first ashes enshrined here belonged to RAF pilots killed in the Battle of Britain. Their black and white portraits stand beside more recent memorials surrounded by teddy bears and dolls. Amid caskets in coloured stone are urns shaped like trophies, some sections looking like the childhood bedroom of an athlete, perfectly preserved cabinets full of prizes won. The memorials are ageless indoors and the older ones gleam as brightly as the day they were installed.

As I climb the stairs a single fly buzzes in the light well, following me from floor to floor. Its soft, incessant hum in the otherwise silent galleries reminds me of an Emily Dickinson poem:

THE END OF THE ROAD

I heard a Fly buzz – when I died –
The Stillness in the Room
Was like the Stillness in the Air –
Between the Heaves of Storm –

The hall has its own peculiar, oppressive atmosphere. The containers are neat and ordered, consolidating memory and assured of their place. They are so unlike the memorials outside, disassociated from their ashes and scattered in the greenery of the gardens. It's a choice made by those who mourn, whether they prefer to walk the lawns or come here to a fixed altar. To me the enshrined ashes feel curiously trapped, cut off from their natural cycle and prevented from being reconstituted in the open air. The niches remind me of pigeonholes filled with uncollected post.

The top storey of the building is half-empty and the throb of the road leaks in through the single glazing of a rose window. Chinese families have a monopoly up here and their urns are surrounded by an altogether different culture of offerings. Cakes and incense proliferate, and a number of large cactuses have been placed beside the memorials. Tunnock's Chocolate Teacakes seem particularly popular with the deceased, and their red and silver foil wrappers glow from recesses in the wall. All these items are strictly against crematorium regulations, but the rules seem to have been waived in this eternal penthouse.

The installing of memorials has been the crematorium's bread and butter, even more so since an inventive undertaker in the 1960s came up with the system of leasing space. What was once sold in perpetuity was transformed into a rent roll. The Hall of Memory, though, has many vacant niches, a suggestion that the crematorium is suffering from a drop-off in business. Increasingly, people would rather carry their fathers, mothers and friends home with them, to be scattered in some favoured spot or kept on a mantelpiece or bedside table.

Two older columbariums are only opened on request. I walk over to the crematorium reception and queue behind a man waiting for his mother's ashes. There seems to have been a mix-up on delivery and he argues with the woman behind the desk as she scrolls through a digital register of the recently cremated. Eventually I'm motioned forward. When I ask about a tour I'm told to take a seat by the window. Outside, a dozen figures in black are being ushered into a funeral service.

Lulled by the hum of a drinks machine, I've begun to doze off when a small, animated figure bursts through the office door. A man wearing a black polo shirt, black jeans and heavy black boots approaches me. Around his waist hangs an enormous bunch of unlabelled keys, jingling merrily as he walks.

Eric Willis looks after maintenance at the crematorium. He is also its unofficial tour guide and archivist. He has the energy of a small bird, the same constant flick of the head and a nose like a long beak. As we shake hands he eyes me inquisitively, perhaps imagining my bones reduced to ash and wondering what urn would suit me best.

We begin at the East Columbarium, the crematorium's oldest, built in 1902. Eric releases a series of locks on the door and I'm ushered inside a small room that's been boxed into the original structure. This is the 'Shrine of Remembrance', a dedicated area set aside for Jewish memorials, and the walls are covered with neat rows of wooden plaques recording their names. Eric moves across and pops one of the panels out from the wall. As with the urns, he explains that space on the wall is leased. Some of these contracts last as little as ten years.

Eric prepares and varnishes the individual panels himself. He used to use plywood but has switched to doing veneers on MDF. He shows me a stack of old memorials under a table, kept in case a family member should return to collect the expired inscription. As I read through the names on the wall I think what a wonderful impermanence there is to this place, the dead revolving like the numbers on an old flip alarm clock.

The corridor that leads to the stairs and the upper levels is blocked by an enormous plastic swan. Filling the space behind it are fake flowers, glittering wreaths and a large, sequined cloak. Some of these lie on the floor and others are propped against the wall, obscuring urns and caskets on the shelves behind them. Eric deftly manoeuvres the swan to one side.

'It's all Marc Bolan's stuff,' he says by way of explanation. 'We have a service every year on the anniversary of his death. Loads of fans come. It seemed a waste just to chuck it all.'

I pick up another smaller swan that's been placed beside a casket covered in tinsel. Eric lifts a candle from a stack of inflatable guitars and invites me to sniff it.

'Gardenias. Bolan's favourite flower.'

I follow Eric up the stairs, ducking and weaving through the tributes, the lyric *I danced myself into the tomb* echoing in my head. We enter a gallery containing some of the very first bodies cremated at Golders Green. Here, too, the walls of urns are overshadowed by furniture piled on the floor and covered by shrouds. I can't escape the feeling that the older columbarium has effectively been turned into a storage depot.

On the top level many of the urns are hidden behind traditional gravestones set into the shelves, a relic of people's distrust of what was then a 'new' mode of burial. Eric lifts the lid of several caskets, revealing a mixture of bones among ash. I'm surprised by the fragments of bone. My guide explains that once the ovens reduce a body, the larger bones still have to be broken up. Today this is all done by a grinding machine, or 'cremulator', producing ash in various grades from granulated to icing sugar. Before this technology appeared, cremated bones had to be taken into a basement and pulverised by a man wielding a sledgehammer.

Once I have Eric going on the subject, he is unstoppable. From one of his many pockets emerges a laminated flipbook of pictures taken during a cremation. Photographs through an oven's observation window show a body subjected to increasing heat, a red-hot skull with flames licking through its eye sockets. A final picture shows the remains being raked out and ground in the machine. My education complete, Eric returns this grim pocketbook to his belt. I wonder who gave permission for their body to serve as an illustrated guide to the science.

Before leaving the first columbarium I'm shown a polished stone casket halfway up one wall. A few years ago a Russian family contacted Eric concerning a relative cremated at Golders Green in 1925. The iron casket in which the dead man's remains were housed had rusted badly and his relatives wanted to provide a new receptacle, fashioned from stone quarried in Russia. This was duly done, but when the new casket arrived it was found to be too small. Nearly a century after his death, the man's remains were cremated for a second time, further reduced until they could be accommodated in their new home.

We walk over to the next columbarium, completed a decade after the first. The interior is grander and more austere, white arches rising from a floor of marble. It's immaculately clean and well lit, feeling more like an art gallery than a house for human remains. By the time this repository was built, the act of cremation had shifted from dubious practice to increasingly fashionable alternative, and dozens of new styles of urn populate the shelves. Several have been cast in clay with lead clasps, while others are made from exotic types of marble. Any attempt to mimic the gravestones of traditional burials is long gone.

Eric points out some notable urns: Bram Stoker, Sigmund Freud and a box containing the inventor of the bus ticket machine. Freud's Grecian urn is encased in glass following a recent attempt to steal it. The urn was shattered and the ashes of the noted psychoanalyst and his wife had to be swept up off the floor.

Many of the urns are enclosed behind ornate ironwork, like the entrance gates of grand doll's houses. All are locked, but occasionally distant relatives rediscover tiny keys and

Eric is obliged to grease the hinges and try to reopen the gates.

Back outside on the cloister, the door to the crematorium's largest chapel is closed with a 'Service in Progress' sign illuminated outside. Duty calls Eric elsewhere, but before we part I ask him how many people have been cremated here. He pulls out a scrap of paper from his waistband.

'Well, it was 332,004 this morning.' He does some quick mental arithmetic. '332,010 as of now.'

Eric hands me his business card, then disappears through another door and back into his labyrinth of brick. The card bears his title, *Head of Maintenance*, but it does him an injustice. He is gatekeeper, storyteller, poet and historian, a grand archivist of the dead.

I return to the hearse and sit leafing through the crematorium brochure in the front seat. Change is coming to Golders Green. Eric's old boss was a 'traditionalist', but the new administration has plans for a virtual video tour of the crematorium and soon people will be able to visit the dead from the comfort of their own sofas.

I watch another funeral procession draw up in the courtyard. We are now a nation of cremation. As of 2018, over three-quarters of us choose to be turned to ash. It's frightening to consider the extremes our cadavers undergo in their final days. From the cold chambers of the mortuary to the incendiary ovens of the crematorium, a human body is subjected to a temperature range of nearly one thousand degrees.

* * *

After the ranks of memorials at Golders Green, the next stop on my journey is more personal. From the crematorium I head south, skirting the fringe of Hampstead Heath and then turning down Highgate West Hill, a steep road that seems to fall away into the city centre. I park up as the first street lights flicker on in the dusk. Somewhere close by lie the bones of an ancestor, buried in a peculiar tomb.

Downhill from the hearse a long line of sports cars gleams in the twilight. I have no faith in my handbrake and picture a cataclysmic descent, Porsches and Bentleys piled one into the next. Grabbing a lump of concrete from a neighbouring flowerbed, I drag it under the front wheel.

Continuing on foot I come to the grand gates of Highgate Cemetery. The cemetery is one of London's 'Magnificent Seven', a collection of Victorian burial grounds that ring the inner city. Within its walls lie colossal arcades and mausoleums, all hemmed in by two centuries of rampant weeds. Among its countless tombs is the grave of George Wombwell, a long-dead celebrity who shares his name with an uncle on my mother's side. It was through the living George that I discovered the dead one, the shoemaker-turned-lion tamer, and the owner of Britain's most famous travelling menagerie.

Wombwell collected exotic animals and toured them around the nation. His first purchase was a pair of boa constrictors bought in the London docks, and from there he expanded to apes, rhinos, golden eagles and every kind of wild cat. Some of Wombwell's animals were reportedly so bizarre they couldn't be identified at all.

While his beasts were popular, Wombwell himself does not seem to have enjoyed such good press. A contemporary described him as 'undersized in mind, as well as in form, a weazen, sharp-faced man, with a skin reddened by more than natural spirits'. My bosom swells with pride at being related to such a man.

Unfortunately, the main cemetery is only open by booking a guided tour or to those with relatives buried here. My tenuous connection to George Wombwell does not prove a persuasive argument at the gatehouse (after all, the man's been dead for a hundred and sixty-eight years), and the day's last tour has long since departed. I return to the hearse in a huff. My tomb itinerary is an exacting one and I seem to have missed the chance to visit my illustrious ancestor. Sulking in the driver's seat, I fall asleep. When I come to again, the summer evening has turned to night.

With nothing else to do I walk back to the cemetery gates. The longer I stand beside the gateway, the more determined I am to see inside. I scan the perimeter for a point of entry, like a child looking for a door into a secret garden. The worlds of the living and the dead have been well separated and the walls rise high above the lane. The parapet is capped with thick steel spikes.

This seemingly impregnable necropolis has one weakness. Every twenty feet or so the wall steps up to match the steep gradient of the lane, like the crow gables on Elizabethan houses. Each of these steps represents a low point, almost within reach.

I walk back up the hill. Near the north end is an enormous glass mansion built inside the walls on land the cemetery sold when it was flat broke. The mansion has a security camera overhanging the lane and, close by, the parapet dips to within a foot or two of my outstretched hand.

Crossing over the road, I lean nonchalantly against the wall, hands in pockets, waiting for a couple with a dog to pass by. When they've rounded a corner I take a running jump at the wall, miss the parapet completely and land on my arse back in the street. I grin awkwardly at the security camera then glance up and down the lane.

On my second attempt I scrape my knees on the brickwork but manage to grab the lip of the wall and hoist myself up. A cyclist comes freewheeling down the hill and I freeze on top of the parapet, like the silhouette of a grossly inept ninja. I've succeeded in getting one foot either side of the spikes but am stuck half-in, half-out.

Trying to shift my weight, I immediately lose my balance, see-sawing towards the graveyard and dropping with a thud into the cemetery undergrowth. I find my head resting against a stone cross and give myself a quick autopsy, feeling for broken ribs or twisted ankles.

Getting to my feet, I strike out among the graves, the dark canopies of trees interrupted by the hard outlines of the tombs. Inadvertently I've timed my trespass with the full moon, and its pale light aids my way through the jungle of memorials. It's a strange transition, stepping from the world of streetlights and cars into these still avenues. The cemetery is a popular location for horror films and dozens have been shot here, from *Tales from the Crypt* and *Beyond the Grave* to a slew of Hammer horrors (*Taste the Blood of Dracula!*,

Frankenstein and the Monster from Hell!). In spite of the scenery I have no dread of what lies beneath me; I'm only wary of being chased through the tombs by a cemetery warden wielding a torch.

The moon disappears behind a cloud and I turn on the feeble light on my phone. I have a vague notion of where Wombwell lies from a map of the grounds, but the further in I go, the more confused I become. Fortunately, I'm saved by the lion.

The statue lies with its chin between its paws, a long scar running down over its right eye. In the moonlight it seems almost alive, as if it might yawn and roll over into the grass. The lion is a likeness of Wombwell's favourite pet and rests across the lid of his tomb. He named it Nero, after the Roman emperor famous for murdering his mother and beating his pregnant lover to death. It's an odd name for an animal that was reputed to be as tame as a house cat and to have slept at the foot of Wombwell's own bed.

Nero's docile nature once caused him to be substituted in a dogfight. Wombwell had agreed to test his lion against a pack of bull terriers but the lion ignored them. Another of Wombwell's pride, Wallace, entered the ring and immediately tore the three dogs to pieces. This fearsome lion's own memorial can be found in Essex, his carcass stuffed (rather badly) and now sitting like a boss-eyed teddy bear in a cabinet in Saffron Walden Museum.

I reach forward and rest a hand on Nero's snout. The night air seems much cooler inside the cemetery; the masses of ivy-clad trees and shaded paths have not retained the heat of the day like the city beyond the walls. The sweat from climbing over the parapet has gone cold on my skin and I shiver in the dark.

Lions were not just Wombwell's favourite pets. Of all the creatures in his menagerie it was the lions that made his name. They were the central attraction when his show rolled into town and crowds swarmed around them. More than once the public suffered injury, such as a child who strayed too close and had its arm bitten off through the bars. The obvious danger of the animals only served to bring more people to see the show.

A regular event wherever Wombwell stopped was a performance by his 'Lion Queens', women who would enter the animals' cages and appear to tame them. Few lasted long in this hazardous profession. Wombwell's own niece was the last of them, mauled by a tiger in an impromptu exhibition. It is a measure of the man's character that he continued to exhibit the tiger after her death, with a sign advertising it as the same that killed the Queen.

A branch snaps somewhere in the undergrowth behind me and I leapfrog the tomb in terror. Crouching behind the lion I scan the moonlit path. After five minutes I decide I'm still the only living thing in the vicinity and emerge sheepishly from my hiding place.

In November 1850 Wombwell died 'in the saddle', on tour with his menagerie. As his teams of horses dragged caged elephants and tigers into another sleepy Yorkshire town, Wombwell expired somewhere behind the closed doors of his caravan. His zoo staggered on into the 20th century without him.

Wombwell's body was transferred to a most unusual coffin, assembled from the salvaged timbers of his namesake ship, *The Royal George*, sunk off Spithead in 1782. This curious memento is now sealed beneath Nero's stone lid, the circus master entombed in the same oak that imprisoned six hundred drowning men.

As midnight approaches I have a final port of call to make and, after more wrong turns in the dark, I arrive in front of an enormous arch. A giant obelisk rises up on one side, lit by the moon, and tangles of ivy hang down from it in long skirts. The arch is framed by four lotus-bird columns and a path disappears into the darkness between them. As I stand alone in front of this forbidding portal, the ivy sways softly in the breeze. The whole scene is so monumental it seems fake, pulled straight from the set of *Indiana Jones*. I touch the obelisk to make sure it isn't made of plastic.

Timidly I cross into the shadows beyond the arch. The path is hemmed in by stone walls and a series of doors has been set in their face, the entrances to old catacombs. The openings are so regular that they appear like the doors off a hotel corridor, as if the dead have just gone to bed.

At the far end the moon penetrates the ivy and a dark cobweb of branches rises from the cemetery's most photographed feature, the Circle of Lebanon, a ring of mausoleums topped by a gigantic cedar, its arms stretched possessively over the graves. For many years the tree has thrived in a plant pot of human remains, but recently it has been diagnosed as fatally ill and is due to be chopped down. I have come to pay my last respects to the longest-lived resident of the whole cemetery, a tree first seeded in 1739 and now doomed to join the men and women in the soil.

I follow the path to a flight of stone steps that leads out the other side of the circle. With blind luck I manage to retrace my steps to the glass mansion and the perimeter wall. The wall is easier to climb from the cemetery side and I peek over the top to check the coast is clear, before dropping back into the land of the living.

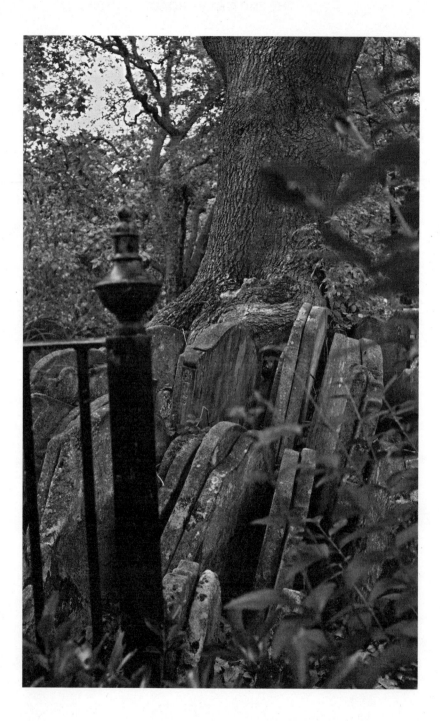

Chapter Three

The hot weather breaks in the night and a storm rages outside. I lie prone beneath the coffin deck, listening to rain running down the sides of the hearse. I wonder what the world would sound like from the inside of a coffin, a lawn mower moving across a graveyard or the feet of a congregation on the grass.

The storm ceases but I can't sleep. I poke my head out through the curtain that separates the underside of the coffin deck and the driver's compartment. The clock on the dashboard has lost several hours, the small hand on eight even though it's the middle of the night. It only keeps time while the engine runs.

Eventually I drift into uneasy dreams. Appropriately for a night spent sleeping in the hearse, I dream of my own funeral. A lonely beach like the shingle at Dunwich stretches into the distance and a line of dim figures processes down to the waterline, men and women surrounding a single coffin. I am borne aloft on the shoulders of old friends then cast adrift, floating on the water while my wife and children bury their faces in the sand, their hair spread out like seaweed. A few feet from the shore my coffin bursts into flame, glowing on a rip tide.

I wake with the guilt of my own unspeakable vanity, cringing at the memory of the crowds of weeping mourners and my family prostrate on the beach. I guess we all want to know we'll be missed.

The dawn casts a thin light under the coffin deck. I pop the tailgate and climb out, stretching on the pavement like Lazarus doing yoga. It's too early for any of London's cafés to have opened their doors, so I make do with a mug of hot chocolate boiled on a gas ring.

I start the hearse and drive into the city. As I pass through empty streets my thoughts return to last night's moonlit cemetery and the lion on the tomb. Considering he spent his whole life on the road, I feel like Wombwell's ghost will fit well in my travelling company.

The sun climbs over the city as I circle King's Cross looking for somewhere to hide an eighteen-foot car. I pull the hearse onto a curb under a railway arch, next to a battered white delivery van. The arch's underside is covered with graffiti, and on one wall *The End is Nigh* has been scrawled in luminous pink letters. The message feels appropriately personal. I cut the engine before carefully arranging the silver screens on the coffin deck and locking the doors, though I'm not convinced anyone would steal a second-hand hearse.

The streets are beginning to fill with commuters as I walk towards my first destination of the day, St Pancras Old Churchyard, tucked in behind the twin train terminals of

King's Cross and the Eurostar. I enter through ornate iron gates.

Near the entrance a man in a suit is using a table-tomb as a desk. He balances a coffee cup and his laptop on the memorial, typing furiously with one hand. Lifting the cup without looking, he spills coffee on the sarcophagus. 'Fuck fuck fuck' greets the morning as he swipes at his suit then carefully examines his brogues, seemingly oblivious to the brown puddle now spreading across the tomb. Such is the living's regard for the dead.

St Pancras Old Churchyard was once on the city's outskirts and the River Fleet meandered beside it, old etchings showing groups of men bathing in the foreground with the tombs fanning out behind them. The Fleet has since been channelled underground and the semi-rural idyll has become one of central London's busiest corridors.

Under the east wall of the graveyard stands an ash tree encircled by a hedge, with a gate set in the middle, and I walk over to peer through the bars. The trunk is ringed with dozens of headstones, stacked tightly together in pairs. The tree rises from the summit of this tombstone mound, its roots so intertwined with them that it's hard to tell bark from stone. Above, the trunk splits and branches out in a tight, symmetrical 'V', like a giant catapult ready to fire corpses across the city.

This strange amorphous mix of tree and stone was the creation of the writer Thomas Hardy. Before he became a famous man of letters, Hardy worked for a firm of London architects. In 1863 the Metropolitan and Midland railways began construction at St Pancras, and their path bisected an ancient burial ground. Locomotives have always had an uneasy relationship with the past, and the laying of the new tracks meant the displacement of old graves. Hardy was assigned the unenviable task of moving hundreds of bodies that the railway uprooted.

The bones were disposed of in mass cemetery graves but the headstones remained. For whatever reasons of his own, Hardy chose to stack them in a circle and plant a tree at their centre. Perhaps he had read of the Yggdrasil, the mythical ash of Norse legend whose 'limbs cover all lands' and whose roots connect worlds.

The outward edges of the graves have numerals etched in the stone, catalogued when Hardy moved them here. With their epitaphs largely hidden only this index remains, whole lives reduced to serial numbers. Hardy's own poem 'The Levelled Churchyard' gives us an indication of how he may have felt about the job:

> O passenger, pray list and catch
> Our sighs and piteous groans,
> Half stifled in this jumbled patch
> Of wretched memorial stones!
>
> We late lamented, resting here,
> Are mixed to human jam,
> And each to each exclaims in fear,
> 'I know not which I am!'

I walk over to the high brick wall hiding the train tracks behind it. Weeds grow tall in its lee and tombs hide in the long grass, leaning against each other like a row of frozen dominoes. A well-weathered skull stares up at me from beneath a rhododendron, eye sockets crumbling as if it were made from chalk.

From St Pancras Old Churchyard I follow the Euston Road to University College London. The university is home to an unusual memorial, the petrified corpse of one of its most famous professors.

I wander through the warren of the university campus, arriving at a building site on Gordon Street. Beyond, the Wilkins Building is a ghost town, but I find what looks like a reception desk. A woman sits tapping a touch screen with fake nails and looks up as I reach the counter.

'Would it be possible to see Jeremy Bentham's head?'

The receptionist blinks, and her mouth opens then shuts again. As I wonder how to reassure her that I'm not a head-hunting psychopath, her colleague wheels his chair over.

'Hold on a minute.'

He leans over his shoulder and shouts into a back office, 'Where's Bentham?'

After a moment's pause, a second woman emerges from within and looks at me apologetically.

'I'm very sorry but he's gone to New York.'

'What? All of him?' I reply.

Jeremy Bentham was in many ways a hero. A philosopher credited as a pioneering advocate of secularism, gender equality, and the abolition of both slavery and the death penalty, his heart seems to have been in the right place. He was also a flagrant narcissist and his celebrated life concluded with a suitably vain bequest.

When he died in 1832 Bentham left his body to science. 'Of what use is a dead man to the living?' he once wrote, and his dissection by anatomists was a fitting answer. But Bentham's will went one step further, decreeing that once his body had been dissected his skeleton was to be extracted from the flesh and dressed in his own clothes. He asked that his mummified head be placed on top and the finished article housed in a glass-fronted cabinet to be put on display.

Bentham was so convinced of his own immortal greatness that he believed his physical presence, even without a pulse, could inspire the next generation. He wrote extensively about his perfectly preserved corpse being brought out at future meetings of friends and colleagues. He even imagined a 'Temple of Fame', where he might sit in state with other mummified men of the future and be admired by passers-by.

Unfortunately for Bentham the mummification was a botch job, an embalming experiment that backfired. Today his head looks like something out of a low-budget horror film, the shrunken skin of the cheeks turned tangerine orange and his glass eyeballs bulging out of their sockets. A replacement waxwork has been added to the display, with a few strands of his hair sewn on.

Bentham's body didn't fare much better. The skeleton had originally been padded out with hay and, in 1939, the university's Department of Egyptology was called in to restore and restuff the professor. His clothes still receive a semi-regular airing, dry-cleaned once every half-century or so.

Alas, this extraordinary mummy is abroad. It transpires that Bentham is on tour, and both the skeleton and his mummified head are currently on loan to a museum in Manhattan. Bentham's is a well-travelled corpse.

I take a chair in the empty reception and read an account of Bentham's last moments. In spite of his faults, the philosopher remained much loved by his friends until the last, and his life's work would echo down the years, helping to spur future reform. John Bowring, who sat by Bentham's bedside as he approached death, wrote a moving description of his final moments:

> It was an imperceptible dying ... There was no struggling, no suffering; life faded into death, as the twilight blends the day with darkness.

Disappointed at having no face-to-face encounter with the professor, I return to the railway arch and fetch the hearse. After straying into a bus lane I join a steady stream of traffic, coaxing the engine up the rise of Pentonville Road.

Approaching the heart of central London the hearse sputters through traffic along High Holborn, the famous landmarks of the city gliding past the window. Enfield the spider seems uninterested, sulking somewhere deep within his web.

I skirt Lincoln's Inn Fields, home to the Hunterian Museum, a strange cabinet of curiosities I visited as a child. As well as specimen jars containing things as varied as a pig's penis and the oesophagus of a whale, the museum owns the skeleton of a famous giant.

My childhood encounter with this goliath is still etched in my memory. I remember the skeleton's unnaturally long neck and the jaw attached with springs, suggesting that it might suddenly snap shut. At the back, a hook and catch held the rear of the skull together, like a trapdoor to the brain. The skeleton stood seven foot seven inches tall in its display case and towered over the rest of the museum's collection.

This is, or was, Charles Byrne, a genetic giant who suffered from the growth disorder now known as acromegaly. What impressed me most about the giant was that he wasn't meant to be there at all. In contrast to Jeremy Bentham, Byrne didn't want to spend an eternity on public display. From the rural Ireland of his upbringing to the streets of London, he had spent his whole life exhibiting himself. People paid to visit him in his London lodgings and he performed tricks in public, like using street lamps to light his pipe. After years of making a living from his remarkable height, he was desperate that his bones did not endure the same indignity. Byrne's will explicitly stated that he wished to be buried at sea in a heavy lead coffin.

Even as a ten-year-old I was struck by the injustice. The Hunterian made no secret of the fact that they'd come by the skeleton illegally and against the man's last wishes. The museum's founder, the surgeon John Hunter, had followed Byrne closely when he moved to London. As the giant's health deteriorated and he began to drink, Hunter moved in like a vulture. When Byrne contracted tuberculosis and died aged just twenty-two, it was Hunter's men who waylaid the giant's coffin on its way from London to Margate. The undertaker was bribed and the body returned to the surgeon. Instead of the anonymity of the North Sea the giant ended up immersed in Hunter's grim cauldron, where the flesh was literally boiled off his bones. Once reduced, the skeleton was pinned together and put on display, black numerals stamped on it like a prisoner's identification printed on bone.

Byrne has endured the ignominy of his glass cabinet for over two hundred years. The museum is currently being refurbished and I fantasise about breaking into their basement and rescuing the Irish giant. I could bundle him onto the coffin deck and then race down river towards the mouth of the Thames. A police chase would ensue, the hearse veering wildly and the giant's bones becoming ever more jumbled with each hairpin turn. If I could make it as far as Margate and board a boat, I might finally give Charles Byrne the funeral he always wanted.

It turns out I'm not alone in my outrage, and there have been many calls for Byrne's skeleton to be laid to rest. Any scientific value the body once possessed has long since been quarried, DNA from the teeth analysed, and countless photographs and X-rays taken to document every inch of the skeleton. Even if the museum one day honours Byrne's final wishes, you could say the damage has already been done.

From Lincoln's Inn I pass under the shadow of St Paul's, guiding the hearse around the cathedral dome and back towards Southwark Bridge. As I traverse the river, the smell of the Thames drifts in through the window: mud, salt and unseen things borne under the piers by the tide. My eyes follow the bend of the river eastward, to the tall spires of Tower Bridge.

Hidden somewhere under this London icon is 'Dead Man's Hole'. The name was given on account of bodies that would find their way there, towed by the river current and caught against the feet of the bridge. It became such a common occurrence that a mortuary was built under the piers, and its white-tiled interior can still be glimpsed from the north bank, along with the boatman's hook used to fish corpses from the water.

Dead Man's Hole is not unique, and the many hollows and troughs in the river's bank have been given names reflecting their grim association. The Thames has a 'Deadman's Dock' and a 'Deadman's Stairs'. Anyone who walks the beaches of Wapping or Vauxhall at low tide is as likely to stumble on fragments of human bone as Roman pottery or medieval coins.

On the south side of the river I slow down at the entrance to a narrow street, running through the old parish of St Saviour's. Redcross Way has the air of an in-between, an alley full of builder's hoardings, locked doors and steel shutters. Most people use it as a shortcut, but halfway along I find a remarkable dedication.

A huge, iron-barred gate sits atop a concrete parapet, every inch festooned with ribbons, bows, beads, paper crosses, flowers, baubles, photographs, figurines and hand-written notes. It resembles something from a forgotten carnival, colours faded and all gaiety gone. A sign fixed at the centre reads:

The Outcast Dead
RIP

These are the red gates of Crossbones, a space that first opened as a burial plot for sex workers, 'a single woman's churchyard', then expanded to become a mass grave for the working poor. From the 16th century onwards, an estimated fifteen thousand bodies were committed here, in a space a little less than the size of a football field.

The gates themselves stand on the threshold of another version of London, an older, anarchic city. They record people whose memory is not cast in stone; there are no generals on horseback or marble mausoleums here. It's as if the tributes have been blown in by the wind, a litter of lives snagged on the bars of the gate.

I try to pick out individual stories from the collage. Several weather-worn photographs are hidden behind carnations, a portrait of eight orphaned children standing at the doors of a Dr Barnardo's home, a photo of a pirate radio DJ beside a golden mannequin. Paul 'The Waterman' and William 'The Lighterman' speak of vanished trades.

The burial ground closed in 1853, and in the years that followed it served briefly as a timber yard, then a fairground. After sitting undisturbed for over a century, Crossbones reared its head again in the 1990s, when a Jubilee Line extension burrowed through its bones. Archaeologists found a hundred and forty-eight bodies in well-preserved coffins, nearly all bearing marks of disease: scurvy, rickets, smallpox and curvature of the spine, a small sample of what afflicted London's poor.

At the same time as workmen were digging up the coffins, a man called John Constable began a small revolution. Much like William Blake two hundred years before him, Constable claimed to have had a vision. Instead of God he saw a dead prostitute, a woman who inspired him to pen a series of plays narrating the graveyard's history. Whether or not you believe in Constable's psychic power, his work was pivotal in raising awareness of Crossbones' past. The playwright still leads a monthly vigil at the graveyard gates, where locals pay their respects to the memory of those buried here.

I enter Crossbones from the south side, stepping into a kind of scrapyard for the dead. Transport for London eventually installed a series of caretakers to guard the vacant ground, one of whom cleared the rubbish and seeded it with plants. This inspired the creation of a garden on the site, breaking up the skin of concrete that had sealed the mass grave. Among the planting, memorials have been forged from piles of brick and steel sheets, all raised over bones found scattered on the surface of the old graveyard. At one end is a pyramid of rubble inset with oyster shells, a shamanic cairn towering over the rest.

Behind a series of wooden crosses fashioned from reclaimed timber, a large chalkboard has been installed for visitors to leave their own tributes. Some are personal, 'Luv ya Mum', others universal, 'We live only to Die'. As I watch, a volunteer scrubs the board clean to make way for new dedications. On the other side, a hoarding separates the garden from a parking lot full of commercial vans.

I sit beside the oyster cairn, a helicopter hovers near the railway bridge and a train thunders past. The current lease from TFL classifies Crossbones as a 'meanwhile garden', and the struggle to preserve it continues, two sides contesting ownership in a tug of war where the rope is made from human bone.

I've whiled away too many hours in the Crossbones garden and have fallen behind schedule. As the day draws in, I go in search of two explorers who came to rest in London's south-west.

Locked in traffic on Lavender Hill, the hearse is mistaken for a black cab and a group of men outside a pub try to flag me down. One crosses over to open the passenger door, his hand pausing on the handle as the realisation sinks in. He grins awkwardly then backs away, the same hand raised in apology. The traffic trickles forward and I leave him standing in the middle of the road.

My first explorer is the famous Egyptologist Howard Carter, the greatest tomb raider of all, whose own remains now lie in Putney Vale Cemetery. I take the turn-off for Putney and glide up a ramp into the car park of an ASDA superstore. The ASDA looms over the cemetery gates, its shadow eclipsing an avenue of freshly dug graves. On the far side, plots full of coloured glass sparkle in the evening sun.

Near the centre of the cemetery a faded council sign proclaims 'The Brighter Borough' next to a map of celebrity dead. Politicians compete for top billing with sculptors, physicians and bodybuilders. Among this roll call is the grave of Bruce Ismay, chairman of the ill-fated White Star Line, which owned and operated the *Titanic*. His tomb floats in a cordoned-off segment of the cemetery, like a lifeboat surrounded by the bobbing headstones of the drowned.

From where I stand, paths fan out in six directions through nearly fifty acres of graves. I pass a tomb 'To Grandad', a handful of lottery tickets stuck to the stone with sticky tape. Following the map, I find Howard Carter just beyond a large family mausoleum with a squirrel grooming itself on the roof.

Carter's grave is simple, a black granite headstone polished to a mirror and reflecting my face back at me. I squat down to read the epitaph.

May your spirit live, may you spend
millions of years, you who loved Thebes,
sitting with your face to the north wind,
Your eyes beholding happiness.

The words are a translation of hieroglyphs found inside the entrance of Carter's most famous discovery, the tomb of Tutankhamun. For three millennia Tutankhamun had been lost in the desert and for three decades he haunted Carter's dreams. Then, in November 1922, Carter brushed sand from the top steps of the pharaoh's hidden grave, briefly becoming the most famous man alive. The treasures of ancient Egypt found within the tomb meant that not only had Carter made the greatest archaeological find of his generation, he'd also enabled the past to speak. It took ten years to catalogue the contents of the tomb, every item shedding light on a buried civilisation.

A German shepherd sits under a tree just beyond Carter's grave. It reminds me of Anubis, the dog-headed god who guarded the pharaoh's burial chamber. In my imagination Putney Vale Cemetery becomes the Valley of the Kings, sand falling in around the graves and a dry desert wind whipping along the avenues. The bulk of ASDA is transformed into a sandstone temple and the sounds of the city replaced with the rushing eddies of the Nile. Someone rides through the cemetery on a moped and the vision evaporates. The owner of the German shepherd gets up from arranging flowers and walks away with his dog at heel.

The premature death of several men associated with Carter's dig led to the media reporting a 'mummy's curse' stalking those who had opened the tomb. Carter himself lived on in spite of ill health, and his eventual obituary in the *New York Times* noted that, after fifty years digging up pharaohs, he 'must have been the subject of the finest collection of Egyptian curses in existence'.

When Carter was laid to rest here in 1939 his fame had waned and few people attended the funeral. At the time of his death he was rumoured to be searching for the final resting place of Alexander the Great, supposedly interred in a gold sarcophagus filled with honey. Carter found his own grave first.

Two jackdaws fly towards me down the avenue of tombs then veer away. Could the archaeologist have resisted keeping some small part of his momentous discovery? Perhaps even now a golden trinket lies clasped to Carter's chest in his Putney grave. I wonder if budding archaeologists make pilgrimages here, hoping the dead man will bless their future digs.

I leave Carter to his millions of years and make my way back to the superstore. From the cemetery I drive across Richmond Park, the hearse suddenly surrounded by ancient oak and fallow deer. I've barely five minutes to settle into this new scenery before being thrust out the far side into Mortlake.

The hearse idles behind the boom of a railway crossing, shaking as a train rattles past. I turn down North Worple Way, a road running parallel with the rails, and the exhaust goes off like a gunshot. A dog chases me along the road, barking, trying to bite the rear wheels. Here, in this innocuous suburb, lies a second explorer whose fame has dwindled down the years.

Outside the church of St Mary's, the hearse takes up two parking spaces. I put a pay and display ticket on the dash then walk back to the entrance. A man hauling carpets out of the adjacent building watches me try the door and then the gate into the graveyard, both locked.

'There's no one here,' he says. 'Who are you looking for?'

I explain I've come to find a dead man, not a living one. The carpet-bearer grins and leads me through the back of an empty building, unbolting a door that opens onto the east side of the church and the graves. The burial ground is dense, crosses and headstones jostling for space with barely an inch of grass between. In their midst one memorial rises above the rest on a great base of sandstone, a life-sized tent serving for a tomb.

Up close, the details of the tent's carving are exquisite. Seams in the stone represent stitches in canvas and the sides of the tent ripple as if flapping in the wind. A marble tablet fixed to the face of the tomb identifies it as Sir Richard Burton's, *Last and noblest of the errant knights ... to whom adventures were as toys.*

Burton was many things – a soldier-turned-explorer, a linguist and a scholar. In the mid-19th century he went where few others dared, leading expeditions in East Africa searching for the source of the Nile, and journeying through the mountains and deserts of the United States before the outbreak of the American Civil War. Burton wrote many books about his travels and pastimes, and their sheer variety gives some impression of the man, from studies of falconry and fencing to the first English translation of the *Kama Sutra*.

Throughout his travels Burton adopted different characters to help him assimilate with those he met, and was seemingly capable of disguising himself at will. A demonstration of this chimeric power was the journey that first made his name, an audacious pilgrimage to Mecca where certain death awaited any non-believer found in Islam's Holy City. Burton styled his facial hair and dress to mimic those he travelled with, even having himself circumcised for added authenticity.

At the rear of the tomb tent, a glass window has been cut into the stone and a ladder allows the visitor to climb up and peer inside. I have to press my nose against the glass and shield my eyes to see into the hollow mausoleum. Under the canopy of stone, two coffins lie side by side, their lids sprinkled with ceiling plaster like a dusting of icing sugar. Burton's steel coffin lies on the right, with lions' mouths for handles, while that of his wife, Lady Isabel Burton, is made from plain wood. On the tiled floor the flowers of a funerary wreath lie preserved inside a glass dome, undisturbed in this vacuum for a hundred and twenty-seven years.

Staring at the steel coffin through the glass, it's hard to imagine a soul as restless as Burton's caged in a box. Much of his life was dedicated to wandering the globe studying different cultures and customs. Burton was reputed to have mastered over twenty-five languages in the course of his travels, from Punjabi to Persian, Arabic and countless dialects. One of his biographers even claimed he kept monkeys in an attempt to learn how they communicated.

In his later years Burton was posted as British consul to Trieste and ill health curtailed his travels. Before suffering a fatal heart attack in the autumn of 1890, he confided a wish to his wife that they be laid together in a tent for eternity, like those they had so often shared. Taking him at his word, Lady

Burton raised the money to build this mortuary gazebo, a tomb for all seasons, in which they could continue their journey into the unchartered territory of the afterlife. Instead of pitching the fabulous tent in the company of other great explorers of his age, Burton's tomb ended up in this small Catholic churchyard in Mortlake. He was never accepted by the establishment, his tastes too diverse, his willingness to 'go native' ostracising him from Victorian society.

On the opposite side of the tent's interior to the window, a mirror covers the wall, creating an illusion of space and some unsettling reflections. Many objects that lie near to the coffins are half-glimpsed: oil lamps, charcoal braziers and censers, all the paraphernalia of a travelling caravan. The ceiling is badly painted with cherubs that seem to be pouring water on the deceased, perhaps intended as a flood of tears. Among these heavenly folk a single line of script runs around the walls. I have to read the inscription backwards in the mirror, one word at a time:

Stay with us, for it is toward evening and the day is now far spent.

Lady Burton struggled to let her husband go, and this haunting line seems to vocalise her sense of loss. In the wake of his death their house became a museum, filled with enormous portraits of the explorer and beautiful editions of his many books. Isabel even dressed a life-size waxwork of her late husband for the newly opened Madame Tussaud's, accompanied by three camels and a painted backdrop of desert palms.

He was clothed in the same robes he wore on his famous pilgrimage to Mecca.

Not long after Burton was laid to rest, Isabel bought a cottage in Mortlake so that she could visit him as often as she pleased. She erected her own tent in the cottage garden and devoted eight isolated months to writing a memoir of her late husband. Never was a biographer so physically close to their subject. I try to imagine her in mourning dress, black with a white veil, turning over her memories of the man and the pages of his manuscripts.

The tent tomb once had a hinged stone door and Isabel regularly visited to sit beside her husband's coffin. There was even a rumour that she invited spiritualists, very much in vogue in late Victorian society, to accompany her into the tomb and attempt to communicate with her husband beyond the grave. Whether or not the tent became a séance chamber, it remained a regular site of pilgrimage for the grieving widow.

When the biography was published, Isabel used the proceeds to add further fixings to the tomb. The strangest of these were chains of tiny camel bells, suspended from the ceiling and, when she died, crossed over the two coffins. The bells are still there, tarnished and joined to a number of mechanisms set into the walls, with bundles of exposed wiring terminating in a large black box at the foot of Lady Burton's coffin.

The box is a 19th-century battery, long since expired. The mechanisms were designed to shake the camel bells when the door to the tent was opened, for visits or private mass, as if Burton continued to travel even after his death. The last time they rang out was when his wife was entombed alongside him, and I wonder if the archaic system could be repaired, the music of the Middle East once more filtering through Mortlake.

A solitary mosquito appears behind the glass, torturing the Burtons in the afterlife, and a sharp pain in my forehead makes me realise I've been glued to the window for over half an hour. I bid farewell to the explorer and his wife, and make my way back across the churchyard to the door in the wall. When I try the handle I find it shut fast. It seems the man who let me in has locked up and left. Having broken into a cemetery the night before, I am now unintentionally imprisoned in a graveyard.

Standing by the bolted gate in the gathering dark it occurs to me to pitch my own 'tent' beside Burton's. The idea of sleeping here would probably offend every Catholic in England, but I think Burton might have approved; unlike his wife he did not believe in any God and once wrote that man worshipped nothing but himself.

I return to the tent. It's a mild night and I have my backpack to serve as a pillow, along with the remains of a half-eaten sandwich – I imagine Burton got by on less in the course of his explorations. Settling down on the grass beneath the tomb, I lie level with plastic vents that have been added to air the insides. The gold-painted crescent and stars on the tent's ridge gleam in the dusk. '*Stay with us, for it is toward evening and the day is now far spent.*' These haunting words now seem an invocation addressed directly to me.

The crosses and headstones of the graveyard press in around the tomb, like unseen animals around a camp fire. I've never believed in ghosts but cannot help imagining them now, encircling me, pulling at my coat and pawing at my feet. I pull out my phone and ring home, but my wife is putting our children to bed and has no interest in voices from beyond the grave when our son is screaming in her ears. I console myself that Burton, travel-hardened though he was, maintained a lifelong fear of the dark, the window cut into his tomb a bid for light even in death. On the far side of the churchyard wall, a street lamp flickers on and tints the glass.

St Mary's lies directly under Heathrow's approach and huge aeroplanes hoover up the sky above me. What would the great explorer make of these machines that have shrunk the world, making his expeditions the work of an idle hour with an in-flight magazine? The regular thunder of the flight corridor keeps me awake, so I turn to examining some photographs of Burton by the light of a torch. Among them is a picture of the man on his deathbed, his sheathed sword hanging over his head in a room wallpapered with maps. He lies propped against the pillows, his hair thin but his dark eyebrows and beard still full and fierce. A crucifix has been placed under his chin and a deep scar runs down from his left eye, the mark of a javelin once thrust into his mouth and out through his cheek.

It's an arresting portrait and remains with me after I've closed my eyes. In the night the smell of the tide drifts into the graveyard, the Thames lying only a street away to the north. As the hum of the aeroplanes merges with sleep, I fancy I can hear the quiet tinkle of a camel bell, calling from the depths of a desert that exists only in my head.

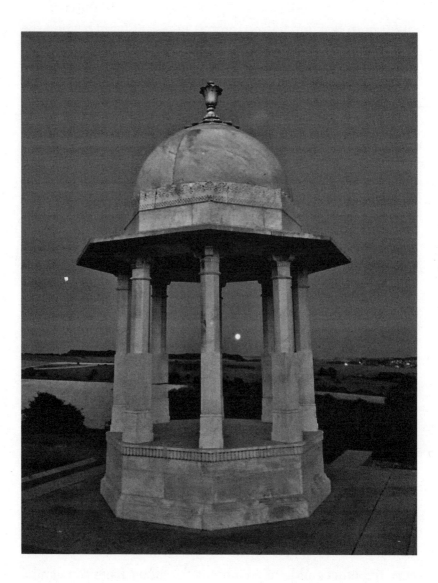

Chapter Four

The sun rises at four in the morning over the spire of St Mary the Virgin. Dew has collected in the stone folds of Burton's tent and the whole tomb has a frosted appearance, as if the great explorer has switched to Arctic expeditions in the afterlife.

A night in a Mortlake graveyard is not as romantic as a night in the Wadi Rum, and the dawn chorus is composed entirely of traffic. Back in the hearse I find Enfield has caught a wasp in his web. The wasp hasn't yet given up, buzzing angrily in the silk strands, and Enfield is busy spinning safeguards to stop it getting away. The little arachnid is earning his keep and I give him an affectionate salute as I start the engine. Before rush hour settles on the city, I plan to strike south through London's suburbs, picking up the route of an old railway that once carried coffins out of the capital.

The Necropolis Railway, or 'black line', was Britain's longest-running funeral train, born out of desperate need. By the early 19th century, London's graveyards and cemeteries had become full to bursting, communal pits reopened time and again to accommodate new corpses. As the city's population swelled, this burial congestion became so acute that parts of coffins were being recycled and old bones crushed for fertiliser. Yesterday's visits to St Pancras and Crossbones had shown me how squeezed graveyards could become, and even the larger cemeteries like Highgate were overwhelmed with new interments. In answer to this crisis a plan was conceived to create the mother of all burial grounds, a cemetery so vast that it might never be filled, and far enough from the city that it would not be surrounded by the living.

As I drive through London's suburbs I watch people going about their daily routines, waiting at bus stops, ferrying children to school. I'm suddenly struck by how small my sphere of human interaction is and how many people I will never meet, people who will remain strangers to the grave.

My map lies open on my knees as I drive, and at traffic lights and junctions I try to plot a course that runs parallel with the old railway cutting. The site for the new necropolis was a small village in Surrey, the charmingly named Brookwood, but it was chosen for its remoteness not its scenery. Brookwood's nearest neighbours were a prison and an asylum, the criminal and the mad clearly being considered appropriate company for the dead. The only way to service such an isolated cemetery was by train.

A new station was built at Waterloo unlike any before or since. Steam-operated coffin lifts bore the deceased from street level through three storeys of mortuaries and waiting rooms to a raised platform above Waterloo's railway arches. A special 'burning chapel' stood beside the platform, named after the French tradition of surrounding dead kings with hundreds of candles. This elaborate room was panelled in oak, with a bier at the centre for coffins awaiting transportation. A train shed was erected, a glass ceiling allowing light in from above but blank walls guarding the mourners' privacy.

The trains themselves were no less elaborate, comprising hearse vans and funeral saloons for different classes of ticket (First, Second and Third). On arriving at Necropolis Junction and the gateway to the new cemetery, the train was uncoupled from its engine and, for the last three-quarters of a mile, the carriages were drawn by black horses along an embankment edged with sequoias and hedges of laurel.

The railway ferried bodies from the capital to greener pastures for nearly a century. Then, in 1941, an incendiary bomb fell on the Waterloo sidings, setting the coffin carriages alight and quickly spreading into the station. The fine plaster ceiling of the 'burning chapel' was consumed by flames and by the next morning the whole three storeys had been reduced to rubble, leaving only the First Class platform hanging above the burnt-out wreck.

Increasingly, coffins were being carried to the cemetery by car, in hearses like my own, and the railway was never rebuilt after the bombing. All that is left of the London terminus today is an office building over the old station driveway, the stone that once proclaimed 'The London Necropolis' wiped clean.

Finally clear of London's grip, I find myself on an empty road following a high stone wall. The hearse has passed this way before, and next to the ashtray a small brass plaque reads

Brookwood Hearse Convention 2003. This morning's visit will be a kind of homecoming. I turn down Cemetery Pales and then into the south side of the cemetery. A sign at the entrance proclaims, *The Song has Ended but the Melody Goes On.*

Once inside the walls I find myself adrift in a wilderness. The interior is a vast plain of scattered graves, great swathes of cemetery grass burnt yellow and littered with pine needles. The planting has grown old and the young rows of sequoias that first welcomed the funeral train are now towering giants.

The hearse bounces down an avenue full of potholes and broken asphalt. I drive past a memorial to an opera singer swallowed by a cypress, its ground-hugging limbs wrapped around the stone in a stranglehold. On the opposite side a floral tribute spells out 'CIAO' above a new marble headstone. The cemetery is a mix of the long abandoned and the recently deceased.

As immense as Brookwood seems, it's only a fraction of its original size. In the 1980s the cemetery fell victim to thieves and many of the memorials were stolen, winched onto flatbed trucks in the middle of the night. This has amplified the sense of a vacuum inside the walls. Brookwood is a far cry from its glory days, when visitors strolled down carefully manicured rides between bubbling watercourses.

As I drive I search between headstones for the terminus of the old railway, the platform where coffins were unloaded for burial. Blue and green dragonflies sift through empty avenues of old mausolea, but nothing else moves. I turn down All Souls Avenue, a track with a strip of grass growing through the middle, but soon get hopelessly lost and end up back where I began.

After another circuit through the cemetery I arrive at my destination, the last stop on the Necropolis Railway. Once complete with mourners' waiting rooms and a fully stocked bar, the station continued to act as a café for many years after the railway was dug up. Then, in 1982, something remarkable emerged in its place.

A small monastic community, the St Edward Brotherhood, established a shrine on the land. The founding monks lived in a caravan while they refurbished the mortuary chapels that had served the railway. The buildings were hidden behind towering thickets of rhododendron, these giant shrubs obscuring the doors and windows, and the monks fought a ten-year battle to reclaim their own overgrown Eden. The station building was demolished but the old platform retained, serving as a quiet garden in which the brothers can wander along the old railbed. At the end of the line is a vegetable garden and a collection of greenhouses.

I step in under the monastery's eaves and ring the bell by the door. A small eternity passes with no sign of life from within, and I reach to press the bell again, pausing at the sound of footsteps. A small man with a long beard opens the door, clad in the traditional black raiment of the Greek Orthodox Church. His beard seems stitched to his eyebrows and spreads out to form a white fan under his chin. He extends his hand with a shy smile, the greeting of one who spends many hours alone. In an almost childlike voice he introduces himself as Father Niphon.

As I follow the monk inside I realise time operates differently for the Brotherhood. My impatience on the threshold stems from the pace of the world I inhabit. Here the days last longer and the whole monastery and its garden seem locked in stasis, alone in the forsaken cemetery.

We sit in a small room where bodies were once placed after disembarking and where the monks themselves slept until they built an extension. I'm offered a cup of green tea and accept gratefully. Our conversation ebbs and flows, any pauses filled by Father Niphon's shy, beatific smile. I cannot tell if the monk relishes the chance of company or is enduring me with saintly patience.

Like all priests of the Orthodox Church, Father Niphon has taken the name of a saint, in his case an obscure Greek hermit who died seven hundred years ago. I ask the Father where he's from, imagining a child raised on the slopes of Mount Athos, and am surprised by his answer.

'Dorset. A small town near Salisbury.'

Slowly the monk seems to find his voice. He tells me that one of his greatest pleasures is to stroll through the grounds at dawn with only the graves for company.

'I used to walk past a splendid tomb on the cemetery's perimeter, a vault with a marble basin on top of it, fifteen feet across. The basin was filled with rainwater and birds used it for a bath, dozens of them splashing in and out. I'd stop and pray there.

'One morning it was gone. Vanished. Someone came and took it away in the night.' Father Niphon pauses and a shadow crosses his face. 'Lots of the monuments have been stolen and broken up.'

Once I've finished my tea we walk across to the second mortuary chapel, now a church, in the shadow of a huge sequoia leaning precariously over the compound. Father Niphon crosses himself as we pass beneath a statue of St Edward the Martyr. The monks are also guardians of the dead, not the many thousands in the cemetery but one special set of bones – the body of a king.

The church doors are wrapped in a cocoon of clematis. As we step inside, the monk apologises for the dim lighting, explaining that the brothers have fallen out with their electrician. He reaches behind beams and screens to switch on individual lights and illuminate the gloom.

The church is crowded with glittering icons, a thousand saints jostling for supremacy on the walls, like portraits in the long gallery of a palace. From their charmed expressions you would not guess at the horror of their ends. Most share a common martyrdom, men and women who were boiled, burnt, hanged, drowned, flayed and, of course, crucified.

Beneath the icons are curious glass exhibition cases, like the cabinets of an antique jeweller. Each one is filled with relics, tiny medallions, and gold and silver crosses containing fragments of the saints. The obligatory piece of the True Cross lies on one shelf, a fairly ordinary-looking splinter of wood.

At the centre of the chapel is a carved shrine glistening with wood polish, on which sits a chest with inset crosses. Here lies St Edward, a Saxon king murdered at the end of the 10th century, then buried without ceremony on a marsh.

From this ignominious end Edward's bones went on a remarkable journey. In 980 his body was dug up and moved to a shrine in Shaftesbury Abbey. During the Dissolution of the Monasteries the shrine was stripped but Edward's bones were hidden before they could be ransacked. They remained buried until 1931, when an archaeologist rediscovered them during a dig, housed in a crude casket.

The finder, John Wilson-Claridge, was unable to persuade a church to accept Edward's relics and honour them for what he believed them to be. As a result, the casket and its bones languished in a Woking bank vault. Finally, the Orthodox Church agreed to venerate the relics and establish a Brotherhood to protect them. Wilson-Claridge brought St Edward to Brookwood nearly fifty years after he first dug him up.

Father Niphon watches me approach the shrine.

'Of course, St Edward is far too precious to be kept in the chest. His bones are hidden elsewhere in the church to protect them.'

He tells me this with the air of someone who is in on a brilliant secret. I glance around the interior. A hollow beam or a loose floor tile?

As we leave the church, we pass beneath an old photograph of the Brotherhood arranged beneath the porch. Father Niphon stands in a group of priests, a much younger man but with dress and posture unchanged, as incorruptible as the relics of the saints themselves. I try to picture him as a boy, beardless and running through a Dorset village, but it's an impossible leap of imagination.

I say farewell to the monk beneath a statue of the Angel of Death, spreading her wings over a family tomb. As I turn to go, Father Niphon gifts me a stack of postcards, each one an icon with the face of an Orthodox saint.

Continuing my journey into England's deep south I have a new set of companions on the dashboard of the hearse. St Erkenwald regards me with sad eyes from above the ashtray, while St Hilda looks furious at having been wedged into the glove box. St Dunstan avoids me altogether, busy with his scripture behind the steering column.

The icons under the windscreen remind me of the enduring faith many drivers put in holy charms to ward off disaster at the wheel, whether it's a swinging cross or a miniature Quran. The popular American ballad 'Plastic Jesus' ridicules the practice, and I silently mouth the lyrics as the hearse pulls out onto the A324.

> I don't care if it rains or freezes
> As long as I've got my Plastic Jesus
> Glued to the dashboard of my car

With my saints to protect me I steer towards England's southern shores, following endless hedgerows and crossing half-seen village greens. The landscape is so typically English I feel as if I'm trapped in a model village, the hearse skirting fields of plastic grass and PVC ponds. After an hour I pull in to the town of Lewes and make for an inviting pub on South Street that sits nestled under chalk cliffs. Father Niphon's green tea is the only sustenance I've had all day.

The Snowdrop Inn is a squat building, overwhelmed by the wall of rock rising behind it. Stepping through the door I glance up, expecting to see a familiar white flower swinging above the entrance. Instead the painted sign shows a row of houses buried beneath snow and figures crying out for help, up to their waists in snowdrifts.

The pub is full of men talking loudly at crowded tables. The clamour of the drinkers seems to come from far away and I start to wonder if I've already spent too long communing with the dead. I walk over to the curve of the bar and reach for a menu. With half an eye on the 'dish of the day', I ask the landlord about the sign.

It transpires the pub was not named after the wildflower. During the winter of 1836 an avalanche of snow fell from the cliffs onto South Street, engulfing a row of cottages, and the whole pub is a kind of memorial to the event, a tribute to what stood here before. It seems ghosts of the past abound, even when I'm not looking for them.

While I wait for my food, the publican directs me to a display case hanging above one of the tables. Awkwardly, I squeeze behind a bench and squint up. Inside the case is a 19th-century account of the avalanche, a sheaf of cut-out pages curling against the glass.

The snows came the day before Christmas. Enormous drifts were soon blocking the roads, some as much as a mile long and twenty feet deep. Coaches became stuck fast or turned over, and horses struggled to stay upright in the storm. In town the snowfall froze to people's doors, forcing them to climb from first-floor windows onto high banks of snow.

Beyond the comforts of home, others died on the roads; a mailman was found frozen to his seat carrying the post between towns.

On the morning of 27 December, the *Brighton Herald* reported that the snow-covered town resembled 'the silence of a tomb'. In Lewes the snow lay so deep on the cliffs above South Street that a frozen cornice hung down over the edge, as if this were the Alps, not sea-level Sussex. In spite of the obvious danger, few wanted to leave the warmth of their firesides.

At around 10 a.m. the cornice broke and an avalanche fell three hundred feet onto the cottages. To bystanders the falling snow appeared like a 'gigantic wave', prising seven homes from their foundations and carrying them out across the road. One chunk of the snow was thrown forty feet over the turnpike and into the river running below, the drift so massive that it filled the frozen riverbed.

I carry my fish pie and chips into the beer garden. With the warmth of the sun on my back, it's hard to imagine that terrible white Christmas of 1836. I wonder again at my unwitting choice of pub and the layers of history that cover this small island.

The people of Lewes rushed to help those trapped beneath the snow. Teams of labourers dug on rotation, one buried up to his neck by a second snowdrop from the cliff. Of the fifteen people buried alive, only seven survived. The last body extracted was a fourteen-year-old boy, still alive but with his leg trapped under a rafter, the rest of him saved by a wigwam of ruined beams. He had lain in frozen solitude for seven hours.

An infant, only six weeks old, was also pulled alive from the wreckage. She was found in a woman's lap, her mother's broken body the only thing between her and the heavy joists of the cottage roof. Everywhere in the ruins lay evidence of the Christmas holiday just passed, '... pieces of cake and plum pudding, intermingled with holly and other evergreens'.

The bodies were carried to South Malling parish church, their coffins being drawn on wagons through a cutting made in the snow banks that lined the road. On their shared grave were placed flowers, maybe some early snowdrops among them. A memorial inside the church proclaims:

An Awful Instance of the Uncertainty of Human Life

I chew my food slowly, staring up at the cliffs behind the pub, their white walls sewn with gravity-defying vegetation. After a meal spent pondering the deadliest avalanche in British history, I settle my bill and leave Lewes through the tunnel under the crag.

My fourth night on the road is not to be spent in a graveyard or under the coffin deck, but on the open slopes of the South Downs. I follow the road from Lewes to Brighton, picking up a tiny cutback lane north of the city, and park overlooking the dual carriageway and the sea. The blue lights of a police car flash in the fold between the hills, and the Brighton observation tower shines like a giant incinerator above rows of terraced houses. I'm preoccupied with thoughts of cremation, having come here to find the remains of a funeral pyre. Somewhere high on these Downs stands a temple of stone in a field of sheep, a memorial to men whose bodies were burnt in the open air.

During the First World War injured Indian soldiers serving in the British Army were sent to Brighton to recover from their wounds. Over twelve thousand men were treated in hospitals around the city, including the great kitchen of the Brighton Pavilion, its many domes like the skyline of an Indian pleasure palace.

Of the thousands hospitalised, fifty-three Hindus and Sikhs died from their injuries. In accordance with the tenets of their faith, they were carried up onto the South Downs and their mortal remains committed to fire, then scattered in the sea. In 1921 a permanent memorial was raised on the site, a domed pavilion designed to be a *chattri*, an 'umbrella' to guard the dead men's memory.

I climb steadily on foot up the hill's slope. A trail like a sheep track winds through the grass and a crow silhouetted on a fencepost turns to watch me pass. The valley below is called Ewe Bottom and is filled with curious raised scars in the turf, long strips created by Iron Age ploughs.

On the outbreak of the Second World War this valley became a military training ground. No sooner had the Chattri been erected than it fell into disrepair, becoming so overgrown that thistles sprouted between its steps. By the 1940s it was in such a poor state that the soldiers on the training ground used it for target practice, pock-marking the stone of its columns, base and steps with hundreds of rifle rounds. No better illustration of the shallow nature of human memory exists than the soldiers of one war using the memorials of the last for a bull's eye.

Gaining the ridge of the hill I can see the Chattri dome in the distance, floating above a copse of trees. I trudge on but it doesn't seem to come any closer, as if the hill is one vast treadmill moving under my feet. Cockchafer beetles spring out of the grass, rebounding against my legs, while gulls circle overhead, diving to catch them.

After what seems like hours I reach a gate. The moon rises behind the hill as I enter the memorial field, its light lending the trees a new, tropical intensity. The dome itself sits on a base of granite, its roof supported by eight columns, and I approach it along a path between ornamental hedges, their yellow flowers catching in my clothes.

On the steps leading up to the dome plastic poppies are clustered in heaps and a laminated verse by the Indian poet Sarojini Naidu lies beside a wreath: *Honour the deeds of the dauntless ones, remember the blood of my martyred sons.* In the late 1940s the Chattri was restored, and on every subsequent year people have processed out here to venerate the fallen.

Daylight is fading and the dome takes on a ghostly cast in the gloaming. The men who were set alight on this hill believed that their souls would be reborn in other bodies, and the inscription on the memorial's base is dedicated to soldiers who 'passed through the fire'. It seems just the spot for the migration of souls.

I unpack my bedroll on the ridge above the memorial with a view of the moonlit sea. Far out across the waves, hundreds of offshore wind turbines flash their red mast lights in unison. I imagine them as the essence of the Indian soldiers, adrift on the water, still waiting for reincarnation.

The Chattri's dead are not the only ash in the Channel's currents. The world's seas teem with human remains, from philosophers to actresses and statesmen. H. G. Wells, the father of science fiction, was carried to sea in a small urn and tossed into the waves off Dorset's Jurassic coast. Legendary American saxophonist Stan Getz had his ashes poured from a saxophone into the Pacific. Colonel Paul Tibbets, the pilot who flew the B-29 that dropped the atomic bomb on Hiroshima, died four thousand miles from here in central Ohio. He too asked for his ashes to be scattered in the Channel, because he remembered it as the most beautiful stretch of water he ever flew over.

I wake to a grey dawn on the Downs and stumble, half asleep, back down the path to the waiting hearse. As I drive towards Worthing I wonder if this scattering of ash is meant to absolve people of their pasts. Adolf Hitler's body was famously disinterred, burnt and scattered in secret on the banks of the River Biederitz, and other Nazi leaders convicted as war criminals were dumped into the River Isa that flows through Bavaria, ensuring they had no fixed memorials. Today, stretches of the same river are flanked by popular nudist beaches and free spirits bathe in the same water that dissolved the nation's past.

Continuing my pursuit of watery graves, I head west along the coast to Portsmouth. The city slowly emerges behind its lagoon, an English Venice down on its luck, the skeletal arm of a dock crane serving as a welcome. As I cross the causeway it starts to rain hard, the windscreen wipers slapping the bonnet. The seal on the driver's door is wearing thin and a rivulet of water bleeds into the footwell, snaking over the door handle and forming a puddle under my feet.

Most people have heard of the Tomb of the Unknown Warrior, the only stone in Westminster Abbey that it's forbidden to walk upon. The body of the infantryman buried there has become a symbol for the nameless dead; an unidentified soldier laid to rest in the company of kings.

Portsmouth has its own nameless warrior, but he was a sailor not a soldier. I coast down Admiralty Road behind the historic docks but get stuck trying to manoeuvre into the visitors' multi-storey car park. After an agonising three-point turn to extricate myself, I leave the hearse opposite *Zooz Tattoos*, before following Half Moon Street to the gates of the dock.

I've come to see a coffin and a body that are no longer together, separated by a quarter-mile of city streets. Portsmouth's unknown sailor was one of hundreds trapped in the wreck of the *Mary Rose*, a Tudor battleship that capsized and sank in the summer of 1545. The pride of Henry VIII's navy, the ship had survived many sea battles, but was finally lost in the Solent when turning to fire at the invading French fleet. When she 'heeled over with the wind' and foundered, nearly five hundred men were on board. Ever since the wreck was recovered, the *Mary Rose* has sat in a purpose-built museum in the old dockyard, periodically hosed with seawater, while the unknown sailor now rests in the city's cathedral.

Inside the museum I bypass displays full of sea-worn trinkets and the barrel of a bronze cannon. The museum has been laid out in such a way that every visitor must pass through a chamber, inside which they're subjected to some mild sensory torture in the form of a video re-enactment. As I stand nervously in the half-dark, one entire wall becomes a cinematic display of the ship's sinking, the room filling with a watery light and the screams of sailors echoing in my ears as broken timbers float towards me.

When I'm released into the main hall, reality continues to be paper thin. The monumental wreck stands with its half-eaten hull facing the viewing galleries while speakers set into the walls play the sound of creaking timbers. Walkways slope to parallel the ship's deck and before long I'm swaying in time with the groaning hull. Only the glass wall of the viewing gallery breaks the illusion, imprisoning the *Mary Rose* like a ship in a bottle.

Despite resting in only fifty feet of water, the mud and tides of the Solent made the *Mary Rose* an elusive wreck for many hundreds of years. The ship was first rediscovered in 1836 but the divers of the day were unable to raise her, contenting themselves with salvaging some of her guns. Soon the wreck disappeared beneath layers of silt, like an old woman reaching for a favourite blanket.

On 5 May 1971 she was found again. After six years of scanning the mud, a team of researchers uncovered three unmistakable portholes in the ship's hull, the eyes of the wreck staring up at them. This time, she would not be allowed to bury herself. The news became a national sensation and hundreds of amateur divers volunteered to take part in raising the wreck. Among those searching for the royal flagship was a young Charles Windsor in his own monogrammed diving suit.

Volunteers and archaeologists worked together to recover all manner of objects embedded in the wreck, from the ship's bells to Tudor cutlery. Their greatest task was recovering the crew themselves. In and around the broken hull were scattered over ten thousand individual bones. Osteologists had the formidable task of reassembling this unique underwater ossuary, one fragment at a time.

From the museum I walk beneath a derelict high-rise slowly being eaten by ivy, huge vines climbing five storeys into frameless windows. Everything in Portsmouth seems to rest on vanished glories and there's an air of a city crowded around the glimmers of its golden days.

Portsmouth Cathedral has no grand entrance but squats behind a line of weeping willows on Lombard Street. Only the clock tower rises above its surroundings, with a golden ship for a weathervane, slowly revolving as if caught in a whirlpool. Once inside, I approach the tomb along aisles covered with memorials to mariners, both ancient and modern. On one wall, a glass case contains a fragment of Nelson's flag from the Battle of Trafalgar. The cathedral reminds me of the Whaleman's Chapel in *Moby Dick*, where the pulpit is shaped like a ship's prow and the chaplain has to climb a ladder made of rigging to deliver sermons to a congregation of fishermen.

The tomb itself is ringed with votive candles and a few globules of wax have bled across the inscription, *Here lies a member of the ship's company of the Mary Rose*. When the grave was dug in 1984, a fully fledged funeral service took place. The service echoed the form of a 16th-century requiem mass, the priests attired in blood-red surplices edged with black and silver, and the service performed in Latin.

The funeral was not just a quaint re-enactment but a condensation of hundreds of years of loss. Many who attended had lost loved ones to the sea and the burial of the Tudor sailor became a collective goodbye to a dozen other men and women. The skeleton was a symbol of a community's shared grief, a talisman reclaimed from the thieving sea.

The service was also attended by the captain's great-granddaughter ten times removed, which must set some kind of inter-generational record for relatives attending funerals. The coffin was small, made of oak and lined with black pitch salvaged from the wreck itself. Inside, the unknown sailor was a mass of 'disassociated skeletal fragments', not one body but a composite skeleton dredged from a mass grave. On top of the bones were placed oak leaves and moss, a long-extinct Tudor burial custom.

From his submarine tomb to a stone berth under a cathedral floor – a stranger journey to the grave is hard to imagine. After four hundred and thirty-nine years lost at sea, the unknown sailor completed his odyssey. As I walk back to Half Moon Street, I wonder if these men would have wanted their bones dredged. As Christians, perhaps a cathedral aisle would have pleased them more than the mud of the harbour bottom, but the majority of their collected bones now languish in museum lockers.

The inside of the hearse is strangely comforting after the chill of Portsmouth's sea front. As I return over the causeway, I think of other drowned sailors still trapped underwater, the sea slowly erasing their remains. It's a fate some willingly elect to share.

While scattering ashes at sea is common practice, few people choose to have their actual bodies committed to the deep. The whole process, like so much about death, is fiendishly complex, and you can't just get your loved ones to row you offshore and chuck you overboard. You can only be cast away in three designated sites around the British coast: the mouth of the River Tyne, the town of Newhaven in Sussex, or, my personal favourite, the Needles Spoil Ground, a dumping zone for dredged harbour material and a popular spot with fishermen. The coffin has to be a specialist affair, immensely heavy to ensure it doesn't wash up. It also needs to be biodegradable and peppered with drill holes to let water in. The body itself needs weighing down too, so it doesn't float to the surface if the coffin disintegrates first. Finally, there's a hefty licence fee to pay for the privilege. With all these hurdles, it's unsurprising that only a handful of people in England choose the sea for a grave, fewer than fifteen a year.

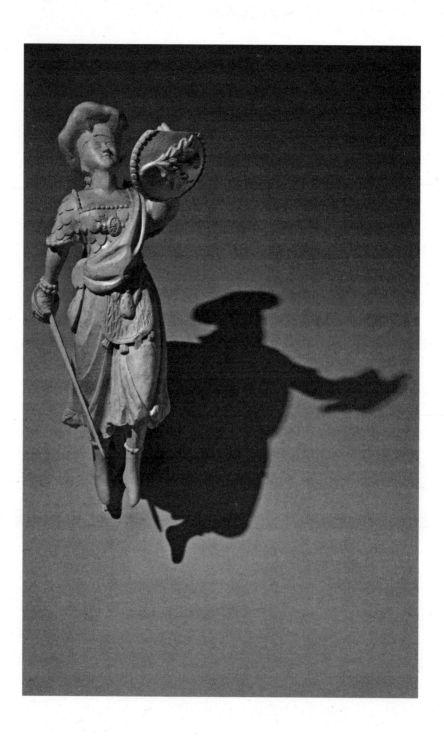

Chapter Five

My journey to date has focused on the tombs of strangers and I've yet to visit the grave of anyone I knew in life. After Portsmouth I'd planned to visit the sepulchres of Winchester Cathedral with my grandmother, a tour guide there for many years. I'd envisaged wheeling her around the aisles while she recited the legends of her favourite dead kings and queens, but, like so many plans we put off, the guided tour never came to pass. My grandmother died in her care home in 2018, at the age of ninety-six.

I plot a course for a small graveyard on the outskirts of Winchester where her ashes lie buried. The churchyard at Morestead stands beside a busy road, with a steady stream of traffic piling off the M3, and it turns out to be almost physically impossible to reach my grandmother's grave. I sit and wait on the verge opposite the church gate, watching cars crest the rise.

I last saw my grandmother two days before she died. She was sitting up in bed doing the crossword, as she'd done every day for as long as I knew her. It was her eternal familiar pose and I found it impossible to believe she was dying. I expected to be asked for the answer to four down, or fifteen across, not summoned for a farewell.

She was frail but composed and perfectly lucid. We talked for a while and then I suggested reading something. Normally I'd pick an article or a book but this time she asked for something specific, a poem I'd never heard of.

Dutifully, I looked up the poem on Google while my grandmother watched me from her pillows. A nurse from the care home brought me a cup of tea. After a while I found the text and began to read, faltering through the unfamiliar verse.

'To Night' is Percy Shelley's ode to the dark. Reading the words out loud I realised my grandmother herself was the poet, weary of the day and longing for the night. The final verse felt as if it were coming from her own mouth.

> Death will come when thou art dead,
> Soon, too soon –
> Sleep will come when thou art fled;
> Of neither would I ask the boon
> I ask of thee, belovèd Night –
> Swift be thine approaching flight,
> Come soon, soon!

As I got up to leave, my grandmother told me to take a book from her shelf. It felt like a last gift, an act of divesting. I was too distracted to choose and snatched one at random, kissed her and fled from the room. It was only sitting on the train home that I reached into my backpack and pulled out *Shelley: The Pursuit*, a biography by Richard Holmes.

I squat in the grass opposite the church for ten minutes before a momentary gap in the traffic appears, allowing me to sprint across the road and up the bank, arriving out of breath among the tombstones.

It's surprisingly hard to find a grave if you have no idea where to look. Even a small country churchyard contains dozens of headstones in no particular order, chronological or otherwise. I start in a corner where a jumble of graves lean against each other for support, a few recent burials dotted at irregular intervals.

Against a tall hedge a number of military men have been buried. My grandfather, whom I never knew, spent his entire working life in the navy and his ashes were scattered here in the 1970s. Perhaps this damp corner of the churchyard was home to my grandmother too, but there's no sign of either among the squat headstones of sergeant-majors and lance-corporals.

Every time I visited my grandmother, I realised how much I took her for granted, her continued presence and her links to the past. My image of her was seasonal, the fireside matriarch with the mellow generosity of old age. I also became aware of how little I really knew of her life. Her past was a series of sepia-toned photographs filled with unfamiliar faces, strangers even though I was related to half of them.

I find the other side of the churchyard equally muddled, cracked table tombs and stone crosses mixed in with gleaming brass memorials. I try to search methodically, working in a grid among the tombstones. Anyone watching from a neighbouring house would have seen me swaying up and down, like someone bobbing for apples in a fairground.

After an hour I've read every stone twice and scoured the grass and the walls of the church. My grandmother's memory is invisible and there seems to be no evidence of her at all. I return disconsolate to the edge of the road and sit down to wait for another gap in the cars, thinking of the old adage that you really can't hang on to the dead. I feel more bereft than ever, the gulf of death made all the greater for want of a signpost.

Back in the hearse my grandmother's ghost reluctantly takes her place among martyrs, knights, shepherds and sailors. She was always a commanding presence and I think I can trust her to keep the others in good order.

The psychological effects of constant traffic, rain and the company of ghosts are beginning to take their toll, and I pull into a McDonald's drive-thru on the edge of the New Forest. The long body of the hearse is a tight fit and comes close to squashing an advertisement for McFlurry® ice cream. I dutifully get in line behind a green Jaguar and place my order at the speaker. When I pick up my chicken nuggets at the window, the man who hands it down to me doesn't even blink. Maybe undertakers come here every day.

My grandmother was a great history lover and she lived it too, having been born in 1922. Her favourite piece of Hampshire history was the life and times of William Walker, 'the man who saved Winchester Cathedral'. She had a photograph of him in her bedroom in the care home, staring at the camera from behind a thick walrus moustache.

At the turn of the 20th century Winchester Cathedral was slowly falling apart. The enormous weight of its walls rested on a peat bog and centuries of poor underpinning, on wood piles or peat, had led to its gradual subsidence. Pillars in the crypt were forcing themselves into the earth, bringing down the vaults they supported. Inside the east end the floor of the cathedral was visibly sinking and, at the west, great chunks of masonry had begun to fall from the façade. Cracks were appearing everywhere, some reportedly large enough for owls to roost in.

An architect and an engineer brought in to avert the crisis realised the only way to save the cathedral from collapse was to underpin it with modern foundations. Unfortunately, this required excavating well below the water table. Any attempt to dig down to the level required for underpinning resulted in a sudden flood of water bubbling up from the peat and filling the pits.

Draining the water would have further undermined the walls, so the engineer came up with an ingenious solution. A diver would be found to descend into flooded holes and lay bags of concrete, enough for the foundations to be temporarily stabilised and drained, thus allowing bricklayers to finish the job. Unlike the divers who salvaged the *Mary Rose*, this job would have to be done in the dark. The peat-filled pits contained syrup-like water with zero visibility.

William Walker was the man they chose, a deep-sea diver who had a remarkable CV, from helping build the Blackwall

Tunnel to rescuing men from flooded coal mines. Walker began his Herculean task in 1906, working for six hours a day in water up to twenty feet deep. He donned an enormously heavy rubber diving suit with a helmet of copper and brass through which air was fed. Bag by bag, he was dragged down into the dark, feeling his way into 'drifts', holes dug through the peat and temporarily shored up so that they wouldn't collapse and bury him underwater.

The diver continued in this lonely task for five and a half years, accruing thousands of hours deep beneath the cathedral walls. He travelled not just downward but also backward in time, working on parts of the building first laid out in the 13th century. I'm not surprised my grandmother idolised Walker. He did not seem to fear any aspect of his work – the dark, the isolation or the repetition – only taking off his helmet to smoke his pipe and 'sanitise' himself between dives. Every weekend he happily cycled the seventy miles home to his house in Croydon.

Sadly, only seven years after he completed his heroic task, Walker was dead, killed by the Spanish influenza epidemic that swept Europe after the First World War. Several memorials to Walker exist, from a diving helmet to a dinner gong. The cathedral installed a statue in his honour in the 1960s but accidently got the wrong man. Instead of the burly-shouldered diver, the sculptor worked from a photograph of the project's engineer. The diocese finally replaced the statue with a new one in 2001, and the real Walker now stands between the bones of King Canute and a shrine to St Swithun.

* * *

Emerging from the shadows of the New Forest, I pull off for Bournemouth at Three Legged Cross. The whole town is wrapped in a kind of sea fog, a thin mist that clings to the overpass. It's an appropriate setting for what I've come here to find, the creator of a famous monster and the heart of the man whose words my grandmother requested on her deathbed.

The Shelley family vault lies behind St Peter's Church on rising ground, and the steps leading up to it are wet with the fog. A dark slab of stone caps the vault's entrance, hiding an underground mausoleum, and beside the grave a number of ballpoint pens have been stabbed into the grass, as if the dead are undergoing acupuncture.

With the air perfectly still and mist clinging to the tomb, I should be feeling the same sense of horror as those first readers who turned the pages of Mary Shelley's *Frankenstein*. She was buried here in 1851 and the vault also contains something of her husband.

Percy Shelley's death is legendary, lost to a storm while sailing off the coast of Italy, but what became of his body is the subject of some dispute. Ten days after going missing at sea, Shelley and his two companions were washed ashore near Viareggio, their bodies partly eaten by fish and rendered almost unrecognisable. Italian quarantine regulations demanded that they be buried in the sand where they were found, and it was not until almost a month later that Shelley's friends, Lord Byron, Edward Trelawney and Leigh Hunt, had him exhumed. There can have been nothing romantic about unearthing a month-old, half-eaten human corpse. What was left of Shelley was cremated on a pyre beside the water.

As the fire died down and the poet's remains smouldered, Trelawney claimed to have thrust his hand into the embers and extracted Shelley's heart, untouched by the flames. The heart passed from Leigh Hunt to Mary Shelley, and, when she died, it was found in a silk pouch in her writing desk. Her son had the organ encased in silver, and when he himself died thirty-eight years later, his father's heart was buried in this same family vault.

The chances of Shelley's heart having survived the fire are slim. An article in the *Athenæum* contended that a hollow organ such as the heart would soon be consumed by the heat but that the liver, being larger, denser and most probably waterlogged, would have been the last part of Shelley to burn. The writer concludes that the heart encased in silver by Shelley's son may have been another organ altogether.

Shelley's ashes had no less of an adventure. While the majority were boxed up by Trelawney and sent to a freshly dug grave in Rome, some portion of them returned to England. In the endless shelves of the British Library's basement is a leather-bound book with a small glass window inset in the cover. The book contains letters by Shelley's wife and friends, and the window is in the shape of an urn. It looks like an old snow globe, a scattering of white flakes behind the glass. Here lies a pinch of Percy Shelley, waiting for some future scholar to shake him up.

Back on the street, a blue plaque on the churchyard wall proclaims the proximity of the Shelleys' mortal remains to any curious passer-by. Mary Shelley's name lives on in a dozen of Bournemouth's businesses and landmarks: a skin clinic, a park and a primary school, among others. The most obvious namesake is right next to the church, the Mary Shelley, an enormous Wetherspoon's pub with the same footprint as the graveyard. A two-faced portrait of Frankenstein's monster hangs over the entrance, its malevolent eyes following me through the door. Inside, Shelley 'memorabilia' is sandwiched between the usual meal deals and slot machines; J. D. Wetherspoon hasn't missed a single opportunity to promote the pub's proximity to the grave.

I buy a drink at the bar. A local artist has produced a series of murals for the walls, titled *The Mary Shelley Suite*, and I take a seat beneath an allegorical scene of Percy Shelley's death. The poet's face floats above a tangerine sea, his fateful sailing boat foundering in the distance, while a disembodied Mary invades the canvas from above like a terrifying puppet.

The room is slowly filling up, the door swinging to and fro and the fog pressing against the windows. There's a curious mix-up of online reviews between those coming here and others visiting Mary Shelley's tomb. Hence under the church-yard listing next to pictures of the grave we have, 'Very good breakfast', 'Amazing ribs' and 'Good place for a quiet drink'.

A band starts up at the other end of the pub, a cover of Sonny & Cher's 'I Got You Babe', and I raise a pint to Mary's memory. Although it's tempting to settle in for the evening, I've another heart to find, the heart of a man who has already crossed my path.

* * *

Thomas Hardy was well acquainted with the Shelley family. Among the bodies he moved from St Pancras Old Churchyard, where I visited his extraordinary tree, were Mary Shelley's mother and stepfather; Hardy supervised their cross-country shipment to the vault in Bournemouth.

As I approach Stinsford, a sign on the road advertises 'The Hardy Experience', a two-in-one chance to see his birthplace and sample the cake in the visitor centre. I bypass these temptations and make for the Church of St Michael, where the poet's heart lies entombed.

I park in a slot marked *Reserved for Clergy*. The other bays are taken and the sun has set; I'm sure the vicar wouldn't mind being temporarily usurped by a hearse. The gate is flanked by enormous urns, and stepping between them I pass into the most perfect churchyard I've ever seen. A well-mown lawn slopes gently away in the dusk and a colossal plane tree cascades over the graveyard wall, its trunk like ten trees welded into one. The whole place is manicured but ancient.

Hardy had the unusual distinction of being buried in two places at once. When his family bowed to 'the wishes of the nation' and agreed that his ashes should go to London, a local doctor came to remove his heart so that a part of him could remain in Dorset. On 16 January 1928 Hardy's ashes were carried up the central aisle of Westminster Abbey, accompanied by the literary giants of his day, while his family buried his heart here in the churchyard at Stinsford. In contrast to the great and good assembled in the abbey, a crowd of village locals paid their respects to 'plain old Tom Hardy', a man they once knew as a boy. The two burials, ashes and heart, were almost synchronised.

I walk on through the graveyard. Not far from the urns, beneath the grave of Hardy's first wife Emma Gifford, an inscription reads, *Here lies the heart of Thomas Hardy*. Into this same plot the poet's heart was placed in a casket of wood. At the church door, I enter on a clever timer mechanism that electronically unbolts a latch and then closes again behind me. Presumably after a certain hour it locks for the night. I have a vision of being sealed inside, forced to subsist on a diet of wafers and communion wine.

St Michael's has a tunnel-like feel, a squat nave with dark furniture. In spite of Hardy's own agnosticism there are countless tributes to his memory, from a stained-glass window to a gleaming brass plaque. I open a visitor's book that lies near the organ and discover a record of pilgrims from Japan, Australia and British Columbia, all come to pay homage to the writer.

In the chancel there's a memorial to the vicar who carried Hardy's heart through the graveyard on that January afternoon. A photograph shows him walking up the path, his eyes fixed on the tiny casket in his hands. Perhaps he was affected by the solemnity of the occasion or just desperate not to drop the great man's vital organ in front of a crowd.

There might be another reason for the vicar's studied concentration. When the doctor removed Hardy's heart the day before his burial, it was quickly wrapped in a tea towel, then placed in a biscuit tin in his bedroom to wait for the undertaker's arrival the following morning. The story of what happened after this has become the stuff of funereal legend.

When the undertaker turned up the next day he found the lid of the biscuit tin on the floor, the tea towel on top of it, and one of Mrs Hardy's cats licking its lips beside the bed. Without hesitation the undertaker grabbed the cat, broke its neck, stuffed the body in the tea towel and put the lot back in the biscuit tin before securing the lid.

The story has clung to Hardy's heart ever since it was interred and seems to have been quietly believed by members of his immediate family. The only sure way of obtaining the truth would be to open the grave and extract the box, which may by now be occupied by nothing but the bones of a cat.

When I step outside again the stars have come out over Stinsford. The great hero Hercules is peeping over the church-yard wall and the bright lights of his right arm hang above the village. The celestial view has competition from a flood-light illuminating the church tower, the bulb flickering and the graves dancing in the shadows like a disco for the dead. I'm reminded of my own village churchyard, where one head-stone is lit up by a spotlight every night, its occupant endur-ing a blinding eternity.

I crouch behind a tomb to block the light and get a better view of the stars. Hardy lived in a golden age of astronomy when the first giant telescopes were being built and light pollution was virtually non-existent. Contemporaries like Isaac Roberts were resolving distant galaxies on their photo-graphic plates, still unaware of what the swirls of far-off star-light actually were. Four years before Hardy's death, Edwin Hubble discovered that our own Milky Way is but one galaxy among billions.

Hardy would no doubt be pleased that the same stars are still visible from his grave, even with the glow of Dorchester on the horizon. I watch Rasalgethi rise behind Stinsford vicarage, the brightest star in the whole constellation of Hercules. As a child I experienced vertigo looking at the night sky, my sense of gravity skewed as if I were falling head first into space. As an adult my perspective has changed, and I take solace being belittled by the stars and a time scale that dwarfs our own.

I retrace my steps up the line of Hardy's descendants. At the far end of the graveyard lies another writer, Cecil Day Lewis, a poet laureate and father to the Oscar-winning actor. His neat tombstone has a single verse from his poem, 'Is it far to go?'.

> Shall I be gone long?
> Forever and a day.
> To whom there belong?
> Ask the stone to say.
> Ask my song.

The poet's plaintive questions are all the more poignant with the stars wheeling overhead, distant suns that have risen over every grave, from the dawn of man to the first night Day Lewis lay here. Leaving the churchyard, I reflect on how many stars have already been extinguished, their light only reaching us years after their death, in the same way that dead men and women can resonate after they've ceased to draw breath.

A week's camping has left my body and soul in need of a wash. Back in the hearse I make for the nearest B&B in Dorchester, a stone's throw across the Frome Valley from Hardy's grave and the town in which he spent the last years of his life.

The proprietor is a man of many handshakes. I have my hand firmly gripped at the door, on the stairs and in my room. A final handshake is administered as a firm goodnight. I'm the only guest, and it seems the owner is trying to reassure himself that I won't vanish in the small hours.

Undressing, I climb into the bed and am instantly swallowed whole, the mattress folding in the middle like the jaws of a dragon. The leather headboard sticks and unsticks from the wallpaper as I struggle to free myself. Eventually, I'm resigned to being slowly digested in my sleep.

Breakfast begins with another vice-like handshake, to celebrate my loyalty. After a meal that would happily have sustained several Arctic expeditions, I sit at the table with my road map spread among the scattered dishes.

Today takes me across Dorset towards the lonely reaches of Dartmoor, a landscape encompassing nearly four hundred square miles of moorland, woodland and wetland. It's a setting enduringly popular with the writers of mystery stories. Celebrated authors like Agatha Christie, Dorothy Sayers and Arthur Conan Doyle have all set novels against its forbidding backdrop. Today I'm going in search of a mystery that outdoes them all.

Within five minutes of setting off from Dorchester I'm
holding up the traffic. Everywhere I go my pace and agenda
seem to be a road block to the living. I turn off down a narrow
lane and find myself alone and unhurried, sheets of rain
sweeping the hearse from either side of a wooded verge.

The scenery is becoming progressively wilder and I'm
surprised to find a Starbucks looming out of the drizzle.
Unable to resist the two-tailed mermaid I pull in under her
green and white banner. I wonder what Thomas Hardy's
drovers would have made of a skinny vanilla latte with a
pump of caramel sauce. With my cup wedged in the ashtray I
continue on my journey, buoyed by three different sugars
competing in my bloodstream.

I pass through Bovey Tracey, the 'Gateway to the Moor',
and soon find myself in a landscape befitting the dead, a maze
of bracken and stone walls, with lone sheep grazing the roadside. The last houses on the moor's edge have names that
evoke shelter, 'Home Orchard' and 'Old Haven', before all
gives way to the wild and the impossible shapes of the tors
emerge, enormous stacks of rock piled one on top of the next.
Here nature has built a last defence against mankind, her very
own prefabricated castles complete with rocky ramparts and
tottering keeps.

The moor has a long history of burial, from ancient *kist-
vaens* where the bones of the Bronze Age were laid to rest,
to the tiny churchyards of its isolated villages. Near
Moorhayes the lane narrows as it descends to a stream,
rocks hemming me in on both sides. Giant frilly ferns stroke
the bonnet as I creep past, the road reverting to nature, and

I feel the hearse is about to become stuck fast. Squeezing out the other end I enter the hamlet of Bone Hill, as bleak as its name suggests.

Deeper and deeper into the moor I go. At Widecombe I pull over beside a church once known as the 'Cathedral of the Moor', two dun-coloured horses standing tethered to its wall. Inside, I leaf through the village Book of the Dead, a burial register that goes back many hundreds of years. The book was once the responsibility of the village sexton, the gravedigger whose house still stands next to the church. It's an imposing building of granite ashlar with a colonnade running along its length and narrow, stone mullioned windows, now used as a village hall. A violent playgroup is in session as I pass the open door, four toddlers wrestling one another beside the hearth where the gravedigger once took his tea.

Nature has its very own sexton, *Nicrophorus vespilloides* or the 'burying beetle'. This insect undertaker, clad in a handsome orange and black suit, digs graves for the corpses of mice and songbirds. The beetle has a powerful set of antennae that can detect a rotting corpse from over half a mile away, and it scurries off to claim the prize then proceeds to bury the recently deceased with a partner, who lays eggs as they excavate. The beetle larvae emerge underground to a ready food supply, and so the cycle of life rolls on.

The story stranger than fiction that has brought me to Dartmoor begins with two farmers hunting rabbits across these hills in February 1914. Pursuing their quarry across the moor, they stumbled across a man in a knickerbocker suit, with long black hair and a blue tie with spots. He was lying face down on a waterproof sheet beside a boulder. When the farmers came closer, it became clear he was dead.

From Widecombe I call in at the village stores in Postbridge. The shopkeeper welcomes me with a broad smile and I ask her if she's heard the story of the body on the moor. 'Which one?' she replies with a laugh, pulling out a map and handing it to me across the counter. I buy bread and cheese then set out, crossing a bridge over the East Dart and making for the hills behind the village.

The rain has not relented and I walk upriver to the sound of falling water. Trees along the riverbank act like sponges, moss-covered and weeping water, and the path is a quagmire. I trudge past two men on dirt bikes, smoking wet cigarettes in their saddles and staring blankly into the rain.

The farmers who found the body on the moor summoned a policeman from Postbridge, and he followed them back to where the corpse lay. In the pockets of the dead man's suit was a purse filled with gold coins (almost £2,000 in today's money), a guidebook to Dartmoor, a razor and shaving kit. A cloakroom ticket issued at Exeter railway station led to the man's other belongings: a pocket watch, a knife, a revolver, and a mourning ring commemorating someone who had died in 1817.

The man had been travelling under the pseudonym Jones but his real name was William Donaghy. Although his possessions sound like the weekend essentials of an international spy, he was a humble schoolmaster, a science teacher. A week after the farmers found him, Donaghy's body was laid to rest at St James's Cemetery in his home town of Liverpool.

I climb steadily to a mass of rocks high above the river. This brooding pile of stones has its own nickname, 'The Devil's Punchbowl', after a hollow cavity at its base. Continuing along the ridge, I make for Dartmoor's roadless interior.

I'm searching for a memorial that appeared on the stone where Donaghy's body was found, but there's scant information as to its whereabouts. Supposedly, it lies somewhere north of the village, beneath Hartland Tor and close to a holly tree. I've gleaned that the stone itself is some three metres wide by two metres tall, a description that fits almost every boulder on the moor.

The slopes below me are covered with gorse in full flower and its coconut scent drifts up on the wind. The house I grew up in was surrounded by gorse and it's a smell laced with memory, like my grandmother's hairspray or seaweed in tidal pools on the beach. Eventually the thickets peter out to reveal the steep side of a valley strewn with boulders and the lone holly tree. On the face of one of these rocks is William Donaghy's memorial, but I hardly know where to begin.

I try to work methodically, but soon find myself dashing from one rock to the next, running up and down the hill. The more tired I become, the more the stones assume sinister shapes, changing into anthropomorphic visions of cadavers. Every blank face seems to sneer at me, mocking my flesh and bone with implacable granite. I pause to wipe the rain from my eyes.

Donaghy's post-mortem revealed nothing suspicious. There was no trace of violence or a struggle on his body, nor was there poison in his veins. He had been in the prime of his life, and the mystified coroner could only rule that he'd died from exposure.

One detail of the story haunts me more than any other: the mourning ring found in the station cloakroom. Such morbid jewellery had fallen out of fashion by the time Donaghy died, yet he still carried a gold band commemorating someone he could never have known. Was it bequeathed by a great-grandfather or simply a curio he'd taken a fancy to? I searched in vain for police records of the ring but it seems to have disappeared. Perhaps someone is still wearing it today.

These thoughts and others assail me as I search hopelessly for the elusive rock. Eventually, I realise the memorial must lie on the other side of the holly in the tall thickets of gorse. I button up my coat, make a mental note of the nearest boulder, and plunge into a dense wall of yellow flowers and barbed twigs. Slipping out of sight, I struggle through a suffocating understorey of cobwebbed branches. Before long I'm pouring sweat, my face and hands lacerated by the thorns.

After a few more faceless stones I stagger into a clearing in the gorse. A large rock has been freed from the undergrowth so that it stands alone. Cut into the base and streaked brown by rainwater is a memorial composed of lead lettering, the only clear view of it afforded to birds passing overhead:

IN MEMORY OF
WILLIAM DONAGHY
OF LIVERPOOL
WHO DIED BESIDE THIS STONE
FEBRUARY 1914

Donaghy walked here in the bitter cold of February, a few months before the outbreak of the First World War. Whatever his motive, he was exactly my own age when he laid himself down in this lonely place. I lean my back against the rock and let the sweat dry on my face. In front of me the gorse tumbles into the river valley, the East Dart flowing around the contours of the hill then disappearing from sight. This was Donaghy's final view, quite probably the last thing he ever saw, and the bend in the river is overwhelmingly poignant, as if Donaghy walked just far enough to be alone before stepping out of life. All in all, I can think of worse places to die.

On my way back to Postbridge I drop down to the river and quench my thirst, wondering if Donaghy did the same a hundred years ago. The memorial has left its mark on me and for some reason the schoolteacher's memory seems precious, an obscure dedication lost in the middle of the moor. How long will it be, I wonder, before it is grown over and forgotten?

Back on the road the hearse meanders in harmony with another river, the Tavy slowly curling towards Cornwall. The Postbridge bread and cheese is still squashed in my coat pocket, and I try to fashion a ploughman's sandwich while keeping one hand on the wheel.

If this never-ending rain is a harbinger of the next Flood, I think the hearse will make a poor Ark. I drive through a deep puddle and water bubbles up through the floor, sloshing about underneath the coffin deck. In Tavistock, the clock of the abbey church glows orange through the afternoon deluge. I slow down to offer a wet hitchhiker a lift but he backs away from the road, waving me on with downcast eyes. The hearse is not the most inviting free ride but it seems a terrible waste of space. Enfield and my ghosts remain the sole passengers.

Beyond Botusfleming I pass a sign for the Pentillie Estate. If you have the spare change you can spend a night in Pentillie Castle's luxury B&B and take a stroll in the gardens, home to Sir James Tillie's mausoleum. Tillie built the castle in 1698, and his will decreed that when he died he be bound to a chair in his best clothes, placed in a stone folly in his garden and that his servants should leave him there with his books, his pipe and a glass of wine. According to legend his faithful retainers brought him daily refreshment for two years but, unable to bear his decomposing body any longer, finally had him interred, replacing his corpse with a statue. When the present owners restored the crumbling folly they found Tillie's body still in situ, hidden beneath the floor, where he remains to this day.

The winding lanes of north Cornwall go by in a blur as I head towards Bude and the Atlantic coast. The empty void over my shoulder seems to fill once more with all the characters I've collected on my travels. The numbers have swelled and it's getting crowded, the master gunner of the *Mary Rose* playing with a cannonball while Percy Shelley's corpse seems perplexed by the cavity in his chest.

When I finally arrive in the coastal hamlet of Morwenstow, I feel as if I've driven into another country altogether. In St Morwenna's churchyard the rain clouds have evaporated and the slate headstones glisten in the evening sun. A line of beech trees bow their heads over the perimeter wall.

Among the numberless graves stands the white figure of a woman. This is no graveyard ghost but a statue, its feet embedded in the grass and its face upturned to the sky. The white woman holds a shield in one hand and a cutlass in the other, her vital pose defying the scene that surrounds her.

Beyond the graveyard wall the land falls steeply towards the sea. In the autumn of 1842 a ship was wrecked on rocks that lie at the valley's bottom, where the fractured Cornish coast meets the Atlantic. The *Caledonia* had been sailing home from Odessa when it became trapped by a midnight storm, its crew of ten and its cargo of corn cast among the rocks. Save for one man the whole crew were drowned, crushed by the fury of the waves.

The vicar at Morwenstow on that stormy September night was Robert Hawker. At dawn he pulled the sailors' bodies from the surf, placing them on broken spars flung up on the shore. With the help of his parishioners, Hawker had the bodies carried up from the sea to the church, where they were set down beneath the lychgate. I turn to look at the arch through which I entered the graveyard, where once the drowned men were laid out in lines.

The *Caledonia* was just one of many wrecks that plagued Hawker's parish, and under these trees he buried forty-three sailors in forty-one years. The white woman, the salvaged figurehead of the ship itself, stands above their communal grave as if warding off future storms. Sitting beside her I feel an acute sense of loneliness, thinking of the men and women buried here who set out for so many different destinations but were all drawn to the fatal rocks of Morwenstow's beach.

My momentary isolation is nothing to that which Robert Hawker knew. I could climb back into the car and be back in a crowded street within the hour, or pick up my phone and dial anywhere in the world. Hawker relied on irregular letters to keep him in touch with England beyond Morwenstow, and he was as likely to hear voices in the wind as from human mouths.

In many ways Hawker's isolation meant that he lived his life in the past. The vicar was both terrified and enchanted by the place he came to inhabit, the savage coastline and the remote farms, all cut off from modernity. He adored the mystic origins of his church, the romance of martyred saints and the legends of the land, and as the rest of the world leapt into a frenzy of progress, Hawker's own life went slowly backward into his own imagined past.

The extremity of his home may have contributed to some of Hawker's famously eccentric habits. He dressed more like a pirate than a parson, his clergyman's dog collar matched with a purple velvet coat and knee-high sea boots. He was also said to have been very fond of animals, and was accompanied on his daily rounds of the parish by a pet pig. Much of the legend surrounding Hawker is based on fact, but his unconventional character has obscured the trials of his life, not least of which were the shipwrecks.

From the church I walk through the wooded valley of Tidna towards the sea. Banks of bracken flank the path and the saddle of Higher Sharpnose Point sticks up above the treeline. On the point itself a sheep trail peters out above a beach of black shale washed by the rising tide. I scramble down to the strand, where a waterfall freshens the sea.

Walking along the edge of the beach as the light begins to fade, I find the tideline a litter of indistinct shapes and get a taste of Hawker's dread at the thought of stumbling on another shipwrecked corpse. The parson's faith was bound up with the sea, ebbing and flowing with its tides, tested by its storms, reaffirmed by its beauty. He saw the devil in the waves and God's face in the calm. As I pick my way among giant car-sized boulders and imagine the horror of being cast among them, I feel the void within my own faithless heart.

Back on Sharpnose I climb higher to the bluff overlooking the beach and to 'Hawker's Hut'. The vicar built himself a lookout under the lip of the cliff, a place to write letters, compose poetry and watch for sailors in need of salvation. Sitting in his crude hut, Hawker became a kind of weathervane, waiting for the next storm that might send more poor souls onto the rocks.

The hut is the size of an old-fashioned privy, cut into the side of the cliff with a roof of turf. The whole has been assembled from the broken timbers of wrecks, many from the *Caledonia*, and inside it mimics the shape of a ship's hull, narrowing from ceiling to floor like a wooden keel. Considering its exposed position, the building is remarkably intact, stuck to the cliff like a mollusc to a rock.

Directly below the hut's stable door the cliff falls away to 'Lucky Hole', two tongues of rock that catch incoming waves. Perhaps the name was given because a sailor borne between these rocks had more chance of escaping alive, or maybe it's a cruel irony and to be caught in these sandstone jaws was certain death.

The sweep of the waves draws my gaze out across the Atlantic, with barely a rock between me and the Canadian coast. Just as with Donaghy the day before, I get the uncanny sense of staring through a dead man's eyes. I settle down in my sleeping bag on the hut's bench, the door ajar and the limitless sea before me. The bench sags against one wall and I rest my head against the panels, the timbers covered with the scrawls of visitors. 'Dear Mr Hawker, I hope this place brought you merry solitude from the dreary world.' The rhythm of the tide on the beach below is more powerful than a bottle full of sleeping pills.

Chapter Six

I crawl out of the hut and stretch on the ledge overlooking Morwenstow beach. My bones feel like part of a scrambled Rubik's Cube, disjointed and out of sequence. Returning past the vicarage where Robert Hawker once lived, I admire its chimneys, each carved to imitate the tower of a favourite church. When Hawker himself died, his epitaph was a simple line cut from one of his poems:

I would not be forgotten in this land.

The hearse complains bitterly at being roused from inactivity and I leave a black cloud of exhaust hanging over Morwenstow as I follow the coast road north. A part of me wants to take a day off from the dead, pull over on some Cornish beach and do nothing at all, and yet I'm so far down this road I might as well go on. The tombs seem to draw me against my will.

I pass close to the village of Heanton Punchardon on the Taw Estuary, where postman and poet Edward Capern is buried. His humble gravestone is capped by a hand bell, attached to a shallow niche above the epitaph. This is the same bell the postman rang on his rounds for thirty years, a cheery greeting as he delivered the mail, walking upwards of thirteen miles a day while scribbling his poetry on the backs of envelopes.

Capern's bell reminds me of a sinister funerary fashion that arose from the fear of being buried alive. Beginning in the 18th century, coffins began to be manufactured to incorporate safety mechanisms, devices that would allow anyone accidentally buried alive to escape, or at least contact the world of the living. These ranged from windows cut into coffins to check up on the corpse, to trumpet-mouthed tubes that could be sniffed regularly to ensure the body was decomposing. The most common was a network of cords attached to the fingers of the body and linked to a bell above ground. This design was critically flawed, because if the system was too sensitive any movement during decomposition would cause the alarm to sound.

I pick up speed down a steep hill outside Lynmouth, the wind roaring through the undercarriage and each bend in the road threatening to send me into oblivion. Every hundred yards, escape lanes offer deliverance in case a car's brakes should fail, and I prepare to take evasive action. Mercifully the road levels out and the sea glimmers through the trees.

The waterfront is busy with surfers loading and unloading their boards from roof racks. In many ways the hearse is the ideal surf mobile and you could fit the whole cast of an Australian sitcom in the back. I consider trying to trade it in for a tidy-looking VW van but drive on before temptation can get the better of me.

This morning's grim task is a quest for a child's tomb resting in a small English church, the work of a famous Italian sculptor. I cross the empty interior of Exmoor, headed for the village of Goathurst, though no goats are in evidence as I pass the welcome sign. The red rubble church peeks out from between a cluster of houses and a noticeboard next to the gate reads *St Edward the King and Martyr*. This is the same saint whose relics I sat alongside in Brookwood Cemetery, sipping green tea with Father Niphon.

Inside the gate is a table tomb with a crenellated top like the icing on a wedding cake. It seems to be sinking into the ground, as if its occupant has pressed a lift button and the whole thing is about to disappear into a hidden basement.

When I lift the latch on the church door a disembodied voice cries 'Hullo' from somewhere within, the sound echoing and multiplying as if a phantom choir has struck up a tune. A cheerful-looking man emerges from a side chapel and introduces himself as the church organist, Colin Chalmers.

I explain that I'm looking for a mortuary chapel.

'Of course!' Colin replies, and proudly escorts me up the aisle to a pair of red velvet curtains on the north wall. With great ceremony he vanishes between them, before a hand reappears beckoning me in.

It's icy cold when I step inside. Colin is standing with his back to a baroque memorial, and two fat cherubs hold an hourglass and a skull over his head. To his right a huge Jacobean tomb, shaped like a four-poster bed, dominates the room. Under the canopy lie Sir Nicholas and Lady Bridget Halswell, and around the base kneel their children, six sons and three daughters, each with a character all their own. The tomb is hard up against a window that casts a wan light on the couple's faces.

On Colin's other side is the statue of a small child, lost in shadow and holding a single flower in her right hand. Recognising the object of my quest, I cross to where it lies at the join between two walls.

'Ah yes ... poor Isabella,' Colin mutters.

The statue commemorates Isabella Kemeys, a child who died in 1835 before she was four years old. Colin spoke as if he knew her personally, and I'm touched by his empathy for the long dead.

In fact, Isabella appears not dead but asleep, her head resting on a pillow. The flower she holds is a rose with a broken stem. At some point a mouse has nestled in the folds of her hair and its droppings decorate her marble curls.

The sculptor, Raffaele Monti, was famous for his realism and I expect to feel sorrow at the sight of one who died so young. My own son is the same age as the girl but only the damp stains on her stone knees connect her to the world of childhood, like dirt picked up from a playground. In all other aspects she is an adult in miniature.

Colin offers me a seat next to an old church treasure chest (empty). When he first came here the tombs had mops and vacuum cleaners leant against them, and a huge wardrobe hid Isabella from sight. Water seeped in through the plaster and weeds grew against the warped medieval glass of the windows.

The memorials had been covered over and the chapel appropriated for storage.

When the church tried to raise money to restore the mortuary chapel, the archdeacon discovered that it still belonged to the Halswell family who built it. Their last surviving descendant was found and approached with a large bill for repairs. Wisely, she chose to spend her money on the living instead, and relinquished the family's deed to the chapel.

Even today the room is not reserved for the tombs, doubling as a space for signing the matrimonial register at weddings. Any local couple embarking on married life do so in the shadow of the departed. As we leave the chapel I notice some words etched into the floor, half hidden by a carpet. Colin joyfully peels back the rug for me, revealing an entire row of tombs staring up from the cold floor of the church. The carpet is fixed in place again and the vaults return to their anonymous repose.

Colin's off to play the organ at a funeral down the road. I offer him a lift in the hearse but he points out this might cause some confusion. We shake hands by the gate before going our separate ways, and I drive through the Somerset Levels in an abstracted mood, wondering how many men and women Colin's organ has ushered into the grave.

In Bridgwater old pillboxes line the riverside, a good reflection of the town, which seems to be on guard against something or someone. I pull over next to a 1970s shopping centre, in search of a toilet. The entrance looks like it's been welded shut, but after several attempts I prise it open and enter a no-man's-land of half-shuttered shops. Mo's Emporium of Wonder & Dreams shares floor space with third-hand cookers and a fancy-dress shop selling sex toys. Elsewhere a man laughs quietly to himself behind a window display filled with toy trains.

At the rear of the building is Diablo's Café, an appropriate name as some kind of fat fire seems to be in process. The door to the toilet is hanging off a single hinge but with a padlock and a sign saying, 'Customers only'. I battle my way through a pall of smoke to the till, and try to find something to buy, settling on a 'manchip', a local pastry filled with what looks like raspberry jam but turns out to be some sort of congealed laxative. I leave Bridgwater as fast as the hearse will carry me, the engine giving a satisfying roar as we bounce out of town.

Crossing over the River Spark, I head towards the village of West Camel. My next tomb is a stab in the dark, as records of its existence are few and contradictory. I'm looking for Henry White Parsons, a man much maligned by time, accused of murdering his own brother to take over his family estates and cheating his neighbours out of their land and money. Legend tells of a candlelit burial in a tomb Parsons built on his own property, but I have no idea what, if anything, remains of this edifice.

All that I can substantiate of the legend is what I've gleaned from Henry Parsons' last will and testament. The National Archive has a wonderful service where you can rummage through the wills of men and women who died centuries ago.

Parsons' cost me £2.50, which I considered a bargain until I downloaded ten pages of impenetrable 18th-century longhand.

The will is dated 1798, but there's no mention of burial by night or of a tomb erected before Parsons' demise. It says only that his nephew should see to it that he was 'interred in a handsome vault within my cedar plantation on Camel Hill'. A sum of £200 was to be set aside for a building to be erected over the vault, with an inscription on marble in his memory.

As I drive, I search the wayside for the hill on which the tomb was erected over two centuries ago, turning up a likely-looking lane past a garage forecourt with rusted pumps. The tomb is rumoured to be massive, a ten-metre-high obelisk towering over the surrounding fields, but if Parsons' grave could ever be seen from the road it's invisible today. A series of houses blink from behind thick hedgerows as the hearse climbs the slope, and just as I reach the hump of the hill I pass a gated driveway with a small painted sign on the rails: *Parson's Steeple*. I slam on the brakes, my toothbrush and torch sliding across the coffin deck as the hearse tilts sideways.

Parson's Steeple? Is this a nickname for the lost tomb? Timidly, I open the barred gate and walk along a gravelled drive to a small, unassuming bungalow with a wooden deck. An orchard surrounds the house on one side but I see no sign of an obelisk.

I knock on what appears to be the front door and wait for an awkward interval, praying that someone is home. Finally, footsteps can be heard from within. Instead of the door opening, a frosted glass window is unlatched and a round face peers through a narrow slit. A shy-looking man regards me suspiciously from within.

'Hi,' I begin nervously. 'Sorry to bother you. I was just wondering if you've got a grave in your garden?'

The man's face softens immediately and the window opens wider.

'You'd better come round the back,' he replies.

I skip across some ornamental planting to where he is waiting on the deck with arms folded. He looks me up and down in quick appraisal.

'So, you've come to see Henry, have you?'

I follow my guide into the garden across a neatly mown lawn. He tells me people used to peer over his hedge to catch sight of the tomb but no one has asked him about it in years.

As we round the back of the bungalow the tomb comes into view. At first it appears to be one solid mass of ivy, but approaching closer the form of the memorial emerges beneath the vines, an arch under a broken obelisk and a hollowed-out recess behind it. There's no inscription on the blank wall.

'It fell off before we came here in '77.'

I marvel that Parson's monument is still standing at all. It looks as if the ivy is the only thing holding the stone together, binding the memory of the man with its thick creepers. As we look upwards a squirrel leaps from a neighbouring tree onto the summit, disappearing in a nest of twigs.

While we stand talking several military planes thunder overhead. My companion explains that the bungalow lies on the flight path of RNAS Yeovilton and for years the navy's

Sea Harrier jump jets used to fly low over the roof, blasting the tottering tomb with their engines.

'I wrote to them, but they didn't give a shit,' he says with resignation.

Researching the tomb, I came across the story of a vault under the obelisk being broken into in the 1960s. A local man, William Orel, believed the tomb to be filled with Parsons' treasure but found nothing except a coffin with a broken lid. Inside, the body was curiously well preserved, but when the tomb raider touched the corpse it promptly crumbled to dust.

'Do you think Parsons is still buried here?' I ask.

'Don't know. If he is, he's got company. We've buried five cats next to him.'

Thanking Parsons' keeper for his time, I return down the hill to the graveyard of All Saints in West Camel. On the exterior wall of the church is a large tablet whose face has begun to flake away. *To the Memory of John White Parsons* can just be made out on the surviving portion. Here lies Henry's nephew, the man who was tasked in his uncle's will with erecting the obelisk. His memory has fared little better, and time is running out for those who wish to see any trace of this peculiar family, quietly fading into Somerset's past.

A rainbow floods the hearse as I leave Camel Hill, as if the mythical pot of gold lies stashed under my passenger seat. I drive without pause until Bradford-upon-Avon, where the hearse stalls in a suicidal position halfway up another hill.

The engine refuses to respond to my frantic pedal-pumping and the line of traffic behind me erupts with horns. I release the handbrake, using the slope to turn downhill, and coast silently past the furious motorists with a 'Have you no respect' expression etched on my face. The engine returns to life before the traffic light at the bottom and I gear up for a second run.

I'm headed for Cleeve Cloud, the highest point in the Cotswolds, and a Stone Age grave that's one of the last great barrows surviving in England. The road winds its way skyward until I draw up beside a sawn-off tree stump and a signpost pointing to a path that disappears into a wood.

Tramping through the trees, I emerge beneath the ridge of the hill and sit down to catch my breath. Above me the sun sweeps cloud shadows across a closely grazed hillside. A 'God spot' appears in a bank of cloud behind the wood and briefly illuminates the ground on which I'm sitting – sometimes the weather conspires to make even the most godless of us believe.

Approached from below, Belas Knap, 'the beautiful summit', looks like the hump of a whale breaching the hill's crest. Long barrows are scattered through the English countryside but most have been destroyed by the plough. The Neolithic craftsmen who built them were some of the world's first farmers but modern-day agriculture has levelled most of their ancient monuments.

The mound is a trapezoid shape, and the north end opens in the middle, two 'horns' projecting out with a false entrance tucked between them. Some scholars believe this to have been a 'spirit door', a way for the dead to come and go from the tomb and collect offerings left by the living.

The first burials at Belas Knap date to the tail end of the Stone Age, although the site continued to be used for centuries. It was not a single-use tomb, but a series of vaults regularly reopened to house new members. It may even be a grand barrow built over earlier mounds, enclosing and incorporating several generations of interments.

Up close, the walls beneath the grass banks are composed of intricate drystone, thousands of pieces of limestone placed one on top of the next. No mortar binds them – it's like a perfect jigsaw puzzle without a visible chink.

The men who laid these walls did so as much as fifty-five centuries ago, and yet 'wallers' still exist in the Cotswolds today, those who've inherited some part of this ancient trade. In 1938, *Country Life* magazine described one such craftsman as 'working in a dream with the rhythmic certainty of unconscious memory'. As little as we know about the people who built and were buried at Belas Knap, these modern-day wallers provide an unbroken link between them and us.

Curiously, a modern burial barrow has been built in Cambridge, in imitation of our ancestors. Sacred Stones, a company 'dedicated to creating meaningful final resting places', has planned a number of long barrows to accommodate the ashes of the 21st century. You can reserve a niche for the next ninety-nine years, but if you desire your loved ones to stay put for five millennia there doesn't seem to be a quoted price.

The barrow has been excavated many times, but the chambers where bones were discovered were propped up and left open in the 1920s. Circling the mound, I crawl into one of these open tombs, sitting against a drystone wall at the rear. I lean on the rock and am surprised to find it decorated with stick men carrying spears. Sadly, these are not a rare survival of the stone age but the whimsy of some other tomb tourist who sat here before me.

After the steep climb up the hill, the cool hollow of the tomb lulls me into a doze. I drift in and out of sleep until I'm woken by a sound I've never heard before. It begins softly, a fast, breathless chorus of voices rising in pitch and frequency, but before long it's a great wave of noise, like the sound of something in pain but multiplied. As it draws nearer I don't know whether to hide or run. Cornered in the tomb, I step out to face the unseen cacophony.

On all sides of the burial mound, pouring along the perimeter and plunging into the woods below, is a vast sea of foxhounds. The field is invisible beneath a roiling mass of black, white and brown. Dogs thunder past, intent on finding whatever it is they chase, all emitting the same canine keen.

I've never heard a dog bay for blood but it's a primal sound, a voice that seems well-suited to this ancient place. Instinctively I climb on top of the barrow as if I'm the object of the hunt. The higher ground affords a view of the whole pack and, as I watch, the last tail disappears beyond the treeline.

From Belas Knap I drop out of the hills and make my way towards Tewkesbury and its 11th-century abbey. I pull up in the ecclesiastical car park where a parade of ornamental yews, shaped like cheerleaders' pom-poms, leads the way to the main entrance. On either side, colossal cedars have taken over what remains of a graveyard and their roots have half-digested the headstones. In a few more years any lingering memorials will have been swallowed whole.

The abbey is gearing up for evensong and two choristers push past me in the doorway, sweating in black gowns with ruffle collars. The warmth of the summer evening is banished inside the abbey, and a Victorian boiler labours as it struggles to heat thousands of square feet of stone and marble. I pick up a visitor's brochure and scan through a 'top ten' of the abbey's attractions. The tomb I've come to see isn't listed, so I set off to see if I can ferret it out.

On my way towards the east end I pass the gift shop, where the brochure mentions that the Duke of Somerset is buried under the till. Impressed by this piece of marketing, I stick my head around a stand of postcards to take a closer look. Sadly, there's no evidence of the duke. The gift shop has a poured concrete floor, but every time someone buys a fridge magnet the chime of the till must echo in Somerset's invisible catacomb.

At the very end of the aisle I come face to face with the tomb I seek. Under an arch of white stone a prone figure lies on his back, his face upturned and his arms by his sides. In contrast to the canopy, the statue is a deep golden-brown, polished by the caress of pilgrims past.

The figure is known as the 'starved monk'. It's an outstanding example of a cadaver tomb, a style of memorial intended to show a person's corpse in a state of decay. A half-skeletal body lies with its skin stretched tight over exposed bones, and the view afforded to the passer-by is akin to staring into an open grave. The head is thrust back, the neck arched and the mouth ajar, as if the dead man were lying on a bed of nails.

These grisly keepsakes reached peak vogue at the end of the Middle Ages, usually being installed before their owners had actually died, so they could pass their own lifeless and worm-eaten image on their way to daily prayer.

Speaking of worms, the starved monk has his fair share. In fact, what makes the effigy so remarkable is that no fewer than five hidden 'vermin' feast on his remains. Of the fifty or so cadaver tombs in England, this is the only one with such a level of bestial detail. Somewhere on his body or in the folds of the burial shroud lie a worm, a snake, a mouse, a frog and a beetle.

Hunting for this famous five is a challenge. The most obvious is the mouse, which sits in the monk's chest cavity chewing on a piece of 15th-century intestine. I quickly tick off the worm (exiting the monk's left kneecap), the snake (slithering through the shroud) and the toad (happily ensconced in the hood). The beetle, however, remains a mystery.

I view the cadaver from every possible angle, leaning in over the stomach and squatting down to inspect between the toes. I've almost admitted defeat when I realise that what I'd taken for a large wart on the monk's bicep is, in fact, the elusive insect. The carving is so worn that an entomologist would be flummoxed.

I'm elated at having completed the challenge and involuntarily cry out, 'I found it!', in a loud boast that echoes around the ambulatory. A couple reading a plaque stop and stare at me, perched with my hands on the monk's ribcage, before hurrying towards the nearest exit.

No one really knows who the starved monk was. The tomb is sometimes referred to as the 'Wakeman Cenotaph' after a one-time abbot of the abbey who was buried elsewhere. But the style of the sculpture pre-dates Abbot Wakeman's death and its true subject remains a mystery. Whatever has become of the monk's bones, there can't be much left for vermin to feast on today.

Near the cadaver tomb is a stand of offertory candles. Being a godless sort I've never lit one before, but something about the effigy inspires me to do so now. I choose a red tealight with a golden wick and place it at the monk's feet. Behind the stone arch dozens of floral bouquets have been hidden, intended for an upcoming service and labelled for different parts of the church. They make the tomb look like it belongs to the recent victim of a high-school tragedy instead of a six-hundred-odd-year-old corpse.

Leaving the monk to his jealous vermin, I make my way back to the abbey door as a service starts up in the choir stalls, passing other tomb effigies wedged in niches or lodged in their own private chapels. At some point curiosity over-comes respect, and graves that have been sealed for centuries are uncorked like old wines, antiquarians eager to validate the identities of those within.

One of the most famous of these grand openings was not here at Tewkesbury but at neighbouring Worcester. The tomb of King John, installed in the cathedral in 1232, has twice been opened, and the second time a thorough inventory of the king's body and vestments was carried out.

At five foot six and a half, the king and I would have stood nose to nose. A robe of crimson damask was found on his body and the remains of a sword and scabbard lay in a heap of rust alongside him. An entertaining story that grew up around the antiquarian's study was that, while the tomb lay open, a local man prised off a piece of the king's decayed flesh and used it to bait a fishing hook. He sat on a bridge in Worcester and, on catching a large perch, paraded it through town with a grin, telling anyone who would listen exactly what he'd done.

On my return to the car park I find the hearse being examined by a man in a hi-vis jacket. Thinking I'm about to receive a parking ticket I try to look business-like, although my jeans and T-shirt hardly scream professional undertaker. My fears are unwarranted as the man turns out to be a local with an interest in old cars. He asks me if he can have a look at the engine.

I yank the lever on the dash and the bonnet pops up with the sound of a dinner gong. The man stoops for a closer look, then straightens up.

'You good at mechanics?' he says, with a barely concealed grimace.

'I can fix a bicycle,' I reply evasively. 'I think.'

The man mutters, 'Good luck,' then walks off into the gathering dusk. I take a look at the engine myself before closing the bonnet. Streaks of oil decorate every visible surface and a faint, persistent hiss can be heard escaping from somewhere deep within. I pat the battery for luck, then close the lid.

* * *

Trawling west into Wales, I almost drift asleep on the M4, lulled by light traffic and the evening breeze. I'm only half-awake when I miss the exit for Llantrisant and have to double back on a looping bridge over the motorway.

'The Parish of the Three Saints' lies on a hill overlooking service stations and roadside hotels. I haven't come here to pay homage to any Christian saint but to a Welshman of a different creed.

I park on a steep cobbled street in the heart of the town. A statue of a man dominates the small market square, his arms outstretched to embrace the houses on either side. The figure has a bronze cloak billowing out behind him and the skin of a fox on his head, its eyes set above his own and its legs trailing on either side of his long beard. The headlights of passing cars illuminate a sickle he clasps in one hand while the other holds a firebrand, as if he is about to set the whole town alight. A plaque at the base reads, *Dr William Price, Surgeon, Chartist, and Self-styled Druid*.

The dark draws in as I cross the street and step into the Bear Inn. On another night, in 1884, flames appeared in the fields behind the pub. Townsfolk drawn to the light discovered a figure in white robes on the hill, busy stoking a barrel of paraffin. As a crowd gathered, police arrived and overturned the barrel, out of which rolled the burning body of a child. The man was William Price, the town doctor, and the body was that of his infant son.

The pub is almost empty when I step inside, an elderly couple watching *EastEnders* on a large screen at the rear. I walk to the bar and the landlady looks up in surprise, as if she never expected anyone to ask for a drink.

William Price remains Llantrisant's most famous son, even though he was raised on a small farm some ten miles from here. He came to this quiet hilltop town already middle-aged, a refuge from a world that believed him half-mad.

From his humble beginnings, Price showed promise as a student and became an apprentice to a local doctor. He went to London, where he became a member of the Royal College of Surgeons before returning to Wales to open his first practice. Running parallel with the young man's aptitude for modern medicine was a belief in an older order of healers. Over time, Price immersed himself in the cult of neo-druidism and its practices, peopled by a group of Welsh nationalists who traced their faith back to the bards of the Iron Age. When not treating patients at the Pontypridd Chainworks, he could be found enacting his own rituals among the stone circles and ancient monuments that lie across this stretch of Glamorgan.

Mixed in with Price's druidic beliefs was the philosophy of free love. For years he lived out of wedlock with a woman called Ann Morgan, then, at the grand old age of eighty-one, he finally committed to marriage, to a woman sixty years his junior. The ceremony was performed in the open air on the 'rocking stone', a huge slab of natural slate on high ground overlooking two Welsh rivers.

When his young wife, Gwenllian Llewellyn, bore him a son, Price blasphemously named their progeny Jesus Christ. Tragically, the boy died before he was five months old. Among many Christian precepts rejected by the doctor was the idea that the body must be buried whole, and he adhered instead to the pre-Christian tradition of burning the dead. This led to the attempted cremation of his son on the hillside at Llantrisant.

Price was eventually acquitted of all wrongdoing as the act of cremation had no statutory law against it. The old man returned home to cremate his son's body at the same spot. From then on the field became sacred to Price and central to his religion. Reports of him walking naked through the grass reciting poetry and followed by his cows fuelled the legend that was steadily growing around him.

I preside over a cold plate of scampi and chips, occasionally glancing up to find myself being closely observed by the couple watching the soap opera. To hide myself from their inquisition I open the first pages of a short story inspired by the events of Price's extraordinary life.

The Bloodstone Tragedy was written by a twenty-five-year-old Arthur Conan Doyle, yet to invent Sherlock Holmes. It tells the tale of a hiker who strays into a narrow gorge in the Welsh mountains and is captured by a madman, who attempts to sacrifice her to his pagan gods. As he drags his victim to a pyre to burn her alive, he's stopped at the last moment by her rescuers, who knock him to the ground. When the druid wakes from the blow he is decreed perfectly sane and reverts to his former life as a respected scientist. The story trades on Price's reputation as a scholar and a doctor but also a man of eccentric dress and occult habit.

I wash the scampi down with a can of Fanta and cross to the bar. The landlady is well acquainted with the biography of William Price and recounts the story of his own cremation. When the druid's health finally failed at the age of ninety-three, he asked to be burnt on a pyre built over the site of his son's. His fame had travelled far since winning the court case that exonerated him, and over twenty thousand people bought tickets to see him burn. He was duly laid inside a stone-walled enclosure and set alight by his friend Dr Robert Anderson, a local hangman. Some who attended had come to think of Price as a kind of prophet, and there were reports of bystanders groping in the hot ash for a fragment of his mortal remains.

I ask if there's anything left of the pyre itself.

'Nothing up there now,' says the landlady. 'I used to rent the field for my horses.'

Thanking her, I walk down behind the pub to the foot of Caerlan Hill. Its dark contours are just visible against the glow of a streetlight and a private drive leads up to a care home for adults with autism. I think this new use would have pleased Price, whose eccentricity often obscured his work as a health pioneer. He believed in a free health service, as well as being vehemently anti-smoking in an age when the whole world smelt of tobacco.

As I make my way back to the hearse I reflect on the legacy of this 19th-century shaman. The case of his son, followed by his own funeral, helped turn the tide in the public perception of cremation. Less than ten years after the doctor druid was immolated, the Cremation Act 1902 was passed, paving the way for the establishing of nationwide crematoria and a gradual popular shift from burial to burning.

Price was survived by his young wife, two daughters and a second son, also named Jesus. Jesus Christ II did not die until the 1960s but, by then, had mercifully changed his name.

From Llantrisant I drive on through the dark to Port Talbot. The whole town glows with the fires of the steelworks, chimneys spouting jets of flame into the night sky. The hearse fills with the sharp tang of smelting and the hulk of a blast furnace stalks the hard shoulder, a shape defined by security lights and smoke. I imagine ten thousand druids cremated in unison, their ash blanketing the motorway like snow.

On down the coast, and the infernal glow of Port Talbot and Swansea slowly fades in the rear-view mirror. Turning off for Rhossili, the road narrows, the dark deepens and the cabin of the hearse shrinks around me. I'm alone with the pale light of the dashboard, suspended, my whole existence contained by three doors and a coffin deck.

Out on the Gower peninsula a strong wind has got up. I've spent too long in the hearse and my fingers have turned china white from gripping the wheel, the kind of industrial injury more commonly associated with operating a jackhammer. A bale of plastic from a field blows across the road, jumping a hedgerow and disappearing again. Every wheelie bin in Wales seems to have blown into my path and I collide with one outside Glynneath, the green plastic popping under the front tyre and leaving a trail of potato peel in my wake.

I turn in for the night in a lay-by somewhere beneath the Black Mountain, a hill divided by old 'corpse roads', paths villagers once used to carry their dead home. Leaning back on the driver's bench I dine on a jumbo pack of Welsh cakes, with 'Made by Welsh People' underlined on the packaging. I devour the lot, covering the black leather of the hearse in caster sugar, as if an undertaker with dandruff has sat here itching his scalp.

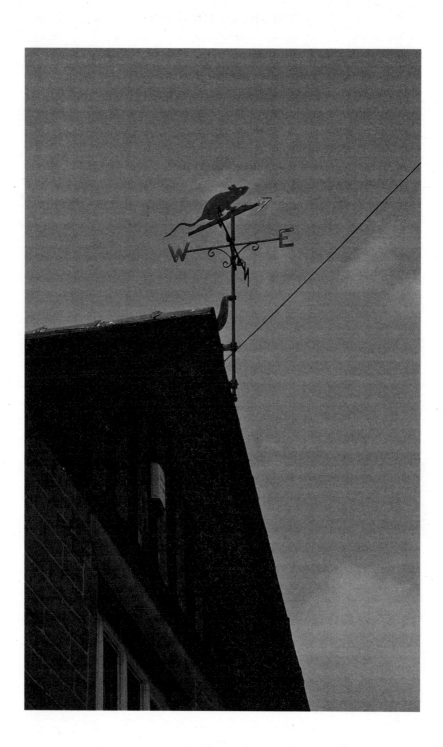

Chapter Seven

In 1984 a film crew arrived in Shrewsbury searching for a location for their adaptation of Charles Dickens's famous novella, *A Christmas Carol*. Nowhere better fitted the bill than the church of St Chad's, with its enclosed graveyard and high brick walls. The crew settled on an 18th-century tomb for Ebenezer's final resting place and asked if they might carve his name into the existing stone. The church agreed, no doubt seeing the tourist potential of having a famous, if fictitious, celebrity added to their burial register.

I wake in the hearse with a crick in my neck. I seem to have rolled off the coffin deck in the night, and find myself lying against one window, with my breath condensed on the glass. As I leave the Brecon Beacons behind me, painted signs on the road read 'Araf, Araf' ('Slow, Slow') and I pass a police van with a camera in the side window. The hearse is barely capable of maintaining the speed limit, let alone exceeding it.

On the outskirts of Shrewsbury what looks like a retirement home stands next to a churchyard. A scattering of elderly residents wander through the garden while graves press hard against the boundary wall. Depending on your point of view, the siting of the home seems completely insensitive or incredibly efficient.

In the town centre I bypass the cathedral and drive towards the sunken gardens of the old quarry and the Georgian façade of St Chad's. The church is an odd shape, a great circle conjoined to a tower at the south end. As well as Ebenezer, St Chad's has other claims to fame, including christening an infant Charles Darwin.

I draw up beside the graveyard railings, and a man scurries out of a booth in the church car park and raps on my window.

'What are you doing?' he says, looking accusingly at the hearse.

'I've come to see Ebenezer Scrooge.'

He nods wearily, as if this is something he hears every day, and I step out of the car and follow him to the graveyard gates. A heavy bolt and chain have been secured across the latch, and there's no other way in.

'Sorry. Looks like they've locked up for the day.'

The gates are ten feet high but with crossbars of iron. They don't look like they'd be too hard to climb.

'Would you mind if I just hopped over for a quick look?'

The man looks at me, mystified. 'As long as you don't nick anything.' After a pause he adds, 'Scrooge is third on the left, flat on the ground.'

Although by this point in my journey I'm practised at breaking into graveyards, I feel a little self-conscious doing so in broad daylight. I haul myself over the gate as quickly as I can and drop down into an empty avenue on the far side.

Without the man's directions I might have wandered the tombs for hours. I find Scrooge exactly where I was told to look, flush with the grass in the graveyard's front row. A large yew tree leans in over him.

In the film adaptation the churchyard is heavily dusted in fake snow as the Ghost of Christmas Future leads Scrooge among the graves. A long skeletal finger is pointed at the tomb, the inscription covered in a drift. Scrooge sinks to his knees and wipes the tomb with the cuff of his jacket, so revealing his own name.

If you have a relatively common name, as I do, it's possible to find your namesake in a remarkable number of graveyards and cemeteries. It turns out I was buried in Norfolk in 1915, Kingston in the late 1980s, and more recently in Bristol and Manchester. On average, a 'Jack Cooke' seems to have been interred in England every thirty years or so, going back several centuries. My mortal remains can also be found in at least ten of America's fifty states, including Texas, Georgia, Arizona and the Carolinas. Never have I felt so little ownership of my own moniker.

I turn again to Ebenezer's inscription, occupying the top half of a cracked slab of stone, the letters fresh against the lichen. The lower half still bears the epitaph of the tomb's actual occupant but it's illegible and I squint at the grave for some time, trying to make out if it belongs to 'Sarah' or 'Elijah', then run my fingers over the words like a blind man reading braille. Whatever poor soul was laid to rest here, their memory has been superseded by an entirely imaginary character. It's a wonderful example of tomb appropriation, but, as a consolation, they receive more visitors to their graveside than ever before.

Rumbling out of Shrewsbury along an arrow-straight road, I head for an airfield and a man who vanished into thin air. The hearse has finally shaken off its daily coughing fit and the engine warms to its task, frightening a flock of pigeons.

I turn down a lane leading to Sleap Airfield. The airfield belonged to the RAF until the 1960s, and the side of the track is littered with the shells of old planes, tarpaulins half-covering cockpits and broken-off wing tips in beds of nettles.

There's no one in the flight control when I arrive, so I make my way up to the members' café. I open the door to be greeted by the smell of frying bacon and fresh coffee. The room is half-filled with groups of men and women sitting at wooden tables, or lounging in easy chairs in what was once the control tower. Large windows frame a view of the runway, where a plane taxies towards a hangar.

Opposite the door is a large charcoal portrait that forms a focal point in the room. A young man in a pilot's jacket surveys me from behind the glass, eyes half-closed. His face looks almost angelic, unmarked by age or worry, and a brass plaque beneath identifies him as Eric Lock, a fighter pilot who lost his life during the Second World War.

Although it's close to one o'clock in the afternoon, I order the 'Flying Start' breakfast, consisting of three eggs (over easy), five rashers of bacon (dead crispy), as well as beans, hash browns, tomatoes, mushrooms, a sausage and some kind of black pudding. I carry my plate over to a free table beneath a number of black and white photographs.

Several of the photographs are of the same pilot, Eric Lock, and the largest shows him posing with his Spitfire. On the side of the aeroplane's nose are twenty-six painted swastikas, one for each of his aerial victories. A true Shropshire lad, Lock was born and raised in a farming family at nearby Bayston Hill. When war broke out he was only nineteen years old but, in spite of his youth, Lock immediately signed up for pilot training. He completed his instruction on the eve of the Battle of Britain, and was hastily posted to an RAF squadron.

From the quiet of a rural upbringing to his first aerial missions, Lock barely had time to turn twenty, and within a few weeks of combat he had gone from nobody to national hero. His strike rate was almost 100 per cent, and it was rare that he returned from the skies without having shot down an enemy plane. By the end of the campaign the farmer's son had become the most successful flying ace in Britain.

In spite of his natural flying talent, Lock did not survive the Battle of Britain unscathed. Bullets from a German fighter entered three of his limbs and he spent months having skin grafts before returning to duty in the summer of 1941. A few weeks later, at the peak of his fame and only twenty-one years old, Lock disappeared over the English Channel. His squadron believed he had crash landed in the sea.

As no trace of his body was ever found, Lock was declared MIA or 'missing in action'. In the absence of a fixed grave, memorials to him are scattered across England. His name is carved on a stone wall in Surrey, in relative anonymity along-side thousands of others, and a street bears his name in Bayston Hill close to where he grew up. Then there is this small bar in a control tower overlooking an airfield.

Eventually I'm defeated by my breakfast, a meal more suited to fuelling war efforts than itinerant authors. As I pay the bill I look around the room once more. The whole place is a kind of shrine, with its framed memories of fallen heroes and its view of a runway that once launched them into the air. As I wave goodbye to the members in their easy chairs, I fancy I hear the dull drone of a plane circling high above the airfield, Eric Lock on his way to fight another battle in the sky.

Somewhere on the outskirts of Birmingham I cross over a canal, part of the enormous network that spreads through the city and across the Midlands. As the hearse passes a canary-coloured narrowboat, I'm put in mind of the story of John Baskerville, printer and type designer, whose body went on a long odyssey after his death.

Baskerville did not believe in God. He asked to be buried in his own back garden on Birmingham's Easy Hill and his wishes were duly carried out in 1775, his body entombed under the lawn in a lead coffin bearing his very own Baskerville font, still in use today.

Not long after his burial, Baskerville's house was sold. In 1791 it was ransacked during the Birmingham Riots and abandoned as a ruin. Eventually a new canal network was built through what was formerly the garden and the surrounding area filled with industrial wharves. In the 1820s workmen dug up Baskerville's coffin and it was passed through the hands of different Birmingham businessmen, who displayed the well-preserved corpse to punters. Contemporary accounts say he was found beautifully dressed in silk, linen and lace, and that the skin of his face was dry but intact, complete with eyebrows and eyelashes.

At some point, presumably after the corpse became too nauseating to exhibit, he was transferred to the vaults of Birmingham's Christ Church on New Street. Another half-century passed before Baskerville was on the move again, this time because the church itself had been demolished to make way for a new shopping precinct in 1899. The bodies from the vaults were relocated across town to Warstone Lane Cemetery and Baskerville was placed at the very centre of the burial ground, in a vault beneath the chapel.

During the Second World War it was not just Birmingham's living who suffered German bombs. Warstone Lane Cemetery received several direct hits, including a bomb that struck the chapel beneath which Baskerville lay entombed. The damaged building was never restored and in 1958 it was demolished completely. The vaults, along with a plaque to Baskerville's memory, were sealed up with brick. Who can say if the printer is finally at rest or whether the turmoil of the 21st century will cause his coffin to resume its travels?

*   *   *

Beyond Birmingham the hearse has another accidental interlude on a motorway, and I hug the hard shoulder as traffic
whistles by. Motorways seem the perfect illustration of the
stark divide between life and death. The verge is erupting
with spring growth, untamed trees and shrubs forming a
dense screen of leaves and blossom. In contrast, the central
reservation is a strip of sickly hued grass layered with dust,
and the asphalt the uniform grey of the grave.

Off the highway and crossing Repton Marsh, the needle
spire of St Wystan's Church comes into view, its windows like
watchful eyes. After six hundred miles on the road, I'm about
to get my first brush with royalty.

In 1779 a workman was employed to dig a hole in the
church floor and make space for a new grave. He dutifully
lifted up the flagstones and began work, sweating as he
broke through layers of stone and brick compacted under
the chancel. With his feet in the hole as he toiled away,
anyone walking up the aisle would have seen a figure cut off
at the knees.

Without warning the man suddenly vanished. Unwittingly,
he had put his spade through the ceiling of a crypt, covered
up and hidden under the church. Man and spade tumbled
through the opening, landing on a partially flooded floor ten
feet below. Bewildered and bruised, the workman found
himself surrounded by carved columns, rising to a vaulted
ceiling through which he had just fallen into the past.

I enter the porch of St Wystan's as the eight bells in the
tower call the hour. A huge clockface has been painted onto
the tower's stonework, a black face with golden roman

numerals. Inside, the way into the crypt is guarded by the statue of a knight. He lies on a raised tomb, his helmet serving as a pillow and his body rigid beneath plate armour. Every single inch of him has been scrawled upon. Across his chest *R S Falcon* stands out in beautiful cursive script, while his legs are so covered with initials they look like the plaster cast of a schoolchild. Someone has even immodestly carved their name across the poor man's crotch.

Although the knight bears the signatures of countless strangers, his own name and origin remain a mystery. For many years he languished in the churchyard, thrown out during refurbishments, but eventually he was brought back in from the cold.

Next to the nameless knight there's a switch on the wall, and when I flick it the stairway below me lights up. The crypt rediscovered by the gravedigger on that fateful afternoon belonged to the kings of Mercia, an Anglo-Saxon dynasty that ruled England for three hundred years. I turn the light off again and commandeer a candle from the church altar. I want to get as close to the original atmosphere of the burial chamber as I possibly can.

Down the steps I go, slipping on treads polished by generations of feet, arriving in a royal dormitory for the dead. The air is several degrees cooler and the candlelight casts shadows on monolithic columns, pitted like acne-scarred skin. Spiral carving twists around the pillars and between them lie stone niches for the kings. Their bodies would have been buried outside in the churchyard until the flesh had rotted from their bones, then brought down here in caskets.

Saxon royalty had wonderful names: Aethelbald, Wiglaf, Wigstan. Each person entombed here believed their bones would be venerated for centuries, but it was the last set of bones that became the centre of attention, the body of Wigstan, after whom the church itself is named.

Wigstan's life was short but eventful. What scant details have trickled down the centuries suggest he turned down his claim to the crown in favour of religious abstinence. His career as a monk was then abruptly cut short by a jilted cousin, who murdered the young man for refusing a marriage to Wigstan's widowed mother. Although he was dead and buried before his eighteenth birthday, a new afterlife awaited this unfortunate soul. Miracles began to be reported about the ground Wigstan was buried in: shafts of light emanating from the soil and locks of golden hair sprouting from his grave. He was soon exhumed and brought here to lie in the mausoleum of his grandfather, and the crypt was transformed into a shrine, new passages cut under the church to allow pilgrims in and out.

Returning up the steps with my candle held before me, I recall the words of another visitor to the crypt, the poet John Betjeman, who came here in the 1950s. Emerging from the sepulchre he wrote a short but memorable review:

Holy air encased in stone.

* * *

I only know of two people who drive a hearse for domestic and social affairs, and they're both fictional Americans. The flame-haired heroine of TV drama *Six Feet Under*, and Harold from *Harold and Maude*, who is so disenchanted with life that he fashions his sports car into a hearse hybrid. As I drive from Repton towards Mansfield I consider what afterlife I might give my own hearse on its return; sell it to a musician as a band wagon or paint it a happy colour to drive the kids to school?

In Mansfield I leave the hearse double-parked at the bottom of Sandy Lane. I've come here to trace the footsteps of a man who, for the last twenty years of his life, walked this road every day.

In retirement Charles Thompson fell in love with the forest of Sherwood that surrounded his home town. A man of routine, he devoted much of his final years to prayer, charity and gardening, but every afternoon, without fail, he would march from his front door across Mansfield to the edge of the forest. There he would sit on the same grassy knoll in a clearing, a spot he promised himself should one day be his grave. When he became too infirm to walk the distance he rode a horse, and when even the ride became a struggle he let a friend lead the horse by its reins.

I cross onto Skerry Lane and then over a playing field that was a racecourse in Thompson's day. An evening breeze blows through Mansfield and I'm glad to stretch my legs after another day in the hearse. Negotiating the Newark Road, I arrive on a small common sandwiched between terraced houses; at its centre is a circular wall of stone with a clutch of holly trees growing inside.

A man with a thick Mansfield accent is yelling at a large dog called Alfie. The dog looks like something out of a police training advert, and I try to give the pair a wide berth. In spite of my best efforts the man spots me and crosses over for a chat.

'Nice dog,' I say nervously as Alfie drools on my toes.

'Thanks,' he says, making no move to restrain the beast. 'He's a cross – Rhodesian ridgeback, Staffordshire bull terrier, a little bit of Dogue de Bordeaux.'

Alfie's owner asks me what I'm doing in Mansfield and I tell him I've come to see Charles Thompson.

'What?' He looks at me as if I've lost my mind. 'You do know he's dead?'

Alfie scents another out-of-towner on the far side of the common and sprints off to investigate, his master grudgingly following along behind him. I hasten over to the circular wall and peer through the iron gate set in the middle.

When Thompson died on 14 December 1784 he was buried here, 'beneath the wild heather of his native forest'. On the morning of his funeral a thick snow fell. The procession followed the same route I've just walked, the hearse carriage making tracks in the snow, and villagers flocked from the surrounding countryside to see off a man who had been a benefactor of the poor. By the conclusion of the service the snow was falling again, thicker than before, and children crying from the cold were lifted into the now empty hearse by the driver and carried back to town.

What made the funeral remarkable was not the weather but the manner in which the grave was dug. Thompson had written in his will that if the gravediggers could make the hole six yards deep they were 'to be handsomely paid for their trouble.' Six yards is eighteen feet, over four times the depth of an ordinary grave. A contemporary account of the funeral confirmed that the depth was reached and that 'A large flat stone was placed over the coffin, resting on a ledge of rock.' In addition, Thompson's will set aside money for a local mason to build the enclosing wall and for a mound of earth to be raised over the grave and planted with trees.

Why was Thompson buried so far from a churchyard and why was he adamant that he should be buried so deep? The reasons for his profound grave relate to the defining event of his life, a natural disaster that he witnessed first-hand.

When he was a young man in Mansfield his mother's premature death caused Thompson to seek his fortune in London. He found work with a cloth merchant who sent him across the sea to Isfahan in modern-day Iran, where for ten years he helped clothe the armies of the Shah of Persia. When the Shah was assassinated and the country descended into chaos, Thompson was forced to flee back to London. He was not long in the city before going abroad again, this time to Lisbon to set up a new arm of the enterprise.

On All Saints' Day 1755, almost five years to the day after his arrival in Portugal, Charles Thompson was at home in his study when a massive earthquake hit the city. The room's door slammed shut with the violence of the first shock. Unable to release it, he staggered to the window and managed to wrestle it open.

The scene that greeted Thompson must have struck a man with his religious convictions as hell on earth. Church towers crumbled before his eyes and whole buildings were swallowed in great rifts torn in the ground, some as much as ten feet wide. The city danced in front of him, then collapsed into a smoking heap of rubble, like an 18th-century Sodom and Gomorrah. Nearly sixty thousand people were killed.

Remarkably, Thompson's own house survived with only minor damage. He attributed this luck to the high ground on which it stood, several streets above the city centre. So haunted was Thompson by the scale of the disaster and its devastation, he chose this elevated park above Mansfield and the elaborate last rites of his own funeral.

Thompson's desire to future-proof his mortal remains against disaster might seem absurd. The very words 'English' and 'earthquake' seem completely incongruous and yet, exactly a hundred years after Thompson's death, an earthquake struck Essex, destroying two churches at Langenhoe and Virley, and damaging many houses in Colchester. Though they are rare, there have been English earthquakes before and since.

I sit on a bench beside Thompson's tomb until the sun sets and the rooftops of Mansfield turn a livid purple. The land is not quite so wild today and Mansfield has outgrown it, the woods of yesteryear replaced with rows of houses. I don't think I can face another night under the coffin deck without a shower and go in search of a cheap hotel. When I pull into Mansfield Travelodge at nine o'clock the reception desk is empty except for a silver bell, and I give it a light tap. Almost instantly a receptionist appears, as if conjured from a hat, beaming at me with a dazzling, tooth-whitened smile. We briefly negotiate which of the dozen available bedrooms I can occupy before realising they're all identical.

The room is basic and has an unsettling aroma, doubly so because I can't identify it. Many years of tired travellers having one-night stands has taken its toll on the furnishings. There is the usual dark stain in the middle of the carpet, inviting visions of axe murderers, but otherwise it's pretty clean. Compared with the hearse, the double bed is the lap of luxury. I think of Enfield in his silk hammock in the car park, and wish him goodnight before closing the window.

Propped against the pillows with the glow of the hotel's security lights filtering through the curtain, I try to imagine the impact of a seismic shock. I picture the Travelodge flung from its foundations and my bed tossed into the neighbouring Tesco Express. In his deep grave, Thompson's coffin is gently rocked by the tremors, like a baby's cradle under its mother's hand.

I wake early and wash. The shower has what can only be described as udders, six little nipples that fire indiscriminate jets of water, hitting me at once in the eye, armpit and groin.

Skipping the Travelodge breakfast buffet, I swing the hearse north-west towards Chesterfield. Near a glittering array of solar panels I halt in a service station that doubles as an adult superstore, already doing a roaring trade at 9 a.m. I drain a cup of coffee in the cab as men scurry across the parking lot, plain bags clutched to their chests.

In Chesterfield, the crooked church spire rises above the car park where I pull in under a cherry tree in full blossom. The spire leans out over the town as if on the brink of collapse, and closer up the angle seems even more extreme, the whole pinnacle twisted like a towel being wrung out to dry.

The spire was installed on top of the church tower over six hundred years ago, but the green wood the builders used wasn't properly braced. When the bottom timbers decayed the structure began to turn. Thirty-two tons of lead tiles speeded the process until St Mary's and All Saints became England's equivalent of Pisa. The spire has warped but remains firmly anchored by its own weight.

St Mary's is the only church I've ever entered through a gift shop. Shelves full of crystal Christ figurines and gilded crosses block my way into the nave. I navigate through this Anglican enterprise, resisting the temptation to buy a pack of holy socks ('*faith on your feet*') or a crotchet Virgin Mary.

I make for the Lady chapel on the south side of the church, side-stepping a cat that slumbers in sunlight beneath a stained-glass window. The chapel is gloomy in comparison with the rest of the church, and a yellow rope cordons off the steps leading up to it like a crime scene. Within, a group of dirty alabaster tombs cluster together, standing, kneeling or lying on their backs. It seems no one's been bothered to take a feather duster to the dead and the effigies have turned the colour of old leather.

The tombs belong to various generations of the Foljambe family. The smallest figure kneels like an afterthought in one corner, a boy in armour who died when he was only thirteen.

197

Scant biographical details have trickled down through the centuries, but the statue is believed to be Sir Thomas Foljambe. In genealogical records he is simply described as *decessit sine prole* or 'died without children'.

There's something seriously wrong with Sir Thomas's tomb. The boy's helmet is out of all proportion to his body and seems to be connected by a ludicrously long neck. The whole statue is being pulled backward off its pedestal and beneath the visor is what looks like the face of a little girl, with strange pinwheel eyes and a tiny mouth painted in red. The church guidebook has nothing to say on this funerary freak, clearly cobbled together at some distant point in history.

Against the back wall is a large memorial, with three figures striding out of the frame. On the right is Youth, looking like a fat farmer in the prime of life, on the left Old Age, a figure bent over itself and using a stick for support. Between them stands Death, with a life-sized corpse in a sack beneath him, wrapped up at both ends like a boiled sweet.

For many years the Foljambe tombs were kept company by the giant rib of a whale. Measuring seven feet long, it stood sentry among the memorials like a lucky charm. This relic of a dead cetacean now lies behind the chancel screen, occupying space usually reserved for the relics of saints. I run my hand along its blackened length where the bone is covered with writing, the work of sailors practising scrimshaw.

Back in the hearse, I remain preoccupied with the effigies in the church. I stretch my thumb and forefinger over the crown of my own skull, wondering if I'd recognise it in a line-up of X-rays. Still fingering my jaw, I look up at a roadside banner advertising a car wash. After many miles on the road the hearse is as dust-covered as the Foljambe tombs and I toy with the idea of taking it in for a hose-down. I'm pretty sure the whole paint job would flake off under pressure, leaving me with the automobile equivalent of a hairless dog.

Driving under a scarp of cliffs outside Baslow, I pass the boarded entrances to old lead mines, once the lifeblood of these Derbyshire villages. At the turn to Eyam, a man stands with his arms folded on a drystone wall, watching each car pass as if looking for someone he's lost. The hearse labours up the hill into the village, overtaken by a blue Robin Reliant on the incline.

Eyam's fame rests squarely on its dead. The Great Plague of 1665 put the village on the map, raging fiercer here than in the heart of London. The capital was the source of the scourge – a bale of cloth sent to a tailor in Eyam carried the disease, and when it was hung to dry in front of his hearth the plague-infected fleas nestled in its folds awoke from the warmth of the fire. Within a week the tailor was dead and the plague was spreading fast through the village. By the following spring, over forty people had died and the villagers were at the point of fleeing.

Their new rector, William Mompesson, fearing thousands of others might succumb, persuaded his congregation with great difficulty to imprison themselves. The villagers pledged not to stray beyond the parish boundary until the plague had spent itself.

Today, the village draws tourists like flies to a corpse, and I follow in the footsteps of a thousand morbid sightseers. The sun is high overhead as the hearse lumbers in to the village car park, and the local museum is capped with a weathervane in the form of a black rat, its nose pointing due east. I use the public toilet next door and find myself washing my hands twice, as though the thought of infection has somehow seeped into my subconscious. The museum is closed, so I set out to walk Eyam's streets and see what evidence of the plague still clings to the village.

The road slopes into the centre of the village and the smell of coal smoke mingled with apple blossom rises up to meet me. I pass a local man walking his dog and whistling in the sunshine. We stop and talk on a street corner, and he tells me he was born and raised in Eyam. Perhaps in a sense he is a plague survivor himself, a distant descendant of those who outlasted the quarantine.

On such a day it's hard to imagine a whole community huddled around the bedsides of the sick and dying. All through the hot summer of 1666 the villagers of Eyam sweated to death behind closed doors, racked by the fever that accompanied the plague. Their only respite was Mompesson's open-air church services, held on the rocks of nearby Cucklet Delf in an attempt to slow the spread of disease. What poignance these services must have held as a dozen new bodies were consigned to the ground every week.

The first house I come to, like the rest of Eyam, is built from blocks of Derbyshire sandstone. It once belonged to Andrew Merrill, the village herbalist, a man who took a pragmatic approach to the plague and secluded himself in a hut on Eyam Moor (with his pet cockerel) until the threat had passed.

Back on the high street a bus unloads fifty day-trippers onto the pavement. They cluster in front of a row of picturesque cottages and take photographs, pulling faces for the camera, trying to evince the physical horrors of the plague. Here is one of Eyam's 'plague cottages', a dwelling in which an entire family was wiped out. A small green plaque attached to a railing lists the names of the victims, and the drawn blinds give the impression that the plague still continues to rage inside, unabated after three hundred and fifty years.

In an age when it's rare to die outside of a hospital, it's curious to walk through a village where hundreds died in their own beds. I touch a scar on my left shoulder, the imprint of past vaccinations and my own protection against 21st-century pandemics.

The next cottage has another sobering roll call of sons and daughters, grandparents and dependants lost. As an antidote, the lawn has been entirely given over to garden gnomes. A hundred bearded men sit, smoke and dig on the grass and gravel, intermingled with regiments of unicorns and fairies. A donations box is nailed to a post by the gate, presumably to fund the acquisition of more technicolour gnomery, the owner turning plague fame into profit.

At the end of the row a woman smokes in an open doorway. I pause to ask if us tourists bother her.

'Not at all.' She smiles and stamps out the cigarette. 'My daughter loves it. Thinks she's a celebrity.'

In the village churchyard a group of children skip around the graves while their parents stand admiring a Celtic cross. The children remind me of a game I used to play with my sister whenever we found ourselves in a graveyard, running down the rows of headstones and trying to spot the longest-lived resident.

The church interior bears witness to Mompesson's tenure and the plague years, both in 17th-century relics and modern additions. The rector's monogrammed chair still sits in the chancel, as if he might sweep back into the church to reclaim it. This is the same seat in which Mompesson would have brooded over the death of his own wife, who succumbed to the disease in August 1666.

High above the belfry arch a portrait of the Grim Reaper stares down at me, its skeletal head touching the ceiling joists and the outline of a scythe in its hands. The painting was covered over with plaster during the years of the Commonwealth and not brought to light again until the 1960s. How sinister that this figure remained invisible within the church walls while the village faithful died in droves.

Further down a side street, George Darby and his daughter Mary lie side by side in a stone-walled enclosure at the end of a row of semi-detached houses. The church is not the sole graveyard – a number of satellite graves fringe the village on plots of land where families buried their own dead in a desperate effort to contain the disease.

Father and daughter have beautiful headstones, their names delicately carved in cursive. When I was eighteen years old I visited a letter-carving workshop in Cambridge, where apprentices tapped patiently at slabs of limestone and slate. I was lent a chisel and hammer, and showed the basic technique. I remember stepping up to a small piece of serpentine, imagining myself a natural. Instead, my first blow split the corner and a large chip ricocheted off the opposite wall.

Beyond the Darbys the road turns to bare earth, and I walk towards a 'squeeze stile', a narrow cleft where the path crosses another stone wall. A sizeable man precedes me and manages to wedge his ample stomach between the stone pillars. I'm at the point of offering to give him a shove when he pops out the other side with a rasp of skin on rock.

We walk together through a landscape edged with stony outcrops and storm-swept beech, passing along Green Leys, a hillside peppered with the old entrances to lead mines. With this industry extinct, Eyam now relies on tragedy to fuel its economy; the worst event in its history has become its primary source of income.

Entering a close-cropped field of grass, we come to a large boulder on rising ground. I defer to my companion and he sits down with a sigh of gratitude. This is Eyam's boundary stone, marking the village limit. It was here that the quarantined villagers left money for food and returned to collect what supplies neighbouring villages had brought them. The boulder has six holes cut into it, supposed to have been filled with vinegar in an attempt to sterilise the coins placed inside.

It seems a fitting place to have my own lunch and I unwrap a sausage roll, laying it out on the stone as a temporary offering. High on the opposite hillside I can just make out another isolated graveyard, a low wall with seven graves inside. This solitary group belong to Elizabeth Hancock, a farmer's wife who buried her six children and husband here in the space of a single week. The scale of her suffering is inconceivable and the small plot is now a listed monument.

All told, two hundred and sixty villagers lost their lives in a little over a year, more than two-thirds of the population. In contrast, the many thousands who died in London made up less than a quarter of the city's inhabitants.

On my return to the hearse I pass a hut of brick and steel inviting me to watch a sheep being roasted whole, an old Eyam tradition. After an hour on the plague trail I don't have the stomach for it. Back in the car park the rat's weathervane has swung westward and a fresh breeze flows down from the hills, as if trying to purge the village of its past.

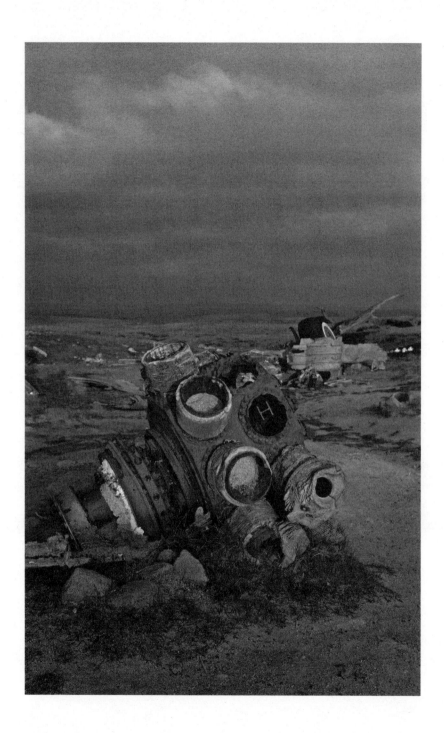

Chapter Eight

On the second day of spring 1959, a young philosopher made his way up a path from the village of Castleton. Neil Moss was twenty years old and a promising undergraduate at Oxford University. He travelled here to join a small team of speleologists, men intent on exploring hidden passages carved through rock by water.

I ascend the narrow streets of Goose Hill to where the tarmac ends and a path climbs into a gorge, the rock dripping wet and sprouting ferns. High above me the ruins of Peveril Castle cap the cliff. The path turns a corner and the mouth of a cave beckons from the head of the gorge, a yawning arch and a roof of black rock. A ticket booth nestles beneath, dwarfed by the span of rock rising above it.

This is the main entrance to Peak Cavern, a network of tunnels extending for over thirteen miles beneath the Derbyshire Dales. As I gawp at the ceiling, a jackdaw swoops in from the cave mouth and disappears into a crevice in the rock. The whole roof of the cavern is a breeding ground for the birds, their precarious nests wedged into rock covered in what looks like black tar. The blackened ceiling harks back to an earlier era when a community of ropemakers lived in the cavern, their tallow candles creating a residue of animal fat, forever stuck to the ceiling.

Moss and his friends came here to probe an unexplored fissure deep within the cave system, over a mile from daylight and beyond a series of intricate passageways and underground hurdles. In contrast I've come to join the last tour of the day, a ticketed amble through the outer caverns.

While I wait for the tour guide to appear, I study a map of the cavern system by the entrance. A labyrinth of tunnels and shafts split from the show cave, descending to chambers with forbidding names: 'Disappointment Rift', 'Swine Hole', 'Ink Sump' and 'Doom's Retreat'. Peak Cavern even has its very own 'River Styx', which seems to lead nowhere at all. Best of all is a dead-end passage some miles into the system, appropriately named 'Deep Thought'.

At the appointed hour our guide emerges from the dark, blinking in the cave mouth like a newly emerged mole. He's a tall man and has to stoop under a rock ledge as we follow him back inside.

The show cave narrows like a funnel and the far end is lit with sporadic electric lights. Vivid patches of greenery grow around them, artificially invigorated even in the total absence of the sun. Our guide points out various film props lying abandoned in the shadows, a statue of St Nicholas from *Clash of the Santas* and a collection of fibreglass boulders from the BBC's *The Chronicles of Narnia*, the producers apparently dissatisfied with millions of years of natural rock formation.

As the cavern floor begins to slope downward, I ask the guide if he's a caver himself.

'If I'm not guiding, I'm caving,' he replies.

'Aren't you a bit tall for it?'

He grins. 'Yeah, there's some places I can't go. Not many, though.' He slaps his thigh. 'The only real limit is this.'

The thighbone is the longest bone in the human body and the one obstacle that no amount of contortion can overcome. I feel my own gratifyingly puny femur.

We come to a passage where the roof suddenly drops and it becomes impossible to walk upright. This section of the cave used to be flooded, and 18th-century visitors had to lie on their backs in coffin-shaped boats, their faces upturned to the ceiling. The ropemakers doubled as their guides, swimming through the passage and dragging the boats along behind them.

I bend at the waist and stoop under the rock, shuffling through like an old man suffering from curvature of the spine. On the far side, the passage opens up then disappears into a void, beyond which nothing is visible. Our guide flicks a switch hidden in the passage wall and we find ourselves huddled at the edge of an enormous cavern, slopes of boulders rising to a ceiling seventy feet overhead. In places the walls bear black scorch marks, the traces of fireworks once used to illuminate the cave. Bygone tourists were serenaded from rock balconies by hidden choirs of the ropemakers' children, but today we have to make do with the echo of our own voices.

The passage continues from 'The Great Cave' and a spray of water seeps from the roof. Many writers came here and wrote about their experience, from Daniel Defoe to Lord Byron, guarding their candles as they were led into the dark. The Prussian clergyman Karl Moritz wrote that the further he journeyed inward, the more he felt 'the thread of life about to be snapped'.

We stop abruptly where the passage plummets into the floor. Below us, 'The Devil's Staircase' disappears into the dark, a steep slope of rock with no visible bottom. I ask our guide where it leads to next.

'Pluto's Dining Room,' he responds, without the hint of a smile. Where else?

This is as far as we day-trippers go.

When Neil Moss arrived at this same point in 1959, his journey had only just begun. From the bottom of the slope, Moss and his companions traversed a passage half-filled with water, then entered another where loose slabs of rock echoed underfoot like a badly tiled floor. They lit their way with carbide lamps, gas-fired torches that burnt with a sooty flame, crawling on hands and knees then slithering full length on their bellies. Progress was painfully slow.

The chamber they sought had a terrible obstacle barring access, 'The Eyehole', a kink in the subterranean geology leading to one of the most beautiful caverns in the whole system. To enter, they had to twist themselves into a tiny opening in the rock, before emerging shoulders first and covered in muck, like overgrown babies climbing out of the womb.

After a final ascent up a steep slope of mud the small team arrived at their destination. A beautiful cascade of flowstone descended from the roof over their heads, like candle wax dripping down the sides of the cavern. The calcite that surrounded them was almost transparent, as if a hand pressed against it would pass right through.

In one corner of the chamber a stalagmitic ramp rose towards the roof, and in its sidewall a tube the width of a man disappeared into the floor. This is what the cavers had set their sights on, an unexplored descent that could lead anywhere or nowhere at all.

Neil Moss was over six feet tall standing in his rubber overalls and boots. In spite of his height he volunteered to be the first man lowered into the chimney, descending with the help of a lightweight ladder. The initial descent was uneventful, but then Moss came to an elbow in the rock where the tube seemed to corkscrew and turn back on itself. Undeterred, the young man managed to manoeuvre around this and continue downwards, now out of sight of his companions. The chimney grew still narrower until it ended abruptly in a choke of boulders.

Moss probed these boulders with his feet, supposing there might be a small cavern beneath him, but saw no way through. Signalling that he was coming back up, he began to climb the ladder. Almost immediately he became stuck. In the narrow chimney, less than two feet wide, Moss was unable to bend his knees or move his hands onto the next rung. A rope was lowered to help haul him out, and although he somehow managed to tie it to himself, it broke the moment force was applied.

As Moss became more desperate his lamp went out, its fumes clouding the chimney. Slowly he began to suffocate, his own breath filling the fissure with carbon dioxide. Before long he had lapsed into unconsciousness.

Several cavers tried to climb down to Moss, belayed from above. A few made it around the elbow to find an object, more mud than man, trapped thirty-five feet down the tube. A caver named Ron Peters actually managed to touch the top of Moss's head and succeeded in dragging him eighteen inches higher up the tube. None of his would-be saviours could stand the lack of oxygen and returned, gasping, to the mouth of the hole.

Twenty-four hours after Moss first became trapped the rescue operation had assumed epic proportions. Hundreds crowded the cave entrance as a thick fog descended on the gorge, and relays crawled with oxygen cylinders, batteries and telephone cable down the long, low labyrinth to 'The Eyehole' and the chamber beyond. Through it all, Moss's ragged breathing could still be heard in the tube, amplified by the narrow shaft of limestone. One witness later described it as 'acting like a stethoscope'. The sound was sporadically interrupted by a desperate team trying to drill their way through the solid rock.

I wonder at the sense of hopeless isolation Moss must have felt even as the cave above him became a hive of activity. He was so close to deliverance and yet so far removed, already doomed from the moment his body wedged in the immovable rock. Doctors had worked shifts from early on in the rescue attempt, pumping oxygen into the shaft and monitoring the young man's breathing. The final medic to be relayed in was Flight Lieutenant John Carter, who listened to Moss's breathing until it gave out at 11 a.m. on Tuesday 24 March, thirty-five hours after he had first entered the tube. The doctor remarked that Moss was the only man he had ever declared dead without examining him first.

Moss's father requested that his body be left where it was, in order not to risk any more lives. Rescuers who'd spent hours underground were hurried to the surface as rain descended on Castleton and threatened to flood the passage-ways to the chamber. The following weekend a last attempt was made to recover Moss in spite of his father's entreaty, but the task proved impossible. Instead, boulders were dropped into the shaft above the trapped body and one of the men scratched an epitaph into the rock beside the entrance, acci-dentally misspelling the name of the deceased:

1959

Niel Moss RIP

Not much has changed in the subterranean sphere, and cavers still descend passages without knowing what lies beyond. The lights carried into the dark have evolved from candle and gas to electric torches, but the men and women drawn to the underground still risk many of the dangers that faced their predecessors. The Neil Moss tragedy did not deter them from continuing to explore Peak Cavern's undiscovered depths. In 1999 Britain's highest vertical rock chamber was found by caver Dave Nixon, who had to crawl through a series of abandoned mines and muddy tunnels, one of which he memo-rably named 'Colostomy Crawl'.

As I walk back into the half-light of the show cave, I contemplate that extraordinary tomb, a thousand feet underground in a natural sarcophagus. For many the idea of remaining in such a place is unthinkable, but for Moss, who loved the underground and all its mystery, his grave is a fitting one. The insatiable curiosity of the human race may eventually cause someone to bypass his bones and probe beyond, but I make a silent wish that Mr Moss never sees the light of day.

Relieved to be free from the bowels of the earth, I follow Snake Pass up through the Derwent Valley towards high moorland. The pass's name is more redolent of Colorado than Derbyshire, and the road twists and turns enough to make me lose my grip on the wheel. The hearse bounces onto a verge of loose rock and I regain control just in time to avoid sliding down a steep embankment. My heart races as dusk envelops the valley bottom.

The evening sun still shines up on the moor as I pull into a lay-by, next to a path striking north through the hills of the Dark Peak. When I switch off the engine the noise of the wind suddenly invades the hearse, moaning through the undercarriage and buffeting the cabin.

On a grey morning seventy years ago, an American military plane crossed this wilderness of heather and gritstone, ferrying thirteen men and a sack full of mail. The day was overcast and a low ceiling of cloud clung to the moor. A few miles short of their destination the captain pushed the plane's nose below the cloud to get a better view, without realising he was perilously close to the ground. The impact was sudden. The plane and its cargo were strewn across Shelf Moor, two thousand feet above sea level.

The lay-by is as close to the site of the wreck as I can get by car. I unload some overnight essentials from the hearse – my camp stove, a sleeping bag, a box of storm matches – then set off up the path. Before long the trail sinks into a deep 'hag' and my view contracts to a high-sided tunnel of peat, like walking through a soft brown canyon. A pair of grouse stalk the rim, hissing at my intrusion then disappearing in a burst of wings.

A small 'x' floats in the middle of my map, marking where the plane came down. I strike off from the path, plotting my own course in the absence of any way markers, tracking back and forth and scanning the ground for wreckage. Finding none, I turn in circles, map in hand but hopelessly lost.

The light has turned golden on the hill as I stumble on again. The whole moor seems to sparkle ahead of me, as if made from glass, and the higher I climb the brighter it becomes. Without warning I trip on an object half hidden in the grass and fall heavily to my knees. Looking down between my legs I find an enormous radiator protruding from the earth, its fins bent from the impact of my foot. The sparkle on the hill suddenly makes sense. I'm surrounded by fragments of the wrecked plane, catching the last of the sun.

The plane was a Boeing B-29 Superfortress, the same type of heavy bomber that was used to drop 'Little Boy' and 'Fat Man' on Hiroshima and Nagasaki during the final month of the Second World War. Its operational nickname was 'Over

Exposed', and for years its turrets had carried cameras instead of machine guns as it photographed the aftermath of atomic bomb tests in the Pacific, before it came to England to take part in reconnaissance operations over Berlin. All thirteen men aboard the plane that morning had been due to finish their tour of duty three days later and return to the US.

I approach the remains of one of the plane's four engines, an oxidised metal monolith to rival the work of any modern sculptor, its eighteen cylinders like a burnt-out Ferris wheel. The wreckage of the Superfortress is spread across almost a quarter of a mile, but most of it lies condensed in the space of two hundred yards. Melted blobs of aluminium, fused by the heat of the fire, are scattered all around and sheep graze among them.

The first to arrive at the scene of the accident were members of a mountain rescue team who had been practising exercises on the moor. They were guided through the mist by the plane's enormous tail fin, standing fifteen feet tall on top of the hill. As they approached, heat still radiated from the burning fuselage and only eight bodies were identified among the smouldering wreck.

The next day the search party returned before dawn and spread out in lines across the moor to find the missing crew members. The remaining bodies were discovered thrown clear of the crash site, one with a blackened wristwatch stopped at nine minutes to eleven. Volunteers carried the dead airmen on stretchers back down the hill I've just climbed. The search party also retrieved the payroll sack containing several thousand American dollars, and letters to loved ones from the mailbag, now scattered across the moor or burnt in the fire.

The density of plane wreckage increases as I approach the hill's summit, the ground beneath my feet turned to bald sand, still scarred by the crash. The split sheets of the fuselage and the landing gear form a twisted heap of folded metal, the name 'Over Exposed' seeming doubly appropriate now. At the epicentre of the debris is a simple memorial formed from wooden crosses and paper poppies, stuck into the soil beneath the shadow of one wing. A brass plaque pinned to a rock reads, *It is doubtful the crew ever saw the ground.*

Leaving the wreckage behind me, I continue towards a great pile of boulders that caps the hill. These are the Higher Shelf Stones, enormous weathered slabs of gritstone shaped by frost, wind and rain. The larger boulders are covered in graffiti, from elegant 19th-century longhand to lazy 21st-century scrawls. One inscription has been cut so profoundly it looks like the author was trying to crack the boulder in two. 'Roy Elliott of Glossop', the letters proudly proclaim, an epitaph that will outlast any graveyard stone. Roy gives his birth date, 19 May 1940, which would make him seventy-nine years old. I wonder if he's still alive.

I unroll my sleeping bag beneath a rock with an overhang, a Star of David chiselled on one side. With my bed protected from sudden showers, I set up my stove on the ridge and cook with a panoramic view of the empty moorland. From a subterranean cave to a hilltop, my tomb tour has taken me to extremes in the space of a few hours.

Thunder seems periodically to roll across the valley. As the sky darkens I'm surprised to see a line of passenger jets pass low over the hill, bound for Amsterdam or Islamabad. The isolated moor lies on the flight path to Manchester airport and the planes seem close enough to reach out and touch, as if they're in danger of suffering the same fate as the American bomber all those years ago.

As I lie awake in my sleeping bag, the sheep huddle closer to me in the dark. In the early hours of the morning I roll over and what I took for a rock leaps to its feet, an old ewe that's mistaken me for a pillow.

Hungry from my night on the Higher Shelf Stones, I steer the hearse into a roadside diner on the outskirts of Glossop. On the side of a phone booth a funeral director has stuck an advertisement, offering to dispose of loved ones for a discounted fifteen hundred quid. The poster reads like a meal deal for the bereaved.

Sitting alone at a corner table I try researching Roy Elliott, the man whose name I found carved on the grit last night. I scan an online phone directory but draw a blank, then stumble on a photograph of Roy aged fifteen on a school trip to Cromer. He sits crossed-legged at the front of a black and white group picture, looking like the kind of boy who might drag a hammer up a hill to etch his name on a rock. Beyond the photograph the trail goes cold. The burial records of the town's graveyards and cemeteries are too dense to wade through this early in the morning.

From the diner I steer the hearse across Manchester. It's Sunday, the Lord's Day, and appropriately I'm looking for a man of God. I stop to check my map next to an electrical substation, the transformers buzzing through the open window, then turn off the main road at Ramsbottom. I drive through the charmingly named Summerseat, where street-lights are still glowing in the middle of the morning.

I'm on the trail of a 17th-century vicar who was remarkable for his refusal to be buried in a churchyard. Somewhere in this landscape of scattered farms and sheep pasture was 'his favourite haunt', a patch of ground where he came to escape life and where he sought solitude in death.

At the post office in the village of Hawkshaw I ask for directions. A woman stands behind the till with a black cat on the counter beside her. It yawns as I approach, staring at me malevolently and showing its teeth.

'I'm looking for Roger Worthington,' I murmur, one eye on the cat. The woman looks up blankly from her newspaper.

I try again. 'The dead vicar. Buried on his own.'

'Oh him,' she responds with a grin. 'Go up Hawkshaw Lane. He's near the top.'

The lane begins with a small housing estate but soon becomes a wide open road, what was once the main highway to the old village. I drive between broken hedgerows, a flock of fat geese threatening to run under my wheels and honking loudly in protest. The lane seems to go on for miles and I slow down, scanning the edges for any sign of Worthington's grave. Outside a stone farmhouse, a lady with a white ponytail watches me approach.

'Are you lost?' she asks as I squeak to a halt beside her.

'Completely. I'm looking for Roger Worthington.'

A long pause follows, in which she seems to examine me more closely.

'What d'you want with him?' she asks, a new note of suspicion in her voice.

Having explained that I'm a humble taphophile, she gives me directions to the last house on the lane, where the late vicar resides in a neighbouring field. 'Stop here on your way back. I've got something to show you,' she adds.

Wondering what lies in wait, I carry on up the lane until the track disappears into a hedge. On the other side a grave is enclosed by a low stone wall, with a stile cut into one side. Climbing over, I stumble and catch my knee on a sharp edge. My first words of greeting to the dead vicar are as blue as the sky.

The grave is a flat slab, edged in concrete and covered over with moss. It seems to have been shattered into several pieces then stuck back together, like broken eggshell. An inscription reads:

Here lies the body of Roger Worthington who departed this life the ninth day of July 1709, about the sixtieth year of his age.

The jigsaw appearance of the grave is the result of a ploughing accident. At some point the tomb was swallowed by a farmer's field and, with nothing to protect it, run over by a horse and plough. The remains languished in the long grass until an absentee landowner gifted the plot of ground to the village, and a public subscription was raised to repair Worthington's grave and build the enclosure. On a hot afternoon in July 1934 a large crowd gathered to rededicate the tomb.

E. S. Armstrong, then Reverend of Hawkshaw, led the service as the congregation sang hymns, and Worthington enjoyed a second funeral service two hundred and twenty-six years after his first. A poem by John Fawcett Skelton was read aloud during the service:

> Next Holcombe Hey a good farm appears,
> A fine substantial house in former years,
> A field away, below the Broadstone Delf,
> In an unbounded cemetery to himself,
> Lies Roger Worthington, an old divine,
> Whose gravestone bears the date 'seventeen nine.'

Someone's installed a picnic table beside the grave and I sit for a while, pondering the chance that stopped Worthington's memory from being erased altogether. Returning down the lane the woman is still in her front yard and beckons me to pull in. 'Come inside,' she says, abandoning her work in the yard.

Jan Barnes is a handsome woman in her fifties who has lived in Hawkshaw for most of her life. I follow her through the rooms of her farmhouse, ducking under low lintels and arriving in an office that faces the lane. She offers me a seat on a swivel chair, then begins rifling through a long shelf of folders bound in red leather.

'I've got Worthington's funeral service here somewhere. Hold on.'

After much rummaging she produces a service sheet with rusted staples in the spine, the cover instructing attendees to meet at 3 pm around the 'lonely old grave in Farm Field'. As I flick through the order of service, I comment on how time-less the whole of Hawkshaw feels.

'It's a very down-to-earth place. People are still living the same kinds of lives they've always done.'

I ask if Worthington receives many visitors.

'Now and again,' Jan replies.

In the summer of 1990, she remembers a thickset man in a suit walking up the lane, his tie loose and his jacket slung over his shoulder.

'He was very hot and bothered. Like you, I asked if he was lost. He was a bit shifty, but said he'd come to see a Mr Worthington. I said he's dead, what do you want to see him about?

'He didn't look very happy about that and said he'd come to see him about paying his poll tax. That made me laugh, but he stomped off up the lane anyway, just to check he really was dead, I suppose.

'A couple of weeks later a white van came racing up Hawkshaw, and they pulled in here and knocked on my door. They wanted to see Mr Worthington too. Again I asked why. They told me he'd ordered an orthopaedic bed and they'd come to install it!'

It seems the poll tax census had been hacked by some opportunistic salesmen, who gambled on an old man living alone but instead found him firmly in the ground.

I thank Jan for her generosity and return to the hearse.

Leaving Hawkshaw behind me, I soon get lost on Lancashire's back roads, steep sided lanes with trim hedgerows, the kind of landscape where you expect to meet Postman Pat around the next bend. In Rossendale this rural idyll gives way to grey industrial estates, and a burnt-out caravan props up advertising hoardings on the side of the M65. I've tied a pine cone from Worthington's grave to my rear-view mirror, an air freshener courtesy of the dead swinging from an elastic band.

From the grave of a man who chose to be buried alone, I'm bound for another entombed far from home, though not through choice. As I approach the coast at Sunderland Point, the roads are washed with sand and a large sign hangs over the verge, 'Road liable to tidal flooding'. I slide onto a causeway that seems to disappear between high banks of mud.

Sunderland Point is cut off by every tide, a village lost among marshes, stranded between the mouth of the River Lune and the sweep of Morecambe Bay. The narrow causeway twists through the mire, mud banks rippling like desert dunes and oystercatchers skimming the estuary.

On the far side of the causeway I park on a steep shingle beach, only the handbrake preventing the hearse from rolling back into the water. Getting out, I find seaweed wrapped around the rear, pulled up by the wheels and draped like a skirt from the fender. The frames of old houses peek from behind pebbledash exteriors and the smell of driftwood fires seeps from high-walled gardens.

The village here grew out of trade, a convenient stop-off for ships – bearing cotton, sugar and slaves – that were too large to dock at nearby Lancaster. I walk along what substitutes for a high street in a community of only seventy souls, the small port having flourished for a century then faded back into obscurity.

One man who landed here in 1736 was destined never to leave. A slave to a captain, 'Sambo' was unloaded with the ship's cargo at Sunderland Point. Brought from West Africa via the West Indies, he was left at an inn where the ship docked to await his master's return. Finding himself alone, in strange company and stranger scenery, Sambo is said to have declined food and water, confining himself to his bed in the inn's attic.

A few days later the man was dead. Oral tradition holds that he died from a broken heart, believing himself abandoned by his master, but it seems more likely that he died of disease, contracted from the European sailors he was forced to ship with. A local magazine, reporting many years after Sambo's death, claimed that others lodging at the inn 'excavated him in a lonely dell in a rabbit warren behind the village, within twenty yards of the sea ... covered only with the clothes in which he had died'.

Mosquitoes drone in my ears as I follow a narrow footpath from the village to the further shore. A brick chapel with sloping eaves stands on one side of the path, a single bell hanging from the peak of the roof and a model of a fishing trawler in the window. The tiny chapel varies its service times according to the tides.

Eventually the path gives way to thorn bushes and the smell of wet sand. Emerging on the peninsula's western edge, I'm surrounded by logs carried here by Atlantic storms, twisted root balls smoothed by the sea. I walk on towards the black and white wick of an old lighthouse, stranded far out in the bay.

Thinking myself alone, I'm startled when a voice from nowhere says, 'Hullo.' I look up and find I've almost collided with a small man sitting on one of the storm-tossed logs. He holds a walking stick across his lap and seems to be wearing clothes several sizes too big.

'Hello,' I reply,

The apparition hails from Middleton and tells me he's been walking this beach every day for the last twenty years.

'It's become a habit,' he says. 'Peaceful place. I don't often meet people.'

Feeling guilty at having disturbed his daily vigil, I try to think of something to say.

'Ever see anything interesting washed up here?' I venture.

The man looks up sharply. 'A dead windsurfer. He was lying in the salt marsh over there. Probably got caught by the current and drowned.'

The story is relayed without visible emotion, as if he were describing finding the bones of a seabird or a stranded jelly-fish. Not knowing what to say to this revelation, I nod gravely and make to move on.

'What have you come for?' he says suddenly, fixing me with eyes the same colour as the mud.

'Sambo's grave. The slave who died.'

He points over his shoulder to where the sea wall turns back on itself.

'You'll find him up there by the hedge.'

Sambo's grave has recently been encircled by a new sea wall to prevent it washing away. At the head of a stone slab lies a Mardi Gras of multicoloured tributes, from painted pebbles and coloured ribbons to a carved wooden ship. The tributes seem to be a mix of passing respects paid by tourists and the product of tradition, regularly replenished by locals. Etched on a tablet at the centre is an elegy written for Sambo sixty years after his death. Penned by James Watson, the brother of a notorious slave trader, it's a romantic ballad that sheds no further light on Sambo or his story. His real name seems lost forever.

Today the grave has become a universal site of memory and a place for remembering the thirty thousand other slaves transported to Lancashire alone. Some of the tributes have been left by people recalling their own stories of immigration, a fine example of the living honouring the dead because they shared something in life.

By the time I make it back to the village the tide has long since turned and the causeway is beginning to disappear beneath the water. Not wishing to be stranded here for another eight hours, I hurry to reverse the hearse and head for the gap between the posts. The rising tide has already exceeded the mark that indicates safe passage but something compels me forward.

A sheen of water spilling across the causeway makes it barely distinguishable from its surroundings, and only sticks in the mud tell me where road ends and river begins. I pass a blue and red boat bobbing alongside and press on, willing the hearse to beat the flood. In the rear-view mirror I can see a shallow wake closing on the causeway behind me. Another mile and I'm safe.

Heading north into the Lakes, I ask myself why I risked drowning in the hearse to catch the tide on Sunderland Point. Something about the place filled me with an intense dread: the air of decay, the man on the beach whose face I already couldn't recall, the grave festooned with bright colours masking its tragic origin. All these had made it worth running the gauntlet to escape.

I stop to refuel in the shadow of limestone cliffs outside Lindale, the cliff faces flowering with yellow gorse. In the village itself I pass a huge black obelisk on the roadside, a memorial that once rose over the grave of John 'Iron Mad' Wilkinson.

Wilkinson was a key figure in England's industrial revolution, his empire of iron furnaces turning out cast-iron bridges and steam-engine cylinders that speeded progress across the nation. In his later years he became so consumed by his iron obsession that he began to produce all kinds of unusual objects, from an iron church pulpit to cast-iron coffins for his friends. He made such a coffin for himself, and when he died it was installed beneath this towering obelisk in the garden of his house outside Lindale.

Wilkinson's fortune soon dissipated among bickering relatives and the estate was dissolved. The new owner took a dislike to the obelisk and toppled it. The twenty-tonne memorial lay hidden in the undergrowth for many years before being re-erected here in the heart of the town where the great man's journey began.

Back on the main road a sign proclaims the borders of 'Lakeland', and my ears start to pop with the rise and fall of the road. Enfield seems to sense we've entered mountain country and abseils down to eye level, as if practising for some great adventure.

We follow a borderless road through Cumbria's high country, successive cattle grids rattling the hearse until it feels like it will break apart. Local drivers speed past, cleaving to corners as if they could steer blindfold. At the foot of Bowerhouse Bank I wait while a farmer feeds his sheep, an inverted breed with black coats and white heads. The hearse idles behind the tractor for a mile, then I turn off at Santon Bridge and head up the valley along the banks of Wastwater.

I book myself into the Wasdale Head Inn, a famous old hotel that squats in the shadow of mountains, Scafell Pike, Great Gable and Kirk Fell all looming over the roof. The inn is sometimes referred to as 'the birthplace of British rock climbing', and the reception desk is approached between panelled walls hung with cracked hobnail boots and old crampons. A number of wiry-looking men queue ahead of me at the check-in, feet shuffling in heavy boots. Once I have the key to my room, I leave the living climbers to visit with dead ones.

Back outside the evening air has cooled. In the valley bottom the tiny church of St Olaf hides behind a cordon of yew trees, their branches bent over it by the wind. The church has long served as a last resting place for fallen climbers, men and women who lost their lives on the surrounding mountains or ascents overseas.

Stepping through the gate, I leave the panorama of Wasdale for a dim world of irregular headstones under the yew trees' canopy. Unlike traditional graves, many here have sloped sides and jagged peaks, carved to resemble cliffs and crags. By the church wall I stop to read the epitaph of a climber buried beneath a stone cross, with a rope tied around it as if he's abseiled into the afterlife.

Several gravestones look about ready to collapse, their bases half out the ground. Churchwardens are now obliged by law to carry out gravestone 'topple tests', wandering around their churchyards and giving headstones a healthy shove to check they're not a danger to the general public.

The door to the church looks like it was made for a child and, stooping inside, I enter one of England's smallest churches. The single room is barely ten feet wide, with oil-burning lamps fixed on stalks and stunted pews wedged in under the windows. Etched on a clear pane of glass in the north wall are the words:

I will lift up mine eyes unto the hills, from whence cometh my strength.

Beneath this is the traced outline of Napes Needle, one of the Lake District's most famous pinnacles, a slender finger of rock projecting from the flanks of its parent mountain.

The low-ceilinged room has a strong feeling of sanctuary, a shelter beneath the fells that surround it. The prayer book beside the tiny altar is filled with memories of men and women whose lives were lived at altitude. Similarly, the windowsills are covered with brass plaques commemorating climbers. *May his memory blow in the winds*, reads one, and *In the echoes of the mountains* another.

Alongside bodies brought down from the cliffs and buried here are memorials to others never seen again, disappeared in high passes or remote snowfields, like that to a man 'lost trekking in Karakorum' in the summer of 1993.

The idea of the vanished climber, last seen heroically silhouetted on cliff or summit, is a sobering reminder that people who die on mountains often remain where they fell. For years climbers on Mount Everest have been forced to confront the corpses of other mountaineers who died on their way up or down and whose bodies now lie at such altitude they are impractical to retrieve. These frozen corpses often acquire nicknames. An American woman who for many years lay a few hundred meters shy of the summit was known as 'Sleeping Beauty' and an Indian policeman's body on the north-east ridge was simply 'Green Boots', on account of his fluorescent plastic footwear.

I sit for a while in a pew at the back of the church. A friend once told me the legend of a young man who climbed a mountain fifty years after his grandfather had been lost on its slopes. Crossing a glacier the climber saw a perfect image of himself locked in the walls of ice, his grandfather's face staring out at him, trapped and ageless, perfectly preserved in the flow.

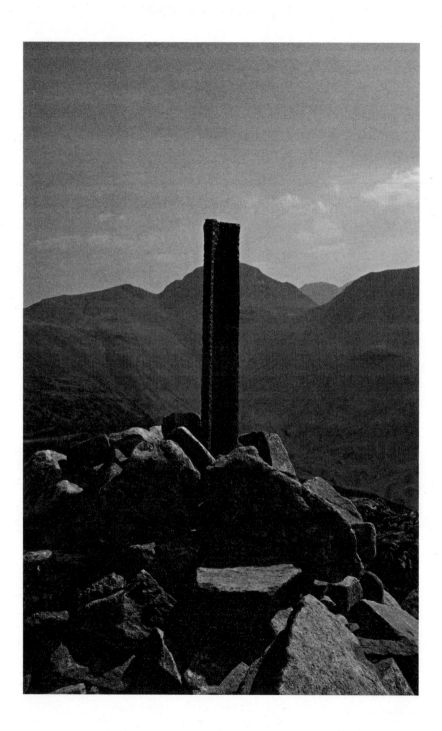

Chapter Nine

· Innominate Tarn ·

· Eternal Vigilance ·

· Necropolis ·

A red dawn breaks in Wasdale, the sun creeping over England's highest mountain and making its presence felt in my boxlike bedroom. After yesterday's encounters with forgotten men, I'm going in search of what remains of a local hero, a man so celebrated he's become synonymous with a landscape.

Alfred Wainwright, walker, author, recluse – a figure instantly recognisable from his white, windblown hair and the pipe permanently hanging from his lips. What outlives Wainwright are his books, obsessive guides to the Lakeland mountains, handwritten and hand-drawn, reproduced in such a way that the reader seems to hold the original in their hands. The books ramble just as he did for most of his life, only held together by his abiding passion for the fells.

On my way out of the inn I check in on the hearse to enquire if any of my dead associates fancy a walk. I imagine the spirits of Thompson, Hardy and Hawker eagerly strapping on boots and gaiters while others turn their backs, content with eternal rest.

I make for the path to the foot of Great Gable, a substantial peak that dominates the dale. The entire range of Lakeland hills, more than two hundred individual fells, are collectively known by summit-baggers as the Wainwrights. Short of spotting a passing comet, this is as good a chance of lasting fame as anyone could wish for.

Passing the final farmhouse in the valley I have an audience of sheepdogs, three heads following my footsteps from a ground-floor window. The path ascends the bare spine of the hill, a slope rising to gullies where snow still clings to shadows. Ahead, the footpath fractures into loose rock, pieces of the mountain that spill over the edge. I sit down on a boulder and pull one of Wainwright's guidebooks from my pocket, intent on following in his footsteps.

The path I've chosen is a circuitous route to the summit. Wainwright describes another, more direct approach, reached by traversing under the crags of the southern face. I break off the path and begin a tentative sideways shuffle, the towering cliffs of Great Napes rising vertically overhead. The slope is steep and the crag seems impenetrable, until I arrive beneath the 'Hell Gates', two narrow chutes that cut through the cliffs and lead directly to the top. Here the scree is coloured a violent orange, as if the devil himself has vomited down the fell.

I begin an agonisingly slow ascent, taking one step forwards only to slide backwards again, a tiny Sisyphus labouring alone. Walkers have slipped here and not stopped until they reached the bottom; one 19th-century hiker slid down the length of one of the Gates, grinding off most of his ear in the process. Eventually I resort to crawling, my hands and feet buried in the scree.

Higher up I pass the famous Sphinx Rock, which Wainwright sketched with his trademark intricacy. Beyond its upturned nose another walker negotiates the slope fifty feet ahead, making ripples in the scree that flow down towards me. His face is turned away, but his flat cap and thick white hair give me an uncanny feeling of familiarity, as if I'm following Wainwright himself. I arrive wheezing at the final crest to find a small group of people sipping tea on the summit, huddled together and basking in the rising sun. The white-haired man is not among them.

On the morning of 8 June 1924, a middle-aged man with an artificial leg climbed up from Wasdale and along the flanks of Great Gable to the mountain's summit, almost three thousand feet high. Unlike me, Geoffrey Winthrop Young did not climb alone but led a congregation of nearly five hundred men and women, come to dedicate these hills to the nation. They carried with them a great bronze plaque on a stretcher, now fixed to the summit cairn.

As a war-stained Union Jack flapped in the wind on the bald crown of the fell, and the crowd's hobnailed boots scratched the rock, Winthrop Young stepped forward to give a eulogy. He spoke of friends who had surrendered 'the fellowship of wind and hill, and sunshine' to ensure the freedom of others. He spoke of all men becoming nothing more than names to future generations, but the splendour of the hills enduring forever.

An extract from the *Journal of the Fell & Rock Climbing Club* of that same year describes the gathering thus:

If there is any communion with the spirits of dead warriors, surely they were very near that silent throng of climbers, hill-walkers, and dalesfolk who assembled in soft rain and rolling mist on the high crest of Great Gable … the service was a tribute to memory.

I cross to where the bronze plaque still sits fixed to the rock. Members of the Fell & Rock Climbing Club bought three thousand acres of the Lake District, dedicating the land to the nation in memory of their brothers who fell in the First World War. Winthrop Young was a fitting spokesman, a life-long climber who started out on the spires of his Cambridge college, scaling them at night without ropes to perch on gargoyles high above the city. Even after losing his leg in the war, he continued to climb with the help of an artificial substitute, to which he strapped crampons and other climbing devices.

Below the war memorial the path drops steeply down to Windy Gap, a saddle between summits where you can stretch out your arms and pretend to take flight. The ghost of Alfred Wainwright leads me to the next hill, Haystacks, an undulating fell capped with heather and sitting at the centre of a circle of higher peaks.

As I descend the ridge, Haystacks seems curiously still, a becalmed place nestled in the lee of the other hills. Wainwright long held Haystacks as his favourite among the fells, and he returned here time and again, sometimes extolling the beauty of the place, at others becoming melancholic ('black are its bones and black is its flesh … gloomy and mysterious even under a blue sky').

I cross a stile and follow a ragged fence line, picking my way among rocks that shelter the path. Before long I arrive on the shore of a large pool of water, Innominate Tarn, like a natural rain gauge collected in a hollow. A few stubby reeds and single boulders break the surface.

Writing his memoirs, Wainwright's thoughts again returned to Haystacks and his deep desire for his ashes to be scattered here:

> All I ask for, at the end, is a last long resting place by the side of Innominate Tarn, on Haystacks … I shall go to it, for the last time, and be carried: someone who knew me in life will take me and empty me out of a little box and leave me there alone. And if you, dear reader, should get a bit of grit in your boot as you are crossing Haystacks in the years to come, please treat it with respect. It might be me.

Wainwright got his last wish and was duly emptied next to this same pool by his second wife, Betty McNally, in the winter of 1991. 'The tarn without a name' seems a fitting place beside which to scatter human remains, a way for Wainwright to be absorbed into the fells he loved so dearly. I stare at the blank mirror of the water. As Walt Whitman once wrote, 'Not a mark, not a record remains – and yet all remains.'

I swim in a smaller, neighbouring pool that feeds Innominate Tarn. The floor is a giant sponge and it bubbles as I wade out. Thinking myself hidden from view, I'm startled when a troop of hikers emerge from nowhere and peer curiously at me, as if I'm part of the fauna. I wait till they've moved on, then hop out and dry myself behind a rock. I watch a water beetle crawl between my toes then scurry away into the heather, wondering if Wainwright ever stripped on his favourite mountain and plunged into its many waters.

Returning, clothed, to Innominate Tarn, its banks are no longer serene but occupied by dozens of hikers converging on it from all directions. Here are the faithful of Wainwright's church, ringing the water's edge and giving thanks to his memory with a Kit-Kat or a ham sandwich. I join a queue of ramblers tramping around the tarn and making for the summit. The difficulty of Wainwright's legacy is that he so popularised the places he loved they're slowly being destroyed. The line ahead of me is more like queuing for a ride at a theme park than climbing a mountain.

A dozen people in front I spy the white-haired walker once more, leaning with one hand on a boulder beside the path. The French philosopher René Descartes believed that the spirits of dead men lived in the craters of the moon named after them. Could the same be said for Wainwright's spirit, still roaming these hills? The man stands out from the crowd, his cap and woollen jumper distinct in a sea of Gore-Tex tops. Again, I wonder how like the dead man this figure is, half expecting to see puffs of pipe smoke drifting down over the rocks between us.

Finally, I reach the steel fencepost that marks the summit. This was Wainwright's holy of holies, and a panoramic view fans out on all sides. The man next to me breathes deeply and sighs, as if the rarefied air will grant him prolonged life. I follow his example.

Wainwright's were not the first or the last ashes to be spread in this scenic spot. The practice has become so common in the Lakeland fells that people have reported finding piles of rich ash in the handholds of popular climbs. Other hikers have been unfortunate enough to be decorated by the dead, the wind wreaking havoc and blowing cremated remains into upturned faces.

Recently botanists have even noticed an environmental impact, nutrient-rich ashes affecting the chemical make-up of the soil at popular viewpoints and allowing common plant species to take over from others that depended on the low fertility of the soil to stifle competition. Whether or not you condone the scattering of ashes, the fells have always offered escape, a place for people to break away from lives lower down. It's hardly surprising, then, that they serve the same function in death, a final flight on the mountain being many people's idea of the perfect farewell.

From Haystacks I return to the inn via Black Sail Pass and sit down on a picnic table with two German men enjoying their lunch. Listening to their strong accents, I can't help being reminded of the war memorial on Great Gable. Whenever I meet Germans of a similar age to me I size them up, imagining what it would be like if we were forced to fight one another across the mud of a battlefield. Judging by the two men's backpacks and appetites, both prodigious, I wouldn't have stood a chance.

* * *

My limbs ache from following Wainwright's spectre across the hills as I steer the hearse back down the dale. For many years Wainwright lived in nearby Kendal, to be close to his beloved fells. On the night of 10 February 1965 he would most likely have been comfortably in bed when a car chase played out on the streets of his home town. Perhaps the roar of engines or screech of tyres disturbed his dreams, as the police pursued their quarry across Kendal and on down a series of narrow country lanes.

The suspect on that fateful winter's night was John Middleton, a serial car thief who had just stolen a Morris Minor. Before long, he lost control of the car and steered it into a ditch. Officers assumed Middleton was trapped inside the wreck, but, when they approached, he fired shots from a window and fled. Gun in hand, he ran through a road-block further down the road, then hijacked another vehicle.

PC George Russell was working night shifts as a patrol car driver. When the alert went out that a man was on the run, Russell and the three officers in his car searched their imme-diate area, beginning with Oxenholme railway station on the town's outskirts. The policemen entered the dark, empty station in the early hours of the morning, the last train having left long before. All four were unarmed. In the waiting room on the southbound platform they could make out a figure lying across a bench, seemingly asleep and matching Middleton's description. One officer returned to the patrol car to summon assistance while Russell volunteered to be the first to enter the room.

Middleton was only feigning sleep and immediately leapt to his feet when Russell entered, pointing a revolver at his chest. The young officer barely had time to utter a word before being shot at point-blank range. The gunman opened the waiting room door and fired further shots across the platform. A second officer ran to tend to Russell and was hit in the shoulder. Meanwhile, PC Alex Archibald had approached the waiting room from the opposite side, clutching his baton in one hand and hoping to surprise Middleton. At the last second the car thief caught sight of him and emptied the remaining rounds from his revolver into Archibald's arm and body, the final bullet lodging close to his spine. As three of the four officers lay prostrate on the platform, Middleton ran off down the railway into the dawn.

Despite the best efforts of his fellow officers, George Russell died in hospital three hours after being shot, just shy of his thirty-sixth birthday. In the wake of the station shootings, a manhunt began to capture Middleton, including the first recorded use of a police helicopter. Two hundred officers, carrying rifles and shotguns, combed the county and, on the following afternoon, Middleton was finally cornered in a small wood outside Sedbergh. With no way of escape, he shot himself in the head. Although he survived, he was unfit to stand trial and spent the rest of his life confined to a prison hospital in Liverpool. To this day, bullet holes from the station shootout are visible in the walls of Oxenholme station.

Instead of making for Kendal and Oxenholme, I head north across Cumbria and enter Carlisle, admiring the local red sandstone that colours the city. I follow the railway line past an old theatre on West Walls, then turn into the cathedral precinct. A powerful organ is erupting inside the building, as if a hundred fingers are being pressed to its keys all at once.

I stand under the spires and buttresses of Carlisle Cathedral, a few people milling around and taking snapshots of the façade. It was here that George Russell's funeral took place, attended by his family and several hundred police officers. From the cathedral his body was taken to Carlisle cemetery, but less than two months later his face reappeared here, high up among the gargoyles and gutters of the south wall.

The cathedral architect, Mr Norman Phillips, had been in the process of planning the building's restoration at the time of PC Russell's death. In the wake of the tragedy he instructed local stonemason Ted Drinkwater to create a likeness of the police officer that could be raised on high, joining dozens of medieval grotesques under the arched windows of the clerestory.

Gazing up at the faces arrayed under the cathedral's lead roof, I can see the policeman's helmet catching the sun near the south-east corner. Drinkwater worked from photographs lent him by the dead man's widow, but he seems to have added some medieval flair, as Russell's strong roman nose is capped by stylised, almond-shaped eyes.

I try to go inside but a crowd is thronging around a bishop in the porch and there's no room to squeeze past. Tombs line the aisle beyond, the effigies of dead bishops surrounding the living one. Clergy and congregation laugh awkwardly at each other's jokes, and eventually I manage to duck past, accidently elbowing an archdeacon in the back.

243

Niches along the walls are occupied by other graves, including an open sarcophagus carved in the shape of a human body, like a mould for casting the dead. Eventually I manage to collar one of the cathedral guides, an elderly man wearing a blue silk scarf, and ask him if he knows anything about George Russell's story. By way of an answer he leads me back outside and we stare up at the bust together. The red sandstone of the cathedral wall is discoloured in places, blackened as if scorched by fire, and my guide tells me the steam trains that once ran on the neighbouring railway eroded the sandstone with their sulphurous smoke. Russell's is one of the few unsullied stones.

Adding modern busts to old buildings has been practised before, but George Russell's grotesque remains unique, a policeman elevated to the ranks of bishops and kings. Perched on high he watches the city's streets and the beat he once trod. His sandstone eyes remain eternally vigilant, a reminder that law and order still abide in the great Border city.

North of Carlisle the countryside is dotted with wind turbines and morose churches with shuttered windows. I pass scattered houses with fantastic gatepost ornaments – a pair of lions, two dragons and a minotaur with an erect penis. Crossing the River Esk, I only realise I've entered Scotland when I pass a saltire on the side of the road, the blue and white flag straining at its post and threatening to take off in the breeze.

In Canonbie, distracted by a light on the dashboard, I narrowly avoid hitting a lollipop man in the middle of the road. The town seems to be almost exclusively lived in by the elderly, standing on street corners, leaning on garden gates, sitting on public benches.

There used to be a bench on the corner of the village I grew up in. Every day for fifteen years the same two men would sit on this bench. I have no idea what they did there, but I'd pass them on my way to school, or coming back from the shops, or going to the playground at the weekend. They never seemed to move, or talk to one another, just staring at the cars and the people passing by. One day there was only one old man and then there was nobody. A few years later the bench vanished too.

The road undulates through the Scottish Borders and the chassis of the hearse lollops up and down, throwing me around like a puppet behind the wheel. Enfield twitches in his web as if travel sick, clinging to his lair behind the sun visor. Huge coniferous plantations cover the country, occasionally giving way to solitary sheep farms. Beyond the trees the landscape becomes a prairie of tussock grass, with a Roman road running straight for mile after mile.

Towards Glasgow the evening light falls on impossible green hillocks, like cartoon hills with nothing but blue sky beyond. The hearse is funnelled onto the M8 motorway on the city's outskirts and I hug the hard shoulder, sidling alongside the wire mesh perimeter of HMP Barlinnie, Scotland's largest prison. The blunt chimney pots of the Victorian jail rise above the motorway scrub and I reflect on the thousands of men who have passed through the doors since 'The Big Hoose' opened in 1882.

The prison holds a number of unmarked graves within its walls. In the final years of capital punishment several prisoners were executed in a purpose-built 'hanging block' inside the prison grounds. Of the ten men hanged between 1946 and 1960, all were buried on site, their bodies considered state property. When refurbishment programmes forced these same bodies to be exhumed, they were buried again without ceremony, remaining inmates of Barlinnie in both life and death. The prison is currently for sale, soon to be rebuilt elsewhere, and the bones of these notorious men look set to become the foundations of a new shopping centre.

As dusk turns to night, I enter Glasgow's famous Necropolis. A hill rises above the city centre, composed of stepped banks overrun with ivy. I leave the hearse on Wishart Street, continuing on foot to an arch at the entrance, erected when the cemetery first opened in 1833. A dedication is slowly peeling from the apex:

> To unite the tombs of many generations who have gone before with the resting places destined for generations yet unborn.

The columns and pinnacles of grand Victorian tombs rise all around me, their stone reflecting the glow of Glasgow's nightlights. It's as if the cemetery is a giant pinball machine, the floodlit monuments doubling as flippers, bumpers and boomerangs, an arcade that's been out of order for years. A silent colony of bats flit along the avenues, diving for whatever hatch of insects has emerged from the undergrowth. One headstone lies flat on its back in the grass, soil blown into the inscription and sprouting wild chamomile.

As I watch the bats pirouette around an obelisk, I think how fickle are the emotions we attach to the animal world. To the Chinese the bat signifies happiness, wealth and serenity, and to the ancient Egyptians it was a cure-all, a way of protecting a house from disease. And yet to me, in a Glasgow graveyard, a bat instantly evokes blood-sucking vampires and unnatural monsters.

Returning to the hearse, I lie back on the coffin deck with the blinds drawn back. Something buzzes around the cabin, flying in one window and exiting another. Under the dim ceiling lights, I turn the pages of an article on the Necropolis written by a local naturalist. In addition to the bats, the cemetery is filled with some wonderfully appropriate residents, from a bulb-fly known as *Eumerus funeralis* to *Ocypus olens*, the 'Devil's Coach Horse', a beetle that hunts earthworms by night.

The air is close and humid inside the hearse. I try to sleep, but my mind is filled with insects, burrowing through the soil, laying their eggs, making their own kingdom under the city. An ambulance wails somewhere beyond the cemetery slopes, and I wonder if its occupant will survive the night.

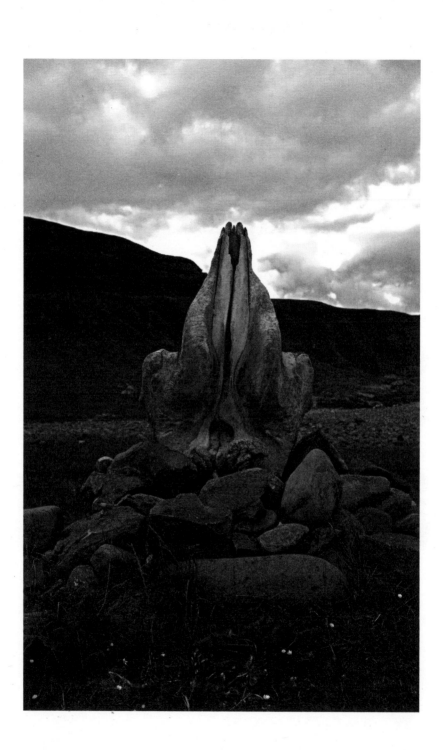

Chapter Ten

Rain sweeps across Glasgow's many spires and citadels, and runs down the sides of the Necropolis monuments above me. I left the passenger window open in the night and a clear puddle of rainwater has pooled on the driver's bench. I brush it out the door with a copy of *Gatherings from Grave Yards*, a completely unreadable account of British burial customs.

Crawling along the banks of the Clyde, my view of the river is through a pall of rain. The Erskine Bridge is empty as I leave Glasgow, and I slowly wake up as the windscreen wipers slap the glass, the hearse cruising three hundred feet above the water. The A82 twists and turns up the banks of Loch Lomond, stands of foxgloves and ferns overhanging the road. A long line of motorhomes and caravans builds up behind me, glued to my tailgate, the more adventurous occasionally sidling into the oncoming traffic in aborted attempts to overtake. I lead them into the Highlands like a merry Pied Piper, my own ponderous procession headed north.

The distances between tombs are greater than before, and my quest is beginning to stretch out across Scotland. I'm travelling into a de-peopled place where burials are not always waymarked, and the next stops on my tour will not be as easily accessed as the plotted graves of England and Wales.

At the top of the loch I pass a fast-food van in a lay-by in the rain, a banner proclaiming 'The Oasis' over a backdrop of painted palm trees and blue skies. I catch a fleeting glimpse of the proprietor staring unblinking through the downpour, like a toy that someone's forgotten to wind. As I watch the van disappear in my rear-view mirror, two ravens sweep down from a hill and fly behind the hearse, like my very own corvid convoy. I'd been waiting for my Edgar Alan Poe moment ever since I set out.

After so many miles of listening to nothing but the engine I've decided to fill the cab with song for the last leg of my tour. I've bought a portable radio and BBC Alba comes and goes over the mountains that line Glen Coe, as one by one the caravans and motorhomes peel off, leaving me alone with Dean Martin's baritone. At the head of the glen, the Buachaille glowers over the road, its slopes covered in loose rock as if the whole mountain is about to slide off its base.

In Fort William I try to use the public toilet but the free stall is blocked, and from the neighbouring cubicle comes a quiet but desperate sobbing. Outside a ten-year old boy plays a fiddle to tourists in the rain. Having stocked up on whisky and apples in the town's grocery store, I take the coast road towards Mallaig.

At Glenfinnan I have to slow through a crowd of people in anoraks milling in the road. They squint through horizontal rain at the high arches of the Glenfinnan Viaduct, forever

4

immortalised as the bridge that carries the Hogwarts Express in J. K. Rowling's *Harry Potter*.

The viaduct has a story stranger than fiction in the form of a missing skeleton. For many years a legend persisted that during construction a horse pulling a cart on top of the unfinished bridge had fallen into one of the hollow piers. The pier was sealed with horse and cart locked forever inside.

One man, Professor Roland Paxton, was convinced the rumours were true and during the 1980s bored a number of small holes in the viaduct piers, inserting a fisheye camera lens to try to locate the skeleton. His search proved fruitless, but a decade later he received a tip that he'd been looking in the wrong place.

Ten miles down the road from Glenfinnan I park on the verge beneath the concrete arches of the Loch nan Uamh Viaduct. The arches were built at the end of the 19th century and converge on an enormous central pylon supporting the trains of the West Highland line.

Paxton came here after his failure at Glenfinnan and, using the same method of bore holes and a camera, resumed his search for the legendary horse. He met with disappointment once more, the camera photographing nothing but rubble in the piers he drilled. Showing remarkable determination, Paxton returned again in 2001, this time armed with a radar scanner. He spent many hours hunting for the horse, passing radio waves through the thick walls until, at long last, an extraordinary image appeared.

The horse's skeleton was discovered standing vertical inside the east wall of the central pylon, the wreck of the cart beneath it. From this evidence it is supposed that the horse's cart was tipping rubble into the cavity when it slipped back-ward and dragged the unfortunate beast with it. I walk in the shadow of the viaduct, crossing a footbridge that spans a swift-flowing burn before pausing underneath the central pylon. I put my hands to the concrete, trying to picture what lies within.

Having paid my respects to this victim of Victorian engi-neering, I rejoin the road and soon arrive in the small seaport of Mallaig. In the harbour, seagulls cluster on the roofs of warehouses, squabbling above a carved wooden memorial to a young fisherman next to the ferry terminal. Lobster creels and fishing nets lie at his feet and a plaque reads, *In memory of those lost at sea.*

In the ticket office I buy a return to the Isle of Rum, an hour's crossing over Hebridean seas. A man in army overalls sits on one side of the waiting room, flanked by an old woman stroking a Dalmatian. Eventually we all file out into the rain and scurry up the ramp onto the ferry.

The hearse remains parked by the pier, and I've left Enfield to guard it in my absence. As the ferry pulls away from the harbour, I wonder if spiders can overheat in airless cars, in the same way as dogs. Rain spots the sea and I comfort myself that Enfield is unlikely to be boiled alive.

The island soon appears over the bow of the ferry, mountains rising straight out of the water like the peaks of some subma-rine range. Nothing moves on the shoreline and I imagine myself aboard Charon's ferry, crossing the divide between worlds, the dark water of the Sound becoming the River Acheron. A loudspeaker announces the price of an all-day breakfast and this underworld evaporates, leaving me with the empty deck and a grumbling stomach.

I've come to Rum to find a temple to the dead, a mausoleum built on the tip of one of Scotland's wildest islands. Disembarking, I walk up the shore path, splashing my way through deep puddles. Not far from the ferry landing stands a castle in which a family once lived in fabulous opulence.

John Bullough had no tie to this island before he owned it. A Lancashire industrialist, he made a fortune radically modernising Britain's textile industry, transforming cotton looms and spindles into mass-production machines. Having accrued enormous wealth, Bullough began to buy sporting estates, purchasing the Isle of Rum in its entirety in 1888. On his death it passed to his son George and, in a classic tale of a fortune made by one generation and spent by the next, George ploughed his father's wealth into the island, building a private paradise for his friends, capped by an elaborate castle.

Kinloch Castle was one of the first private houses in Scotland to have electricity but all its windows are dark as I approach through the rain. The front is curtained by weeds, seeded in the shallow steps leading up to its doors. A once grand colonnade forms a walkway around the perimeter, now barred by a steel fence.

I squeeze through a small gap at one corner and onto a terrace that hasn't seen a promenade in years. The castle is roughly square – two storeys of red sandstone, with turrets on the corners and an elaborate tower rising over the entrance. Above the walkway, the remains of a glass ceiling hang from rotten timbers, panes suspended like guillotines. Warily, I tiptoe around the walkway, peering through the stone-mullioned windows of the ground floor.

The first window I press my face to reveals a double-height gallery filled with family portraits. A row of stags' heads projects from beneath the upper balcony, their bodies cut off at the shoulders and their thick bull necks arching over the room. Glass eyes stare impassively at the opposite wall where a portrait of George Bullough in hunting dress hangs slightly askew. In the middle of the room is a grand piano, a Steinway with a leopard-skin rug spread across the lid. Next to the animal's open jaws is a donation box with the words, *Save Kinloch Castle.*

The castle is a time bomb. In 1967, at the age of ninety-eight, George Bullough's wife, Lady Monica, died and left the entire island to what is now Scottish Natural Heritage. She also gifted them the castle, and decreed that the building and its contents not be split from one another. This left an insurance and maintenance nightmare, a decaying citadel full of valuables that couldn't be flogged.

I continue my morbid investigation of vanished glories, and the next window reveals a mahogany-panelled dining room, crystal glasses laid out on the table as if guests have only to enter and seat themselves. Even after the Bulloughs gave up their castle it continued to receive occasional visitors, one wing briefly becoming Britain's grandest youth hostel. A broken YHA sign lies among the splintered glass on the walkway, and I glimpse a room with mattresses piled to the ceiling, polyester feathers littering the floor like the aftermath of a monumental pillow fight.

On the castle's north side the gates to an inner courtyard lie ajar, cast-iron gutters capped with dragons' heads leering over the quad. The roofline sports an army of tall chimney stacks, one sprouting a silver birch from the pot, and a songbird makes a clicking noise from the branches, as if bemoaning the acres of decay.

The last room I peer into was once Lady Bullough's private drawing room. Silk curtains hang in strips on either side of the window bay and white sofas cluster around a great fireplace, their skirts stained with damp and gaudy purple pillows fraying at the edges. Tarnished mirrors line the walls and the whole room looks as if it might crumble to nothing should anyone dare step inside.

My circumnavigation complete, I wander out into the wild garden, where flights of stone steps lead nowhere and a summerhouse stares blindly at the sea. There is nothing left of the palm houses, bowling greens and fruit orchards once tended by twelve gardeners. The family coat of arms is fixed to the ruins, two bulls bellowing defiantly at the mainland.

This, then, is where the Bulloughs once partied till dawn, a lifestyle scarcely imaginable today. I'm bound for the other end of their story, the family mausoleum, no less grand though far less accessible. I leave the castle and trudge on into the island's interior, a river rushing alongside and the rain falling still harder. The rusted hulk of a stone-breaking machine lies beside the track, a relic of George Bullough's efforts to tame this wilderness with new roads.

A path lined with pink and white orchids climbs steeply away from the road, following the contours of a hill. I follow these small accents of colour as I splash my way through the impenetrable grey of the afternoon. A Highland cow raises its horns so as to see me from beneath a thick, wet fringe, eyeing me coldly as it chews, then returning its nose to the grass. The cow looks right through me as if I have no substance at all.

After a gruelling march across the island I reach its west coast. A swollen burn crosses the path before tumbling into the sea and I have to wade through it above a waterfall. Beyond the next headland I'm rewarded for my efforts with a view of a sheltered cove and a small bothy hugging the shore.

This is Guirdil, a humble dwelling with a roof of tin, maintained by a group of volunteers. It is one of many mountain bothies spread across Scotland's wild quarters, free shelter to anyone prepared to walk some distance from a road. Tonight, it serves as my halfway house between the Bulloughs' castle and their tombs.

Approaching the bothy door, I find the skull of a whale, its lower jaw missing, balanced on a pile of stones. I pick one of the rocks from the pile, its sides bright green in the rain and pitted with flecks of red. This is a bloodstone, and it lends its name to the hill that rises at the far end of the beach, the only known deposit of this mineral in the British Isles. In ancient times bloodstone was ascribed magical properties, including the ability to render invisibility. Perhaps the whole beach and bothy are hidden from the outside world, a blank corner of the map under the protective shroud of the hill.

The insides of Guirdil have a half-lived-in atmosphere, with ashes in the grate and empty bottles of spirits, as if someone has but recently stepped out and not returned. I spread my map on the floor, causing ripples of dust to break like waves against the walls. Flies, disturbed by my presence, crawl across the map's contours and rub their legs in its folds.

Later, I sit by a fire of wet driftwood that spits green flames from old nails, reading a biography of the Bulloughs by Alistair Scott. The author relates stories from the castle's heyday, when the family dined on ten-course meals and listened to an Orchestrion, a fabulous organ that mimicked a forty-piece orchestra. In contrast, the only music I hear at Guirdil is the wind and waves, while I eat a ready meal from a plastic bag.

Outside, the rain has stopped and there's a silver light on the sea. If you're ever truly alone, and I mean completely alone, it's impossible not to hear things. Human voices haunt wild places even in the absence of people themselves, and the wind is full of words this evening, some whispered, others almost screamed, so that I look nervously out of the window.

The English polymath Charles Babbage was taken with the notion of every human utterance being indelibly recorded, forever trapped in the atoms of the air. He wrote a treatise on the subject:

The air itself is one vast library, on whose pages are for
ever written all that man has ever said or woman
whispered. There, in their mutable but unerring
characters, mixed with the earliest, as well as with the
latest sighs of mortality, stand for ever recorded, vows
unredeemed, promises unfulfilled, perpetuating in the
united movements of each particle, the testimony of
man's changeful will.

It appeals to me, this idea of an overloaded atmosphere filled
with the echoes of our ancestors. Out here at Guirdil it seems
a plausible reality.

I return to my book and become so absorbed that only the
bothy's candles burning low rouse me from the page. Slowly
I look up, still lost in a tale of George Bullough's yacht trip
around the world.

To my horror a face has appeared at the window, silhouetted by the midnight glow of a northern summer. A hairy
chin presses against the windowpane and a pair of wet nostrils
fog the glass. I can't see the eyes, but from the forehead two
huge horns curve upward, filling the entire frame.

My first thought is that the devil himself has come to join
me for a nightcap. Awestruck, I rise from my chair.
Immediately, the face at the window vanishes and the sharp
sound of something running across the bloodstone fills the
air. Struggling out of my stupor, I run to the door and open it.

Down on the shoreline no fewer than five faces stare back at
me. They're attached to the bodies of goats not demons, a tribe
of *Capra hircus*, cloven-hoofed but very much of the mortal

realm. The black dresses of their fleece drag on the shingle. They get bored watching me and start to playfully lock horns or shuffle off down the beach to find somewhere to sleep. I bid them good night and return to the embers of my fire.

Before leaving the bothy the next day, I sign the guestbook, damp and curling at its edges. The last visitor left two nights before I arrived, a man named Titus from Freiberg. Perhaps it was his voice I heard on the wind.

The most direct route to the Bulloughs' tombs lies over a saddle between two mountains, a steep climb up from the beach. I struggle through the thigh-high heather, swiping ticks from my chest and legs, and pausing to splash my face in a burn. From the ridge I drop into another glen, onto a patched and potholed track.

This is the broken road that Lady Bullough's coffin was carried down in 1967, having journeyed from Suffolk to Scotland by train and ferry. I try to imagine the lonely procession bouncing down the valley, the Land Rover bearing the coffin and trying to avoid the ditch.

After an hour's walking along the track, I cross a bridge that seems on the point of collapse. The road is prone to washing away after heavy storms and I pick my way among outcrops of tumbled rock. Rounding a corner, I find myself gazing on the last resting place of the Bulloughs of Rum.

A broad bay opens onto the Atlantic Ocean and the outlines of other Hebridean islands to the west. Their contours seem to shape-shift on the horizon, one minute standing tall as volcanoes, then shrinking to merge with the sea. Above the beach a grassy meadow rises to meet the road. At its centre stands a solitary temple, the track petering out between iron posts that once held a pair of enormous gates. Beyond, the temple itself rests on eighteen columns, the Atlantic breakers visible in the gaps between.

Could there be anything more absurd than this model Parthenon beside the sea? When George Bullough first built it here, the pillars and their Doric capitals must have seemed like a flat-pack version of another civilisation. Time and weather have done their dependable work, and the mausoleum has now settled into its surrounds.

I step over a fence of broken chain links to where three sarcophagi lie in state beneath the Grecian canopy. John Bullough occupies the centre ground but his sandstone sarcophagus is dwarfed by the granite tombs of his son and daughter-in-law. The temple's roof is exposed to the prevailing wind and seems permanently damp, the oak beams like a sponge dripping salt water onto the tombs' lids. All will one day melt into the belligerent sea wind, the beams collapsing inward and the slate tiles thrown to the ground, and a few centuries from now I imagine the tombs roofless, surrounded by the stumps of pillars, their stone so smoothed that no inscriptions can be read. The mausoleum remains the only part of the island still owned by the Bullough family, but any memory of them will soon be wiped from the island playground they once cherished.

A man appears on the track above the mausoleum, small and lean, with the leather face of someone who has spent his life outdoors. I wait for him at the temple steps and we start up a fractured conversation, lapsing periodically into silence to stare at the tombs and the sea. I realise I haven't opened my mouth to speak since arriving on the island, and my jaw resists the effort.

David is a rock climber from Cumbria and his accent is thick, hard to hold onto in the wind. Last night, while I was at Guirdil communing with goats, David was camping on the slopes of Askival, the island's highest mountain. Unwittingly, he had pitched his bivvy bag among the burrows of Manx shearwaters, a seabird that stays in coastal waters by day but returns to breed in the island's mountains by night. As David settled down to sleep, thousands of angry avians descended on him, screaming like banshees as they landed and covering his sleeping bag in guano. Looking at his hollow eyes, I can tell he's had a rough night.

David carries on to the beach. Behind the mausoleum the meadow rises to a plateau of rock overlooking the bay. As if this temple tomb were not extraordinary enough, it hides the ruins of another in its shadow – George Bullough's first attempt to bury his father in style.

I climb up through the meadow to where the remains of an arch lie half-buried in the ground. Barely visible behind a screen of grass and wild flowers is a wall of glazed tiles and mosaic, the initials 'J.B.' peeking out through the weeds. This is the rear wall of John Bullough's original grave, a groin vault built into the hillside in the shape of a cross and sealed with an iron portcullis. When his father died in 1891, George Bullough had the vault dug out and glazed by Italian ceramicists at enormous expense. The Bishop of Argyle led an elaborate funeral service.

Here John Bullough happily rested for less than a decade. According to legend, a young friend of George came to the island and was allowed to visit the tomb. Standing in its vault of colourful tiles he made an unfortunate remark that it resembled a public lavatory. George Bullough's response was as eccentric as anything in his storied life. Having first removed his father's sarcophagus, he packed the tomb with TNT and blew it across the hillside.

The blast is still etched into the topography of the hill. Great lumps of worked stone lie concealed in the grass and a finely carved cornice pokes out from between my feet. In among these ruins are thousands of coloured shards, pieces of tile thrown out by the explosion like confetti at a wedding. I pick up a yellow square of mosaic, the glaze cracked and faded.

From the Bulloughs' bones I embark on the long road back to the ferry. I take a detour down a track of pink pebbles to Kilmory, where the old island burial ground stands in stark contrast to the Bulloughs' mausoleum. Here, behind a dry stone dyke, lies a sad collection of stones belonging to the islanders who once called Rum their own. I stand in the ruins of the village that surrounds the graveyard, abandoned in the 1820s during the Highland Clearances. The walls of the houses are grown over with turf and look out at a dark river of peat flowing into the sea.

The ground is lumpen with years of burial but the only legible grave records a household struck down by diphtheria, the names in ascending order of age like an inverted family tree. The headstone is massively thick, as if echoing the weight of grief born by parents who buried six children here. It's a strange sensation to be so alone in a landscape and yet surrounded by a whole community in the ground.

The boat departs the island on time, leaving twenty-four hours after I landed. I sit in the ferry café examining my calves for ticks, like a monkey picking fleas. Opposite me a young man stirs a plate of food with little indication that he's going to eat it. His tired face is filled with some hidden regret and he seems on the verge of tears.

'Are you all right?' I ask, rolling back another trouser leg.

'Fine,' he mutters. 'Had an accident on the hill. Had to come home.'

He produces the hand not stirring his dinner from under the table between us. It's heavily bound in medical gauze and a red stain spreads from his palm to his wrist.

'Jesus. What happened to you?'

With an air of deep despair, the man relays his story. A teacher from the mainland, he'd come to Rum with the intention of spending a whole week climbing its hills. On the very first day he'd fallen off a ridge and cartwheeled down the hillside. The hand had broken his fall.

'It made me realise how fragile we all are,' he says, looking more sorrowful than ever.

I nod silently, sipping my tea and watching him wipe at a line of blood now snaking down his wrist.

Stepping out onto the deck as the ferry rumbles into Mallaig, I search the harbour front for my car. Seen from a distance the hearse is a kind of black hole. It reflects nothing, only visible as a concentration of shadows between the other cars parked on the waterfront. I'm reluctant to get back into the old coach after my footloose hike on Rum, but I haul my belongings off the luggage rack as we dock, saying goodbye to the wounded schoolteacher.

Back on land I open the rear doors of the hearse and notice a hairline crack has developed along one window. Having read somewhere that a cracked windshield can be stalled with a piece of sticky tape, I proceed to cover the glass in strips of silver duct. In the space of five minutes the hearse is robbed of its remaining dignity.

Enfield is alive and well, though he barely registers my return, emerging briefly when the engine starts then scurrying back to bed. I head inland through the night but have driven less than ten miles when I find the road barred. A man in hi-vis clothing appears, looks wonderingly at the hearse and its taped fenestration, then informs me the two lanes are closed for resurfacing and won't re-open until the next day. There's no way around and so, with the deep sigh of one accepting the varied tapestry of fate, I pull the hearse onto the verge and climb back onto the coffin deck. As I strip and crawl into my sleeping bag, the red glare of the roadworks fills the cabin with satanic light. The odour of hot tar completes my own Highland hell.

*　*　*

265

The following morning dawns bright and clear. The hi-vis man has been replaced by another, and he waves the hearse through with raised eyebrows. I pick up the Great North Road towards Fort Augustus, pausing for a cup of coffee on the banks of Loch Ness, where a colourful crowd have gathered on the shore. Tourists rim the water's edge, eagerly scanning the surface or waiting to board boats. They've flocked here to see a mythical monster, more famous than the abominable snowman, more terrible than the deep-sea Kraken. A man in a tartan-skirted 'Nessie' hat leads a parade down to the shoreline, men and women struggling under the weight of their camera lenses, all dreaming of dinosaurs. When a fish jumps, a hundred shutters go off in unison.

The hearse is headed for another, lesser loch, a loch filled with islands but mercifully free from monsters. Bordering an area of Scotland known as the 'Great Wilderness', Loch Maree forms the southern boundary of Fisherfield, a forbidding landscape without human habitation or trees. In contrast, the thirteen-mile loch is a floating forest, a series of over sixty islands carrying some of the last remnants of primeval woodland that once covered much of the Highlands. Far out in the black waters of the loch, stands of Scots pine cling to beaches of golden sand.

The name 'Maree' derives from an early Christian saint, Máel Ruba, who established his own cult here among the pagan people that inhabited this glen in the 7th century. One of the loch's islands also bears his name, a self-contained hideaway where he was reputed to have built a hermit cell and dug a holy well. This island hermitage became venerated, a sacred place where people journeyed in the hope of miracles. Legends of bulls being sacrificed on its shores and pilgrims drinking from the well spring proliferated, and the whole island became associated with a kind of magic, a fusion of pagan lore and Christian piety. Those considered insane were brought here and dunked repeatedly in the water until 'cured', and as late as the 19th century people were being towed around the island to restore their rightful minds. Over time a graveyard was also established on the blessed isle, now filled with a millennium of bones.

Driving through the village of Kinlochewe at the loch's eastern tip, I revisit my plan of attack. I'd intended to bring a canoe and sedately paddle my way out to the island graveyard (motorised craft are banned). A friend in Glasgow had offered the loan of his kayak, but when we tried to load it onto the flower deck of the hearse it slid off and broke in two, a bad omen if ever there was one.

Bereft of a boat, the only way to the island was a solo swim. I'd never been a strong swimmer but the scattering of islands seemed to present a kind of lifeline strung out across the loch. None of the stretches of water looked longer than a swimming pool. If I took my time, I might get to the graveyard by island hopping.

With such visions in my head I find myself on the shoulder of the A832 overlooking the loch, wrestling with a wetsuit that once belonged to my sister. I perform desperate leaps into the air to try to squeeze belly and chest into tired neoprene, the zip constricting my throat so that I can barely breathe. I pull on a rubber hat like a skullcap, then lean against the hearse, sucking air. I'm poorly equipped, but the weather is with me and the sun shines high in a cloudless sky. I set off, an amateur frogman headed towards the loch.

The ground between the road and the loch's edge is a series of dips and hollows, each containing a deep bog. Sphagnum moss springs under my feet as I walk, water oozing between my toes. One moment I feel like I'm skipping across an inflatable floor, the next I'm buried to the waist in fermented water. I heave myself out of the bog with both hands, hoping no one bears witness to my slimy rebirth. On the shore of the loch I sort through the dry bag roped to my shoulders, a heavy jacket and a thermos my only accessories.

As I step into the water my skin is glued to my bones by the cold, my whole body racked with a scrotum-tightening shudder. Casting off, I recall an article I read about happy summer bathers swimming across Scottish lochs, only to suffer heart attacks halfway across. In the space of a few strokes the water temperature can change by several degrees as the loch floor drops to depths of over five hundred feet. In the less conditioned, the shock has been known to prompt hyperventilation and sudden drowning.

The crossing to the first island seems to stretch on forever. The water is black as night but crystal clear, like swimming in outer space. My feet touch land once more and I pick my way, shivering, over jagged rocks, before spreading myself on a large boulder in the sun. I'm suddenly cold-blooded, hugging the warm stone and waiting for the sun to reanimate me, returning to life by slow degrees.

I sit up and look out towards the next island. I can see now how locals might have considered these waters a cure for madness; the extreme cold has focused my mind and everything feels more sharply defined. As I follow the shore to the next outcrop of rock, the air is heavy with the smell of pine, interspersed with willow, ash, holly and oak, not a leaf moving in the still of the day.

The second baptism is not as painful as the first and, eager to reach my goal, I swim fast across the gulf between islands. I walk barefoot along the next shoreline, my dry bag clutched to my chest. This is the largest island and contains its own loch within a loch, a pair of tiny islands floating in its midst. On seeing them I have the same sensation one gets opening a Russian doll to discover ever smaller worlds hidden within.

Finally, I reach a beach facing the object of my quest, the mysterious Isle Maree. A thick fringe of trees drops to a border of pure white sand, the rival of any tropical island. A breeze has got up and small waves sweep the water from the west, slapping my face as I cast off again and causing me to swallow several lungfuls of the loch's black potion. Halfway there and my knees suddenly scrape on something huge lying in the water beneath me. My internal organs do gymnastics and for a heartbeat I've given credence to every monster myth ever told. Looking down, I find myself marooned on a giant rock, submerged in the middle of the channel.

I arrive at the terminal beach and, teeth chattering, dig for my jacket while white fingers struggle to unscrew the thermos. Between the trees, a narrow path leads under low-slung branches to a clearing at the island's heart. A Celtic cross has fallen from its pedestal and lies propped against a perimeter wall. Written in Gaelic on the face are the words, *One who never turned his back on friend or foe*. Beneath the monument gravestones spread out in all directions, a few standing proud but most lying flat and seeming to form a solid floor, the ground cobbled with epitaphs. I stop and listen. Apart from the ripple of the loch water there is nothing, only my own footfall among the dead leaves.

A burial ground this old and isolated has spawned its share of legends. The most popular of these holds that a Viking prince and his bride lie here, side by side under stone crosses, having taken their own lives. I find no evidence of the suicidal lovers and stumble instead on a 20th-century grave belonging to Alexander Robertson. Beneath his epitaph lies a cracked china dove with a hole in its breast. Robertson was proprietor of the Loch Maree Hotel, a guest house that still stands today. The hotel used to be the gateway to the loch's islands, and in the autumn of 1877 it received a very special guest.

Queen Victoria, then in the fortieth year of her reign, was in the midst of a Highland tour when she came to the loch. The monarch and her retinue chartered a boat to row them out to Isle Maree and she set foot here on 'a most beautiful bright morning', perhaps not unlike this one. Her diaries record her wandering among the graves as I have done, but it wasn't the graveyard that left a lasting impression on the queen. Victoria was more taken by the sight of a 'wishing tree', a sacred oak that stood in the woods. She found rags and ribbons tied to the branches and hundreds of coins stuck into the bark. The queen and her companions 'hammered in some pennies' of their own before returning to their boat.

On the south side of the island I stumble on what remains of the wishing tree. Dead limbs surround a trunk, killed by copper poisoning, and every available crack and fissure is filled with coins. There must be thousands, copper pennies that have turned blue with age and the odd glint of silver. A visitor in the 1920s described the tree as being covered in metallic scales, as if it were a dragon, but today the dragon has been hewn into a dozen parts. It strikes me that many of the coins Victoria found embedded here would have borne her own portrait. I wonder how she felt to journey to an island so remote and find the hopes and dreams of other pilgrims reflected in her own image.

Some coins are strewn on the ground and I stoop to pick up a silver Dutch guilder. The face of another queen stares back at me, Juliana of the Netherlands, still on the throne when this coin was minted in 1973. Tempted as I am to pocket the coin, I return Juliana to where I found her. Even though I don't believe in the power of the tree, the accumulated desires of so many people make it a totemic place. Besides, there's a legend that if anything is taken from Isle Maree, the madness it was supposed to cure will return to the world. There's plenty to go round already.

Returning to the beach, I pass a green hollow filled with water and leaves, the remnants of Máel Ruba's holy well. I stoop down and cup my hands in the leaf-dark liquid. The water tastes bitter, definitely not a candidate for mass bottling. The sand and pebbles on the beach are warm underfoot, and, reluctant to begin my long swim back, I lie down and close my eyes. Nothing moves on the loch.

If ever there were a stepping stone between worlds, then this is surely it. It seems an ideal place to be buried, inaccessible and inviolate, yet in a way it's too perfect, a make-believe island that belongs in a book. An hour goes by before I pull my skullcap on again and roll my coat into the dry bag. Wading once more into the waves, the only sound as I pull away from the island is the huff and puff of my own chest.

Relieved to be freed from the undersized wetsuit, I whistle along to the radio as I drive through the village of Poolewe. The road narrows to Scottish single track, a lane picking its way across peninsulas, and I'm forced to spin the steering back and forth around tiny lochans and hairpin turns.

The sky is full of streaks of cloud drawing me north. Near Gruinard Bay, a glimmer from the Summer Isles infuses the hearse and the black curtains and dusty coffin deck suddenly light up, looking almost cheerful. I'm so distracted by the scenery that I fail to check the petrol gauge until it hovers near empty, and have to tailgate a lorry outside Ullapool, praying that its slipstream will buy me a few extra miles. I limp into the town's garage vowing not to make the same mistake twice, buying a twenty-gallon jerry can and strapping it to the passenger seat.

The beauty of Scotland's north-west lies in its staggering age. The mountains here are formed from some of the oldest rock on the planet and I pass through a landscape that predates the birth of many stars. It's a place carved by different forces, most recently the melting of the ice sheets fifteen thousand years ago. The strange volcanic shapes of Suilven and Stac Pollaidh stalk the horizon, mountains whose vertical faces were whittled by ice.

Outside Inchnadamph red deer browse the roadside, the traffic so sporadic they don't even look up as the hearse passes by. I'm headed for a crack in the mountains, a series of caves that hold the bones of animals that inhabited Scotland before humans ever set foot here.

The caves lie at the top of a steep glen, and in the parking circle at the base of the trail two Dutch motorhomes are anchored side by side. A man with a horseshoe moustache sits on the foot rungs of a ladder cleaning his shoes, his wife in the doorway above him. They watch me unpack camping gear from the hearse, but when I turn and wave they scuttle inside as fast as they can. Starting off up the track, I can feel their eyes following me from behind the silver shutters of the mobile home.

The path climbs beside a burn – Allt nan Uamh, the 'stream of the caves' – which drops over shelves of rock into deep, moss-lined pools. The valley is verdant, the underlying limestone making its soil especially fertile, and wild flowers litter the slopes rising on either side. Higher up are exposed ridges of sandstone and quartzite, bare swathes of wet rock that catch the last of the sun, making the whole landscape look like it's wrapped in tin foil. Eventually the flow of water disappears underground and I stumble along a dry riverbed, islands of grass sprouting in the channel.

The path I tread was once a famous battleground for geologists, the Inchnadamph hills possessing a sequence of exposed rock that confounded the scientists of a century ago. To them, everything here seemed out of order, sheets of older rocks overlying younger ones, the chronology of deep time gone awry. The geologists searched every inch of these hills in laborious surveys that lasted for years. What they eventually uncovered was the world's first thrust fault, evidence that the sequence of rocks was the result of a tectonic collision, an anomaly created by forces within the earth.

One of those pioneering geologists was Charles Lapworth. He imagined huge sheets of rocks grinding west, thrusting up and over younger rocks and crushing them in their path. Staying in the Inchnadamph Hotel, he wrote of recurring nightmares where he was squashed in his own bed by this unstoppable force.

I continue following the riverbed and the bluff of the caves comes into view. Three fingers of limestone crown a steep slope, like the clawed toes of a wild animal. Between these lie the cave mouths, their entrances tinged red as if lipstick has been applied to the rock.

In the course of their surveys the geologists also unearthed some remarkable graves, not of men but of beasts. The team that finally cracked the geological riddle excavated a number of these bones, reindeer and brown bears they found in these caves. Laboriously, I climb higher, black slugs lining the well-made path that traverses the slope, hundreds of them inching along as I trudge past. Their collective crawl is like a funeral procession in miniature, mourning the loss of some or other noteworthy mollusc.

Stepping under the stone arch of the first cave, I get a cold shower from water dripping off the overhang. The rock face is tortured, twisted into shapes like curling letters. Inside, the dirt floor is dimpled and surrounded by smooth cavities in the rock, niches where the bones were discovered. Later expeditions turned up many more skeletons in these caves, from Arctic fox and lynx to wolves and wild horses. The bones seemed to straddle the last ice age, some animals returning after the ice sheets melted but others even older, seeking shelter here or washed in by melting ice and preserved. In 1927 the most remarkable discovery of all was made, the partial skull of a polar bear. Thought to be eighteen thousand years old, it remains the only example ever discovered in the British Isles.

Clumps of yellow saxifrage frame the entrance to the second cave. More water drips from the ceiling, the steady tick-tick-tick on rock an ominous reminder of the passage of time, as if I'm hearing my own life ebbing away. While exploring the back of the cavern, I almost trip and fall into a deep cavity. Shining a light into it, I illuminate a pile of toilet roll spread across the rocks ten feet below me. It seems remarkable that anyone would crap in a place of burial, but humans have always sought privacy, both in death and defecation.

I spread out my sleeping bag inside the mouth of the last cave, on a platform of stone with a view back down the glen. I'm dog-tired but it's still too light to sleep, and I feel the same sense of injustice as a child told to go to bed on a summer's night. The cave entrance offers a framed window on the world, and I try to picture a polar bear padding up the glen on its way home from a hunt. I have no such creature to fear tonight, only the slugs continuing their great march across the mountains.

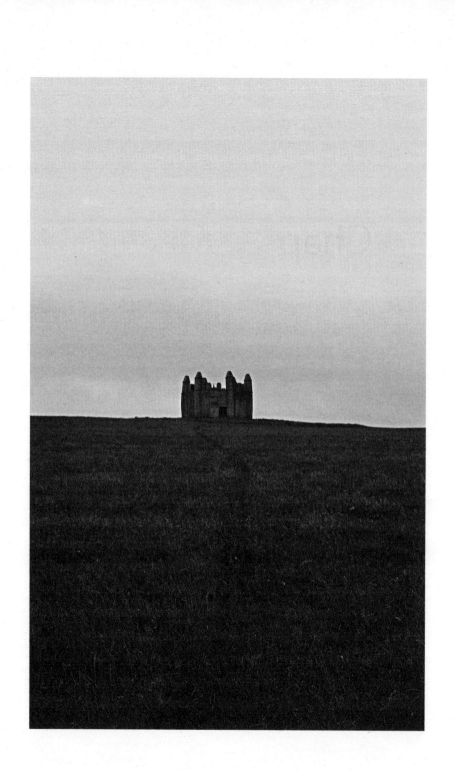

Chapter Eleven

I cook a breakfast of beans and eggs. The sun slowly creeps up the glen and as it strikes the slopes beneath the cave the heather comes alive with thousands of butterflies. Closer up they reveal themselves to be magpie moths, feeding on the heather's flowers as a golden eagle circles high above. The Scottish hills are full of such everyday splendour.

Back in the car park the Dutch motorhomes have vanished, perhaps finding the hearse an uncomfortable companion in the night. I head north from Inchnadamph, with the broken shell of Ardvreck Castle tottering on the side of the road, another doomed dynasty come to an end. I've opened the windows and vents, and the clean, cold Highland air washes through the hearse, invigorating the ghosts collected on my travels. Memories condense and the figures seem to assume solid shape around me, Alfred Wainwright smoking his pipe at my shoulder, a family of Eyam plague victims arguing in the back seat. I may finally be losing it.

In a wide glen I pull over at a viewpoint overlooking mountains, fields of boulders strewn at their base. A campervan with the word 'FREEDOM' spray-painted across the sleeping platform occupies most of the lay-by, and I roll into a puddle next to the crash barrier. After taking a few mandatory and forgettable photos I climb back into the hearse, only to find it's stuck fast in the puddle. When I engage first gear and depress the throttle, the car wobbles from side to side, spraying mud over a sign for Durness.

There seems to be little indication of life in 'Freedom', but I timidly approach the driver's window and knock lightly on the pane. I can hear a shuffling somewhere inside, followed by the sound of something heavy falling off a shelf. A thin, bearded face appears at the window, half-asleep.

The bearded man (Michael) agrees to help me in my plight. He leans back into the campervan and barks something, at which point three more faces appear at the windows, two boys and a woman. We troop back to the hearse and they gather around the rear end of the coffin deck to push. With my foot to the floor and the family of four heaving at the rear doors, the hearse finally escapes the mud. I shoot forwards, then stop to say thank you for my deliverance. The smallest boy salutes.

I reach Britain's northern edge four miles east of Cape Wrath. The Atlantic stretches out before me and I give the dashboard an affectionate pat, proud of the hearse for making it this far. Its aches and pains have multiplied, and a now familiar chorus of loose metal and squeaky springs fills the cabin, rising and falling with the road.

Crossing the causeway at the Kyle of Tongue, I glimpse the town's cliff-hugging graveyard, its denizens fearlessly challenging the worst the weather can throw at them. All of these north-coast towns have graveyards that face the sea, tall obelisks standing like middle fingers to the elements, defying the storms to erase the names of those they commemorate.

I stop for lunch in the tiny hamlet of Betty Hill, about as far from anywhere as you could hope to be. Amid the scattering of houses is a sign for 'Farr Bay'. I wander down a track from the road and over a wooden bridge onto the beach, where a wide cove of white sand stretches before me, decorated with clumps of seaweed and stranded jellyfish. I sit down in the tall marram grass sprouting from the dunes.

Something about the view suddenly clicks into place, like two halves of an old photograph reassembled. A door in the wall of childhood memory opens, and I realise that I've been here before. A sequence of bright images parades across my mind: a never-ending car journey, the smell of heather through an open window, and then the bridge and the beach, a long-awaited release running into the waves with my sister.

The sensation makes me momentarily dizzy, as if caught between past and present, unsure of which is real. How many more of these hidden afternoons exist in our subconscious, memories that define us but lie buried in the morass of the mind? A child jumps from the sand dunes onto the beach, the sand softening the thud, and I wonder if I'll ever return here again.

Still disorientated by flashbacks, I drive on towards Thurso. Warnings of sheep in the road crystallise around a sharp bend and I nearly plough into a line of them strung out across the two lanes. I pass the decommissioned nuclear plant at

Dounreay, golfers playing beneath the shadow of the reactor's sphere.

Approaching my last stop on the British mainland, my journey seems to spool out behind me, a black thread winding from Suffolk to Sutherland. I've visited graves high and low, grand and humble, and yet I've passed uncountable others without a backwards glance. It would be easy to turn around and begin again, choosing another cast of ghosts to chase to the grave.

I press on, determined to finish what I started, branching off on a smaller road and driving until it dwindles to nothing. The hearse bounces across broken ground, coming to rest in front of a barred steel gate. Beyond, a field full of fat spring lambs rises towards a strange, lonely tower, the parapet buckling while the walls bulge outwards.

Rain is falling in thin sheets, coming and going as I climb the gate and cross the field. Ancient sagas record that two armies once met on this same hill, the lambs frolicking on ground formerly covered with the bodies of soldiers. In 1196 Earl Harald Maddadson, ruler of Orkney and 'a great chief, obstinate and hard-hearted', crossed the Pentland Firth and waged battle against Earl Harald Ungi, the rightful heir to the island kingdom. They met on Clardon Hill and their struggle raged back and forth, Ungi's men gaining the upper hand only for their leader to be slain. The tide of the battle turned and Maddadson ran amuck, routing his enemies and wreaking vengeance on the surrounding villages of Caithness. When the dust settled, a few surviving men loyal to Ungi returned and buried him where he fell.

Much later, locals erected a shrine to mark the grave of this fallen warrior, but in the 18th century the landowner, Sir George Sinclair, destroyed what remained of it. Alexander Pope, the local minister and antiquary, was outraged, and after Sir George's death wrote to his son, Sir John, petitioning him to preserve the sacred ground. The young man humoured the elderly minister and erected a tower over what was believed to be the site of the original grave. Rather than rededicate it as a shrine, he put it to use as a family mausoleum, though he himself was never buried here.

I reach the hill's summit and the foot of the strange tower, which is folding in on itself like a castle made of jelly; the whole structure looks as if one firm shake would reduce it to a pile of rubble. A building inspector's report from work carried out in the 1980s stated that the 'burial vault (was) broken into and the coffins displaced', and today the tower seems to be shedding its skin, the harling wall peeling from the stone and two sheep trying to shelter from the rain by pressing themselves against it.

The main entrance to the mausoleum floats six feet off the ground, the steps removed and the opening filled in with breeze-block. To the south a studded steel panel blocks another doorway, above which a stone tablet is topped with the remains of a heraldic device. Carved into the stone are the words, *The Burial Place of the Sinclairs of Ulbster*.

I circle around the tower a few times, disturbing the sheep but failing to find any means of getting inside. Returning to the gate, I meet a man leaning on the bars, a collie dog at his feet. I take him for the farmer and prepare to apologise for my trespass.

'Thought the bulls might get you,' he says as I reach him.

'What bulls?'

He points along the fence line to where two enormous bovines, one orange, the other a dirty white, lean against the wire. Hurriedly I scramble back over the gate.

'They're no bother most of the time, but the white one's got a mean streak.'

I ask him if he farms the land.

'Oh no, I just come up here to feed the bulls.' He pulls a half-empty pack of chocolate digestives from his pocket. 'I call the orange one Jack.'

I turn back to the beasts. My namesake looks reassuringly passive, no doubt drugged with biscuits and regular affection. The man introduces himself as Donnie, and we stand and talk with the rain dripping in our eyes and the dog circling our feet. When I ask about the mausoleum, Donnie says he used to clamber over the walls as a boy, sitting between broken shelves stacked with coffins.

'So there really were coffins in there?'

'Oh aye. The Sinclairs buried their dead here for years.'

I ask Donnie if he knows when they gave up on the place. He's not sure, but thinks funeral processions still came here in the 19th century. At some point the tower was finally sealed up, with a new roof and the steel door to stop vandals.

Donnie stares over my shoulder to where the rain is clearing off the face of the sea, perhaps lost in memories of his childhood séances in the mausoleum. A living Sinclair still lives in the ruins of the castle at the bottom of the hill, the former Liberal MP Lord Thurso. Donnie remembers sitting on cannons by the castle steps, now all washed away by the waves. The collie pulls impatiently at his trouser leg.

'Nice meeting you.' Donnie reaches into his pocket and the voice of a small radio fills the damp afternoon. Man and dog slope off down the road to the sound of the shipping forecast.

In Scrabster I have an hour to kill before the ferry to Orkney. I sit alone in a café on the harbour front, chain-drinking coffee and thinking of all the miles and tombs that have passed since I set out. At some point I wander into the toilet and find the cubicle door covered in graffiti. Among the usual telephone numbers and promises of free sex are four words that make me laugh out loud: *Lord Lucan was 'ere*.

Lucan makes an interesting entry in the annals of the dead. Accused of murdering his children's nanny on the night of 7 November 1974, he promptly disappeared from the face of the earth. His car was found abandoned near Dover but Lucan was never seen again, convicted of murder in absentia. A quarter of a century later he was declared legally dead. A death certificate was issued in 2016, at which point Lucan would have been eighty-two years old.

Endless theories abound as to the British peer's ultimate fate. Did he kill himself or flee the country? The idea that he ended up in a toilet in the arse end of Scrabster is an appealing one. I try to imagine him boarding a boat for the far north, vanishing into an Arctic fog.

Losing track of time, I end up having to run down the pier for the ferry and lean breathless on the deck rails as it separates from the dock. The ship manoeuvres its way out of the harbour mouth in a flurry of miniature whirlpools, and Harald's Tower comes into view on its hill, looking more like a toy castle than ever.

Crossing the Pentland Firth, the ferry breaks free of the weather, a veil of rain clinging to the mainland even as the sun illuminates the islands that lie ahead. In the eyes of ancient cartographers, Orkney was a candidate for the mythical land of Thule, a place beyond the borders of the known world. In the 21st century we have a different idea of scale and our modern-day Ultima Thule is an island in space, a rock drifting on the outer edge of the solar system. Seen from the sea, though, Orkney still retains something of its old magic.

Out of the shelter of the land, a fierce wind sweeps the deck and a lady standing next to me loses her hearing aid, caught in the long white strands of her hair. Automatically she reaches back and replaces it. Noticing me watching she smiles.

'It's OK,' she says. 'It sings to me when it's lost.'

The ferry approaches Orkney from the west, cliffs of red sandstone rearing out of the swell and black cormorants skimming the waves. Spread across the archipelago's seventy islands are the graves of fishermen, farmers, sea kings and poets, from Neolithic tombs to last week's obituaries. Orkney has a long history of habitation and a varied roll call of the dead.

At Stromness I transfer to a fishing vessel headed for the 'High Island'. Hoy stands proud above its low-lying neighbours, humpbacked and rising to sea cliffs that fall over a thousand feet into the Atlantic. The small boat crosses Scapa Flow on an ebb tide, bound for the harbour of Moaness, a sorrowful-sounding destination, though the island is awash with sunshine. We chug slowly past rocky headlands: Sow Skerry, Sandside, The Lash. Birds nest in old gun emplacements fixed to the cliffs, a legacy of Scapa Flow's wartime history, and fifty feet below us the wrecks of battleships lie in the sand. Their steel hulls are wrapped in 'dead man's fingers', a soft coral waving in the harbour currents like an endless farewell.

As we approach the Moaness pier, a woman waits impatiently for the boat to draw alongside, craning her neck over the harbour rails. The helmsman fastening ropes to stanchions catches her eye and dives back into the boat's cabin, emerging with an armful of parcels that the woman hoists ashore. No sooner is the post delivered than our captain is bridging the steps to lend passengers a hand as they disembark. He is all things to all people.

On the edge of the harbour a graveyard gives straight onto a beach. Several boats lie upturned, their hulls flaking paint the same colour as the sky, and in among the graves the smell of seaweed is overpowering. The whole place has a limpet-like atmosphere, the graves clinging desperately to the land even as one corner of the churchyard wall slips down onto the shore.

Many of the epitaphs tell of death by drowning, as if the abandoned boats belong to those now underground. The headstones all lean away from the wind and the church itself is roofless and forsaken, the only decoration an 18th-century memento mori set in one wall. Beyond the ruin a row of 21st-century graves have been cordoned off with breezeblock, turning their backs on the old churchyard, and a young man angrily throws wooden pallets off the flat bed of a trailer, cursing his work.

I follow the coast road on foot, a single track that skirts the inland hills. The sun has softened the asphalt so that my boots sink into it, leaving sporadic footprints like cat's paws in concrete. The island bus comes speeding around the corner, empty save for a driver with distracted eyes, and I have to leap into the roadside to avoid being run down. The sea-corralled motorist is a dangerous animal, beholden to no one.

I sit down in the heather to gather my wits and rest my legs. I'm on the trail of Hoy's most famous burial, the grave of Betty Corrigall, but it's also the island's most remote, a body buried on the boundary between two parishes.

Marching on, birds contest ownership of the hot air above me, a curlew and a black-backed gull duelling in the sky. I crest Lyrawa Hill and come to a crossroad, where a sheep track snakes away over moorland. In the winter of 1933 two men cutting peat here came across one corner of a wooden box. Peeling back another layer of turf, they exposed a coffin.

Terrified by their discovery, the men summoned the island postmaster. The coffin was duly opened, revealing the preserved body of a beautiful woman, with locks of curling hair falling over her shoulders. So immaculate was her appearance that the postmaster called police from the Orkney mainland to inspect the corpse. After examination it was determined that the body was over a century old, and the woman was reinterred in the peat.

The body belonged to Betty Corrigall, laid to rest here in the 1770s. Her miraculous preservation was attributed to the ground in which she was buried. Peat bogs are nature's answer to mummification, a delicate balance of saturated soil and acids, deprived of any oxygen, combining to slow the process of decay. The outward appearance of those buried in the bogs can remain unchanged for centuries.

Examples of such naturally preserved men and women are nicknamed 'bog bodies'. They all share a common side-effect of their exposure to the peat, the dyeing of their hair and skin to various shades of orange. Face, torso and limbs emerge from the ground looking as if they've been covered in tanning solution. An ancient 'bog dog' found in Lower Saxony had fur that was a beautiful russet red.

The extraordinary preservation of such corpses often starkly highlights the ways in which they died. One of the most famous of all such discoveries, the 'Tollund Man', came out of the ground with the remains of a hanging noose still fastened around his neck. He was murdered over two millennia ago, and yet his face looks as if he's only just been cut down from the rope.

Betty Corrigall was also hanged, but by her own hand. In a tragedy as old as time, Betty fell for a sailor who fled to sea as soon as she conceived a child. Pregnant and unmarried, Betty was ostracised by her neighbours, the whole island seeming to turn against her. Twice she tried to take her own life in desperation. On the first attempt she walked into the sea, only to be dragged back to land by a villager. The second time she left nothing to chance and hanged herself from the rafters of a barn.

I continue down the planks of the boardwalk to the corral of wooden stakes and wire that bounds Betty's grave. A small freshwater lochan trickles through the exposed layers of the peat banks, and the handiwork of the men who stumbled upon Betty's body is still clear to see. Beyond the crude fence a thick white headstone bears a simple inscription, *Here lies Betty Corrigall.*

The outcast's grave is starkly beautiful and the bare scenery magnificent. Behind the picket fence a heather-clad hill rolls away to the west, decorated with no other landmark. Describing another lonely burial, the author John Galsworthy wrote, '... no clammy sepulchre among other hideous graves ... just the wide sky and wayside blessings'. Betty Corrigall's grave enjoys a solitary majesty.

Unfortunately for Betty her accidental exhumation in 1933 was not to be her last. Less than ten years later, soldiers stationed on the island during the Second World War came across her coffin while cutting peat from the same bank. They too were struck by her remarkable looks, nicknaming her the 'Lady of Hoy'. Word of the beauty lying under the moor soon spread through the barracks of other soldiers. Time and again, they dug Betty up to gawp at her face or play practical jokes on one another. As in life, she had become the plaything of heartless men.

Eventually an officer put an end to these unearthings by

burying Betty fifty yards from her original plot and ordering a slab of concrete placed over the coffin. Betty hasn't moved since, her ethereal beauty long destroyed by exposure.

Crouching down beside the fence, I examine some strands of flowering heather that have been twisted through the wire. One man who made the pilgrimage to this grave was Kenwood Bryant, an American minister who arrived here after the end of the war. So struck was he by Betty's story that he held a small service in her memory, erecting a wooden cross at the grave's head. The bog soon swallowed this tribute, and the problem of a permanent marker wasn't solved until 1979, when local carpenter Harry Berry made a headstone from fibreglass, impervious to rot and light enough not to sink into the ground.

The grave is remarkably realistic and already has the appearance of well-worn stone. I tap it lightly and the illusion is shattered, the fibreglass sounding hollow like a fairground prop. A second service was held in Betty's honour to inaugurate this ingenious device, and from the grave of an outcast to two funerals in the space of thirty years, a lasting memorial had finally been established. If it does ever need replacing, I wonder if this story will still have a place in the islanders' hearts.

Retracing the coast path, I come to a junction with a smaller road, which tapers into a wide valley and is soon lost in its immensity. A hut stands beside the meeting of ways, its roof built from massive slates the size of bathtubs.

I start down the road as shadows begin to lengthen on the hills, the sun setting at the valley's west end. The whole glen seems splintered, as if the forces of nature waged a battle here but neither side won. To my right, Ward Hill rises into a cloudless evening sky, and burns tumble and converge down a steep corrie in its flank. Over the road lies a near-featureless peatland, empty save for a slab of stone lying stranded in the bog, a great tabular erratic plucked up by a shrinking glacier and carried here on a sheet of moving ice.

This freak in the landscape has drawn people to it for thousands of years. I follow a rough path across the peatland, the rock growing in stature until I find myself standing beside a colossal piece of red sandstone, almost thirty feet in length. An entrance has been carved into one side of the rock and a boulder that once served for a door lies a few feet away, like a cork unplugged from a bottle. I poke my head through the opening, and a hollowed chamber is revealed within.

In folklore the stone is known as the 'Dwarfie Stane', a reference to the dwarf who supposedly once made it his home. Other traditions abound of giants living here and haunting the neighbourhood. Although no body or artefact has ever been recovered from its hollows, the stone's internal layout conforms to that of a tomb, making it a curious anomaly among the chambered cairns that dominate the rest of Orkney's archipelago. It is the only rock-cut tomb in the British Isles.

I take a seat on the boulder that once sealed the entrance. Rolled back from the hole, it has all the drama of the biblical resurrection, as if Jesus has just woken up and wandered off down the glen, although the Dwarfie Stane is at least three thousand years older than the Gospels.

In the entrance passage the stone is warm to the touch, as if someone has installed underfloor heating. On either side shelves that may have contained the bones of our distant ancestors now lie bare. The tomb is like a small off-grid apartment, the shelves providing convenient stores for sundries, and at one end there's even a complimentary stone 'pillow', carved with the names of visitors who came before me.

I shuffle to the back of the tomb and place my rucksack against the rear wall, running a hand over the deep scars in the ceiling. These are the maker's marks, the rock shaped with nothing more than the point of an antler or sharpened stone.

In 1846 another man lay here as I do now, tracing these same carvings with his fingertips. Seeking refuge in the tomb during a thunderstorm, he carefully added his own name, 'H Miller', to the stone pillow as rain lashed the glen.

Hugh Miller arrived here, as I have done, at the end of a long journey. He was a man with a deep interest in the landscape, a stonemason who taught himself science and walked thousands of miles across Scotland, studying its rocks and fossils. Lying on his back as the storm continued to rage outside, Miller described the 'luxury of listening', the joy of hearing rain patter on stone and the wind blowing through the valley. Of the graffiti he left in the Dwarfie Stane he later wrote:

In what state will the world then exist, what sort of ideas will fill the head of the man who, when the rock has well nigh yielded up its charge, will decipher my name for the last time ...?

I try to answer these questions posed across a hundred and seventy-five years. In what state will the world then exist? If Hugh Miller magically returned to this glen in another clap of thunder, he might not suspect the world had changed at all. In a way it hasn't, and his beloved bedrock still underpins us. As for his second question, my head is filled with desires, not ideas. A desire to be done with the dead, to go home, to see my wife and children. I'm weary of chasing men and women whom I can never catch.

When Miller himself went home after his long geological journey, his health steadily declined. He had lived and breathed stone all his life, working as a young man in quarries that filled his lungs with a fine crystalline dust. Ten years after he lay here scratching his name into this tomb he began to experience psychotic episodes, most likely the result of silicosis. Fearing he had become a danger to his family, he took his own life by shooting himself in the chest. It was a tragic end for a brilliant man, a seeker always curious about what the future might bring.

The light in the doorway has been reduced to the dim glimmer of a summer's night. There's a long tradition of sleeping in the Dwarfie Stane, and I arrange a neatly made bed before stepping outside to brush my teeth in the gloaming. Near the entrance an inscription left by another temporary tenant reads, *I have sat here two nights and so learned patience*. It's unclear whether the author was referring to the solemnity of the spot or the abundance of midges.

Nightfall brings a rising wind that scours the glen, the high-sided valley acting like a wind tunnel. There's no shelter but the tomb in this solitary place, and I watch gusts of wind flatten the grass that frames the door, the 'Jesus' stone lying close enough to deflect the worst of the weather. With my feet stuffed in my sleep sack and steam from my kettle condensing on the ceiling, I feel protected. I pull a blanket across from the shelf now bereft of bones. I'm at my farthest point from home, alone in a tomb belonging to men and women who lived five thousand years before I was born.

Having laid my head on the pillow, my affection for the grave is tempered by a feeling of slow suffocation. I'm dragged back from the frontier of sleep by the horrid notion that someone might replace the stone in the door and seal me inside. I sit up and stare at the boulder's stark outline in the entrance, then call 'Hello?', my voice bouncing off the roof. I call out again, and my throat feels as if it's lined with cotton wool. When I finally slumber, no phantoms of the past nor visions of the future invade my dreamless sleep, no monstrous troll creeps in to lie beside me in the half-dark. Whatever spirit of the Neolithic still dwells in the stone, it is mute and the story spent.

The following morning dawns with a barely perceptible brightening of the tomb's entrance. I shuffle out of my sepulchral crib and blink at a low ceiling of cloud that clings to the glen. I'd imagined the final sunrise of my tomb tour as a blaze of glory and an affirmation of life. Instead the sun is invisible, and a pale light suffuses the world as I roll up my sleeping bag and sweep the tomb's floor. Walking back to the road, I cower as two great skuas swoop down from the cliffs on the hillside, dive bombing my head as if to say, 'Begone.'

All things come to an end. I've visited my last tomb and finished paying my respects. Retracing my steps to the harbour at Moaness, I stand beside the pier for the boat to come in, a sense of relief mingled with regret. As others passengers arrive one by one at the harbour rails, I think of Mr Miller, waiting for the same boat to carry him home.

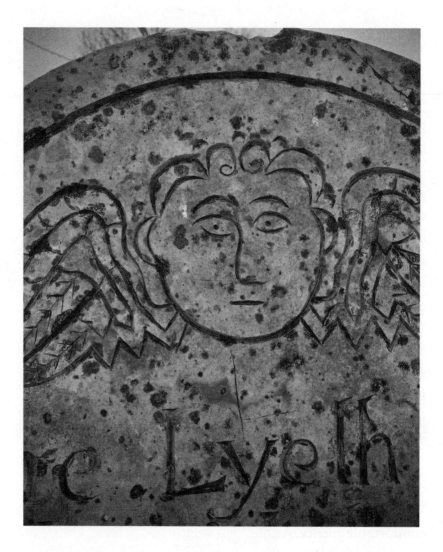

EPILOGUE

The hearse never made the return journey. After the dark miles of Sutherland's endless moors and the salt winds of Orkney, it limped a short way south before coming to a halt on a hard shoulder. This time no amount of persuasion would revive it. For a moment I hoped my old friend would burst into flame, a roadside pyre a fitting end to its final procession.

A man from the RAC came and picked me up. Before he winched the long black carcass onto his trailer he examined the engine, trying to revive whatever vital organs had expired. He asked me how far I'd come, and I told him. There was a pause while he stopped what he was doing and stood up.

'I wouldn't have driven it to the end of the road.'

I sat alongside him in the truck's cab as we headed towards Aberdeen. He didn't once ask me why I was driving a hearse. We talked about the living not the dead, and then sank into a comfortable silence. As the road went by with unaccustomed speed, I had time to reflect on my journey.

I'd travelled close to two thousand miles in my pursuit of the past. From the first grave balanced on the cliff edge in

Dunwich to the final night inside a tomb of sandstone, I'd spent nearly a month of my life in the company of ghosts. My whole journey now seemed like an act of remembrance, a trip down memory lane where the present had receded ever further each day. The idea of returning to the here and now was daunting; the country of my birth was no longer defined by the living but delineated by the dead.

From churchyards and cathedral aisles to those buried on moors and mountains, I found solace in the knowledge that our ancestors underlie us all. Standing so close to the physical remains of these men and women had brought their stories to life; they continued to be present and absent, their memory flickering among us.

And what of my own interment, whether death came tomorrow or fifty years hence? Encountering remnants of other lives had made me more thankful for my own. After returning south I bought myself a 'do your own' will; a thick, plastic-wrapped booklet costing £5. I was surprised to find I cared what became of my bones, shuddering at the memory of 'the cremulator', the machine grinding human remains to dust at Golders Green. I also reasoned I'd spent enough time in a hearse to forgo the expense of being carried to the grave in one.

The romantic in me searched for alternative endings. One obituary I read told the story of a middle-aged piano tuner who, in the autumn of 1992, strapped twenty-six helium balloons to a home-made gondola and took off from a lake in central Japan. Yoshikazu Suzuki set out to cross the Pacific Ocean and was last seen five hundred miles off the coast, waving and heading east into the sunrise. He never made landfall in America, nor were his remains ever found.

Similarly, I read stories of men and women who chose to blast their remains into space, escaping the earthbound condition entirely. But if my journey had taught me anything it was a love for the British landscape and its layered history. Ultimately, I desired nothing more than to be laid in the garden compost and covered over with the grass cuttings, absorbed back into my native soil.

Filling out my will, I wondered what the tomb tourist of the future had to look forward to. The last half-century has given us new ways of remembering our loved ones but also better means for erasing their physical remains. The hallowed ground of yesteryear is constantly being repurposed and whole graveyards disappear beneath new developments; ancient barrows are stranded on roundabouts and mass graves buried under golf links. Churches are turned into hostels, pubs or nightclubs, the bones of the dead reverberating to the rhythms of the living. Such is the shortage of space and the shallow nature of human memory.

As for the hearse, it had been rolled into the back of my neighbours' cow shed, awaiting collection by a man who agreed to pay cash for her remains. The night before the car was due to be collected, my wife walked to the end of the garden and looked at it long and hard. A cow farted in the adjacent stall. Solemnly, I took a heavy piece of tarpaulin and drew it gently over the black livery, as if pulling a shroud over a body.

Later, lying in bed, a terrible silence settled on the house. I lay flat on my back and wide awake in the dark, listening to the suffocating sound of nothing at all. Then, just as sleep beckoned, a strange and ominous noise entered the room, seeming to emanate from oak beams in the plastered ceiling. A knocking, ticking noise like an irregular clock fell upon my ears, swelling then fading. I had never heard anything like it before. Some arcane prior knowledge floated up from the bedpan of my brain and I realised, with a terrified certainty, that I was in the presence of the deathwatch beetle, quietly chewing our house as it probably had been for the last four hundred years. With a curious sense of closure I recalled the origin of its nickname, so given because it would often be heard in the silence of the deathbed vigil, just before the sick man or woman expired.

The following morning the buyer arrived to pick up the hearse. As he secured it to another trailer, I thought of the 'rolling junk' that F. Scott Fitzgerald drove a thousand miles across America in the summer of 1920. When the old wreck was finally disposed of, he wrote, 'Perhaps it is resolved into its component parts and has lost its identity and its mortal soul – or perished by fire or been drowned in the deep sea.'

As the truck began to pull away from the shed, I realised I'd forgotten Enfield. Frantically, I ran out into the road and flagged the driver down. He stopped and watched, uncomprehending, as I climbed up onto the trailer and prised open the passenger door. To my relief the spider was still alive and preoccupied with his dinner, spinning a small fly into a neat silk bauble. Under the scrutiny of the man behind the wheel I transferred Enfield to the pocket of my coat.

THE END OF THE ROAD

I dismounted and the truck moved off again, leaving a cloud of dust hanging behind it. Slowly, I carried Enfield back to the house, holding my pocket shut to prevent him from climbing out. I released the spider on the doormat and he scurried across the kitchen and into the shadow of the fridge. The wanderer had found a permanent home at last, here to live out the remainder of his days.

ACKNOWLEDGEMENTS

Many debts are owed for the writing of this book.

First, to my long-suffering wife Jennifer, for letting me abandon our children and disappear in a hearse. Also to my agent Claudia, who encouraged the original idea, and Jack Fogg at HarperCollins for his patience and wisdom. Thanks as well to Clemency, Adam, Bud and Pamela, for reading the unreadable, and especially Mark Bolland, for raking through the manuscript and removing the loose stones and weeds.

Researching so many past lives led me to some brilliant authors. In particular, I'd like to acknowledge my debt to Piers Brendon's biography of Robert Stephen Hawker, and Alastair Scott's book on the Bulloughs of Rum. I'm also grateful to local historians for their research, namely R. L. Rimell's account of the Theberton zeppelin, Geoffrey Probert's history of St Stephen's Chapel, Bures, and James Lovelock's first-hand experience of the Neil Moss caving tragedy.

Finally, a book about the dead would be nothing without the living. I'd especially like to thank Eric Willis for his fascinating tour of Golders Green Cemetery, Father Niphon for his time and green tea, and Jan Barnes for sharing her archive and memories.